NATURAL RIVALS

NATURAL RIVALS

John Muir, Gifford Pinchot, and the
Creation of America's Public Lands

JOHN CLAYTON

PEGASUS BOOKS
NEW YORK LONDON

NATURAL RIVALS

Pegasus Books Ltd.
148 W 37th Street, 13th Floor
New York, NY 10018

First Pegasus Books cloth edition August 2019

Excerpts from the John Muir Papers, Holt-Atherton Special Collections,
University of the Pacific Library. © 1984 Muir-Hanna Trust

Interior design by Maria Fernandez

Library of Congress Cataloging-in-Publication Data is available.

ISBN: 978-1-64313-080-4

10 9 8 7 6 5 4 3 2 1

Printed in the United States of America
Distributed by W. W. Norton & Company
www.pegasusbooks.us

To Charlie "Chasmo" Mitchell,
teacher, scholar, inspirer, friend

CONTENTS

Cast of Characters   ix

Timeline of Key Events   xi

Prologue   xiii

PART I: NATURAL PROPHET, NATURAL STATESMAN   1

1: Gramercy Park   3

2: "Radiate Radiate Radiate"   15

3: The Tragedy of John Muir   34

4: "Sufficient Confidence in His Own Wisdom"   59

5: The Tragedy of Gifford Pinchot   83

PART II: THE BIRTH OF PUBLIC LANDS   101

6: Bigger Stakes at Play   103

7: Free Land for Many Uses   125

8: No Trespassing   140

9: Lake McDonald's Delight   159

10: The Public Good Forever   180

Epilogue   207

Acknowledgments   217

Notes   221

Bibliography   259

Index   267

CAST OF CHARACTERS

On the 1896–97 National Forest Commission:

John Muir (1838–1914), (nonvoting) naturalist, wanderer, writer, activist, evangelist. Defender of Yosemite National Park, cofounder of the Sierra Club.

Gifford Pinchot (1865–1946), (secretary) forester, politician, administrator. Founder of the U.S. Forest Service, advisor to Theodore Roosevelt.

Charles Sargent (1841–1927), (chair) horticulturalist, botanist, head of Harvard's Arnold Arboretum. Friend of Muir, mentor to Pinchot.

Arnold Hague (1840–1917), geologist, Yellowstone expert. Imagine John Muir crossed with a Washington, D.C., insider. Ally of Pinchot.

William Brewer (1828–1910), botanist, proto-forester, taught Pinchot at Yale.

Henry Abbot (1831–1927), civil engineer, streamflow and reservoir expert, ally of Sargent.

Alexander Agassiz (1835–1910), zoologist. Did not participate.

O. Wolcott Gibbs (1822–1908) (ex officio), chemist. President of the National Academy of Sciences.

Magazine editors:

Robert Underwood Johnson (1853–1937), associate editor of *The Century*. Muir's close friend and political collaborator.

William Stiles (1837–1897), editor of *Garden and Forest*. Charles Sargent owned the magazine, but Stiles was chief writer and lobbyist.

George Bird Grinnell (1849–1938), editor of *Forest and Stream*. Aristocratic hunter-conservationist and friend of Theodore Roosevelt.

Supporting players:

Frederick Law Olmsted (1822–1903), landscape architect, park planner, mentor to Pinchot.

Bernhard Fernow (1851–1923), forester, Pinchot's predecessor as chief government forester.

William Kent, (1864–1928), philanthropist, congressman, donor of Muir Woods National Monument.

William Holman (1822–1897), Indiana congressman. Rural cheapskate and anti-monopolist.

Relevant U.S. presidents:

Benjamin Harrison (R), in office 1889–93. Created first Forest Reserves.

Grover Cleveland (D), 1893–97. Convened the National Forest Commission.

William McKinley (R), 1897–1901. Little interested in the natural world.

Theodore Roosevelt (R), 1901–09. Nature lover with charismatic personality.

William Taft (R), 1909–13. More timid than Roosevelt but charged with carrying on his legacy.

Woodrow Wilson (D), 1913–21. Little interested in the natural world.

TIMELINE OF KEY EVENTS

Before Muir and Pinchot meet:

1838: John Muir is born

1864: Yosemite Valley: California state park

1865: Gifford Pinchot is born

1868: Muir arrives in the Sierra

1872: Yellowstone: national park

1880: Muir marries Louie Strentzel

1889: Muir and R.U. Johnson in Yosemite

1889: Pinchot graduates Yale

1890: Yosemite, Sequoia, and General Grant: national parks

1891: Forest Reserve Act (Section 24)

1891–93: Pinchot at Biltmore

1892: Muir organizes Sierra Club

1893–94: Pinchot–Laura Houghteling romance

Muir–Pinchot collaboration (climax of this book):

1893: Pinchot and Muir first meet in New York

1895: *Century* symposium, "A Plan to Save the Forests"

1896: National Forest Commission trip

February 1897: Washington's Birthday Reserves

March 1897: Civil Sundry Appropriations Bill

June 1897: Forest Management Act (Pettigrew amendment)

1897–98: Muir's *Harper's* and *Atlantic* articles

June 1897: Pinchot offered federal job

Later events:

1898: Pinchot becomes chief forester

1901: Roosevelt becomes president

1903: Muir and Roosevelt in Yosemite

1905: Pinchot founds U.S. Forest Service

1906: Yosemite Valley added to national park

1907: Muir and Pinchot at Sierra Club board meeting

1910: Pinchot is fired

1913: Hetch Hetchy dam is approved

1914: Muir dies

1946: Pinchot dies

PROLOGUE

O n a springtime drive from my home near Yellowstone to Glacier National Park, I tumbled across rolling green foothills and then crested a snowcapped mountain pass where evergreens blanketed bustling creeks. As my eight-hour route spooled along rural two-lane roads, I enjoyed changing patterns of landscape: varied geology of mountains and plains, varied ecology of woodlands and grasslands, and varied land use of ranches and small towns. Behind those patterns, visible only on specialized maps, was the fact that some of this land was privately owned and some was public.

My house looks out on public land managed by the U.S. Forest Service. Glacier is public land managed by the National Park Service. Between the two, I drove through lots of public land administered by the federal Bureau of Land Management.[1] I also drove within view of national wildlife refuges, dammed reservoirs, an air force base, designated wilderness areas, and lands administered by the state of Montana. In effect I was on a tour of public lands: different uses—such as recreation, habitat, or economic development—managed by different agencies, reflecting different sets of societal values. An extreme example came during the hour I spent driving across the Blackfeet Indian Reservation. On these lands, a sovereign nation sets the public-land priorities—a Blackfeet nation that for centuries did not concern itself with "ownership" of land. In the late 1800s, whites demanded that Blackfeet recognize property rights and organize their lives around private land. Then whites also started talking about "public land."[2]

When I was growing up in Massachusetts, most public lands were recreational destinations, such as a beach, a woodsy trail, a city park, or an athletic facility. In 1990, I moved to Montana, where public lands are both ubiquitous and multifunctional. In addition to recreational destinations such as Yellowstone and Glacier, Montana has public lands managed for a variety of purposes by the Forest Service and Bureau of Land Management. Indeed these *multiple-use agencies* seek to balance logging, grazing, habitat, recreation, and other uses—on acreages twenty times greater than that of the Park Service.[3] Their processes to achieve that balance aim to give all members of the public a voice in decisions. Those decisions affect Western landscapes' magnificent wide-open spaces—and the economic livelihoods of ranchers, loggers, guides, and others who work the land, as well as the self-identity of hikers, hunters, bikers, Jeepers, skiers, snowmobilers, and others who play on the land.[4]

Managing public lands is thus complicated. Each interest group pursues a different deep-rooted passion, but furthermore each stretch of land boasts different characteristics. Matching everything up is like putting together a jigsaw puzzle—except that ongoing political developments keep changing the sizes of the pieces. Furthermore, although assembling a jigsaw puzzle is a fun family activity that merges interests to assemble a beautiful vision, on public lands the puzzle-work is a tedious prerequisite for people's true interests, which are the activities that take place on the land.

My drive to Glacier in the spring of 2017 followed a series of controversies suggesting that the nationwide public-lands jigsaw might get entirely swept off its table. The reigning Republican party platform called for federal lands to be returned to states. Congress changed accounting rules to make such land transfers easier. The administration of President Donald

Trump began a review designed to shrink national monuments. All this developed soon after the acquittal of militants who took over Oregon's Malheur National Wildlife Refuge to protest the very idea of federal land ownership. In opposition to these trends, public lands became a major wellspring of the 2017 #resistance to Trump. A popular rallying cry held that these lands were our citizens' shared inheritance, which the corrupt administration intended to destroy.[5]

I had trouble with both sides of the debate. The arguments for *federal land transfer* relied on naïve fantasies in which well-paying rural jobs would magically appear and litigation would magically vanish, despite everything we know about our economic and legal systems. Meanwhile, many defenders of public lands ridiculously overstated the bogeyman, acting as if America's crown jewels were already on the chopping block.[6]

To alleviate my frustration, I asked whether deeper values were fueling the clash. And I realized that when people talk about *public lands,* what they really want to talk about is *lands that demonstrate our society's relationship with nature.*[7] That's why people care so much about these issues: they're fighting not only over acreage but also over a relationship. Indeed, the relationship contains spiritual components—some people's almost-religious faith in nature and its systems is conflicting with others' faith in technology, enlightened bureaucrats, or free markets.[8]

Antagonism toward Trump's interior secretary, Ryan Zinke, provided a simple example of the intertwining of public lands and attitudes toward nature. Zinke favored large increases in drilling, mining, and other development on public lands. In other words, he wanted public lands to reflect a more resource-extractive relationship to nature. Personally, I disagreed; I even saw his position as a betrayal of the public trust. But I couldn't call Zinke an enemy of public *lands,* because he did believe in federal ownership of the lands to be drilled. He even resigned as a delegate to the 2016 Republican convention over its public lands disposal platform. Indeed, there's no reason for public lands to be exclusively associated with nature-friendly outcomes. Actions on private lands can benefit nature, as when Ted Turner runs herds of bison, the Nature Conservancy funds conservation easements, or Michael Bloomberg proposes business stances to fight climate change.[9] And some public lands have little explicit effect on nature, as when they are used for streets, plazas, libraries, military facilities, rodeo grounds, or museums.[10]

The real wonder of public lands is less about outcomes than it is about process. On public lands, we as a democratic society get to decide collectively what happens. We can come together to articulate our relationship to nature. Bike trail here, elk habitat there. Logging here, grazing there. Scenic pullout here, oil rig out of sight behind a hill. Even if putting together the jigsaw puzzle can feel like a tiresome chore, it's a privilege. And its results, though far from perfect, are almost always better than a pile of jumbled pieces. In short, although we often speak of public lands as if they're *nature's lands*, what makes them profound is that they're *democracy's lands*.

That's why the public land debate was resonating so deeply: it captured both conflict about America's relationship to nature and conflict about the structure of America's democracy. Although those conflicts felt as in-the-moment as a Trump tweet, they had deep metaphysical roots. Does nature provide humans with essential resources, or is it bigger and more holy than corrupt human society—and what process do we use to find a balance?

When phrased as such a philosophical conflict, the divide might seem impossible to bridge. Yet the historical evidence says otherwise. We bridged the divide, once. America embraced public lands throughout the twentieth century. America created the varied land-management agencies whose work I had witnessed on my drive. Americans started calling public lands a *birthright*. I'd seen—and even taken for granted—the results on the landscape: somehow America once established a public land ideal. Why didn't I know more about how that had happened?

I was driving to Glacier to research a story. On the shores of fjord-like Lake McDonald, where unending forests spill from bare pointed peaks all the way down to impossibly clear waters, two renowned individuals had once taken an unheralded camping trip. In 1896, when they visited,

Glacier was not yet a national park, and part of the purpose of their visit was to decide its fate.

One of the men was John Muir, the most well-known naturalist in American history, often called the "father of the National Park Service." In part through his successful efforts to enshrine Yosemite, Muir brilliantly articulated the principles of protecting national parks as places where nature can provide people with spiritual renewal. The multitalented Muir was also a groundbreaking scientist, much-lauded author, and founder and longtime president of the Sierra Club, one of America's first environmental advocacy organizations.

Staying with Muir at Lake McDonald was Gifford Pinchot. Today Pinchot's name isn't as widely known as Muir's. But many who know it hold him in similar regard. In 1905, Pinchot founded the U.S. Forest Service to chart a sustainable course for America's timber while also yielding benefits such as clean water and forest recreation. Pinchot's principles and leadership were almost singlehandedly responsible for the organization's success. Meanwhile, Pinchot served as President Theodore Roosevelt's chief advisor on environmental issues, including the massive expansion of public lands that may be Roosevelt's greatest legacy.

In some circles, Pinchot is also famous as a counterpoint to Muir. Many historians use the two men to embody opposing philosophies. The romantic Muir is *preservation*: leaving nature alone so as to benefit from its holistic wonder. The practical Pinchot is *conservation*: using natural resources sustainably to serve what Pinchot called the "greatest good for the greatest number in the long run." [11] To regular folks, *preservation* and *conservation* may seem like similar ideas, especially in contrast to wanton exploitation of natural resources for short-term gain. But to some scholars, the difference between these near-synonyms helps explain America's twentiethth-century environmental history. [12]

From 1905 to 1913, the two philosophies clashed over plans to dam a remote Yosemite valley called Hetch Hetchy. Because the dam would provide drinking water to a great number of people in San Francisco, Pinchot saw it as good conservation. Because it would devalue natural conditions in a national park, Muir saw it as an affront to preservation. Muir lost that battle, but his disciples used it to inspire a crusade.

Ever since, almost every dam, mine, grazing allotment, timber sale, proposed wilderness area, national park, or national monument—every decision about priorities on public lands—has been argued as an expression of this preservation-versus-conservation divide. How much use is necessary for human needs, and how much degrades the sanctity of nature? Although each situation differs slightly, each is fueled by that same basic question. Each thus plays out predictably. Conservationists get accused of too much compromise with short-term extraction; preservationists get accused of elitist and out-of-touch disdain for human society. As the battles rage within bureaucracies, on election days, and in courthouses, the negativity stymies meaningful action. The preservation-versus-conservation stalemate leads to outcomes bad for nature and society both.[13] When experts try to explain why this happens, the easiest way to illustrate the divide is to describe Muir and Pinchot at Hetch Hetchy. But the danger in telling a story like that is that it can end up implying that Muir and Pinchot themselves *caused* the stalemate, that their actions split the environmental cause. That was the lesson I'd taken from college classes, occasional readings in environmental history, and popular treatments such as Ken Burns's documentary *The National Parks: America's Best Idea*—the two men were implacable enemies.[14]

Under that assumption, once I discovered that the men had spent time together on the shores of Lake McDonald, I could imagine their interactions making for good drama. Lots of bickering. Maybe Pinchot would point out the first trees to cut and the first valleys to dam. Maybe Muir would fulminate that none of it should be touched, for any reason, ever. I could write a book titled Natural Enemies, with a plot in which the heat of their arguments grew to a boiling point.

But by the time I drove to Glacier, that vision was already in trouble. In real life, my research showed, Muir and Pinchot didn't argue very much. For example, both men used the same word to describe their interactions at Lake McDonald: *delight.*[15] Living on opposite sides of the country, they wrote many letters—and most of those letters were warm, enthusiastic, affectionate, and supportive. One of their most famous arguments, at a Seattle hotel in 1897, was later shown to have never happened. And even Hetch Hetchy is often misunderstood: it was not a straightforward clash between preservation and conservation, nor were Muir and Pinchot its primary antagonists.

How would I come to terms with fact that Muir and Pinchot didn't act like enemies? I achieved a breakthrough when I came to think of them as *rivals*, the way 1980s basketball players Larry Bird of the Boston Celtics and Magic Johnson of the Los Angeles Lakers were rivals. Bird and Magic exhibited different playing styles that embodied different philosophies about basketball. When they competed against each other, the rivalry challenged both to greater heights. But they weren't mortal enemies. Growing up in Massachusetts, I'd been a huge Bird fan, but I didn't see Magic as evil. I knew that Magic's talents were equally deserving of triumph—that's what made it a great rivalry.

If Muir and Pinchot were rivals rather than enemies, then they simply offered alternative paths to articulating a constructive societal relationship to nature. The paths were like different approaches to the summit of a mountain: like Charlie Chaplin and Buster Keaton making funny movies, Ernest Hemingway and William Faulkner writing fiction, the Beatles and the Rolling Stones making rock 'n' roll, Betty Friedan and Gloria Steinem fighting for feminism, or Malcolm X and Martin Luther King Jr. advancing civil rights. The rivalry of Muir and Pinchot offered different reasons to move beyond short-term exploitation. If different people preferred one to the other, that was a productive expansion of the audience for their shared passion.

Then I remembered the climax of the Bird-Magic rivalry, in 1992. They joined together on the U.S. Olympic Team, the "Dream Team." Their styles turned out to be complementary. They delighted in each other's skills and character. They took basketball's beauty and joy to an international stage. Their legacy: basketball was propelled from an American-only sport to one of the world's most popular.[16]

What if John Muir and Gifford Pinchot had likewise been collaborators who created a useful legacy? What might that look like?

This book tells how the Dream Team interactions of rivals John Muir and Gifford Pinchot contributed to establishing the public lands ideal. We start with the moment the two men met, at a Pinchot mansion on a private park in New York City. To understand their rivalry, we then look at Muir's life, the way his prophet-like ambitions turned him into a political activist—and led to disappointment over Hetch Hetchy. A similar narrative of Pinchot's life shows how his statesmanlike ambitions led to similar sorrow. Then we return to the late 1800s. We bring in additional characters to examine not only individual ambitions but also societal ones: the need for new expressions of Americans' collective relationship to nature. As we watch Muir and Pinchot share outlooks with each other at Lake McDonald, and then communicate and enact that shared vision, we see how they convinced Americans to embrace public lands.

This angle on Muir and Pinchot is unusual. It doesn't talk much about *wilderness*, nor about their individual activities with the Sierra Club or Forest Service. Without diminishing the importance of those angles—certainly wilderness is central to Americans' ideas of nature—this book is telling a different story, one about public lands in general.[17] Notions of a Forest Service, a Park Service, a Bureau of Land Management, or a government-designated wilderness area depend on a broader ideal of public land. Public lands are, in essence, a prerequisite to most of today's perspectives on environmental issues. These perspectives, and the agencies charged with implementing their results, exist only because Americans understood the purpose of public land far differently in the 1910s than they did in the 1880s. The collaboration of Muir and Pinchot helped make that change happen.[18]

Muir and Pinchot did not *invent* public lands any more than they invented a preservation-versus-conservation divide. Indeed they were just two of many individuals involved in this culture-wide change, and any attempt to rank those individuals' contributions would be both impossible and foolish. Maybe the role of Theodore Roosevelt was more important, or Frederick Law Olmsted, Robert Underwood Johnson, Charles Sargent, Bernhard Fernow, or George Bird Grinnell—either as individuals or while engaged in rivalries of their own. Or maybe if none of these people had existed, wider forces of economics, demographics, and technological development would have elevated others to play their roles.

However, there are three good reasons to look at these changes through the lens of John Muir and Gifford Pinchot. First, we've already told so much environmental history through these two men—projecting back onto them so many of our own assumptions about wilderness and spirituality and economic development—that it's worth looking at their relationship in a different light. Second, in the current moment, as our longstanding debates about the environment intensify around issues of climate change, we are also having debates about how our democracy functions: about how people relate to each other, as well as to nature. As ever-more-divisive rhetoric threatens to split the public, it's worth looking back at how Muir and Pinchot saw "the public" in "public lands," and whether rivalries such as theirs can sometimes be productive rather than divisive.

Third, and most fascinating, is the way the Muir-Pinchot rivalry mirrors the deeper rivalries that fuel the American character. Americans love to see life through nature-versus-civilization contrasts: country versus town, spontaneity versus planning, heart versus head. We are relentlessly practical innovators who are also among the most religious people in the developed world. We pride ourselves on classlessness but honor inherited wealth. We claim to be outsiders and self-made even when our success relies on insider networks. We crusade for fairness even while hopelessly entangled with self-interest. We hate elitists unless they agree with us. We admire statesmen until they are vilified by our favorite prophets. Our hunger for community is second only to our individualism. Our values are always coming into conflict—sometimes in the form of a person such as Muir versus a person such as Pinchot, and often within our own individual souls.

My visit to Glacier was memorable. I took the official Lake McDonald boat cruise on a perfectly still blue day without a single other craft on the water. Early one morning, avoiding the crowds, I followed Muir's steps to the stunning, glacier-fed Avalanche Lake. I dug through old documents to learn about Lake McDonald in 1896. I camped on the lakeshore and watched the sunset the same way Muir and Pinchot had. I found the joint legacy I had hoped to.

But the story of that legacy ended up bigger than I expected. Where Natural Enemies would have been a sometimes-depressing story of two men's lives and the enduring quarrels they spawned, with *Natural Rivals* I instead discovered the birth of public lands. I hit upon the story of a country founded on seemingly unlimited natural wealth bumping up against those limits, and finding its character in how it responds. I saw it as the story of a society maturing into adulthood, learning to appreciate and balance its profound blessings. It was the story of America, told on and through the lands we collectively own.

NATURAL RIVALS

PART I

NATURAL PROPHET, NATURAL STATESMAN

1
Gramercy Park

When they first met, at an 1893 dinner in a New York City mansion, John Muir and Gifford Pinchot would have struck anybody as almost comically mismatched. The fifty-five-year-old, five-foot-nine Muir had graying, untrimmed hair and a huge, unkempt beard. Sensitive lines surrounded deep-set, kind-looking eyes. He had a gentle, firm self-possession. But he rarely gave much thought to his clothes or grooming, and could almost look like a wayward scrap of the wild frontier. [1]

By contrast, the twenty-seven-year-old Pinchot was six-foot-two and gaunt, barely over 150 pounds. He wore a brushy, well-groomed mustache under a patrician nose and high forehead. At Yale, where he was nicknamed "Apollo," he'd been voted most handsome. He had the cockiness of privilege, but was often quiet, a good listener. [2]

Those differences in appearance represented a genuine gulf in wealth and class. Muir had grown up a poor immigrant. His family moved from Scotland to a farm on the Wisconsin frontier when he was ten years old.

His father, Daniel, an itinerant preacher, made John work hard to clear forests and raise crops, while discouraging John's interests in science and literature. By contrast, Pinchot had been raised a blueblood, in New York City and in Europe. He attended Phillips Exeter, the New Hampshire boys' boarding school. At Yale, he joined Skull and Bones, the elite secret society.

They were raised in different religious traditions: Muir evangelical, Pinchot pious. Daniel Muir was a Campbellite, a sect that later evolved to the Disciples of Christ and Churches of Christ. He took an impossibly strict approach to salvation. To get to heaven, he preached, you needed endless discipline, relentless toil on the farm, and free time devoted solely to Bible study. Stern and humorless, Daniel saw non-religious books or music as frivolities. By contrast, Pinchot's devout mother was descended from Puritans, who saw the individual as less important than God and community. To glorify God, you should live a useful life. Your purpose on Earth wasn't so much about achieving individual salvation—for yourself or others—but about driving yourself to improve others' material conditions. [3]

Muir and Pinchot both led lives shaped by intense relationships with their fathers. In Muir's rebellion, he escaped the farm and rejected Daniel's joyless, workaholic approach to spirituality. John not only embraced science and books, but also spent years performing no visible work at all. By contrast, Pinchot's choices were shaped by his public-spirited father. When Gifford was a teenager, the two of them together decided that he would be a forester, and that they would use the family fortune to help achieve his aims.

Muir's work life was driven by individualism, Pinchot's by community. A self-made man, Muir in his twenties forged a promising career as a solo inventor of machines in factories. Then he became a self-unmade man: in his thirties he tossed all that aside to instead wander in nature. In contrast, Pinchot was a systems thinker who saw how people and organizations fit together. He moved among the rich and powerful—over the course of his life, he would be personally acquainted with every president from Ulysses Grant to Harry Truman. [4] In his circle, it was expected that he would build a career by building networks and systems—and then would continue that career in order to share his expertise and extend the privilege to others.

Muir and Pinchot moved differently across the introvert/extrovert scale. Muir, the self-taught boy from the remote frontier, was at first painfully shy, overwhelmed by society. But gradually he found his voice and became a champion talker. By contrast, Pinchot started out popular and self-confident, engaged in dozens of athletic and social activities in school. But as he aged, he would come to prefer fly-fishing and other solitary pursuits; colleagues would sometimes complain that he could be socially stiff, prone to staring off into the distance.

They had opposing relationships to power. Muir had no interest. He rarely joined institutions or sought prestigious positions, rarely put himself in situations where social status mattered. To the extent that he sought to influence other people, he wanted to do so by telling them stories, inducing rather than commanding them to change. By contrast, Pinchot was ambitious. He wanted to change the world, and wanted to be known for doing so. If that involved emphasizing social status and pursuing powerful jobs—even president of the United States—he would relish the challenge.

There's no end of ways to describe how they differed: Muir was an outsider, Pinchot an insider. Muir had the heart of a poet, Pinchot of a missionary. Muir was the West, Pinchot the East. Muir embodied the amateur tradition, Pinchot the professional. Muir was still stumbling into his life's calling in his fifties, Pinchot had known his since his teens. If not for his boundless charm, Muir's passion could seem self-absorbed and thoughtless; sometimes forgetting to turn on his charm, Pinchot's dedication could seem calculating and egotistical.

But for all their contrasts, they did share one great love: nature. Even here, however, they came from opposite perspectives. Muir saw nature as an expression of divinity, with possibilities to change people's relationships to their God and their inner selves. Pinchot saw nature's resources as a potential source of wealth that, if distributed fairly, could change people's relationships to their outer world.

What happens when two such rivals meet? One might expect that they would fail to connect. Instead, at that dinner, they formed an auspicious bond.

A normal person in John Muir's shoes might have been nervous, on that evening in June of 1893, as he approached the mansion at 2 Gramercy Park with his odd shuffling gait.[5] One of the most prestigious addresses in Manhattan, it was not Muir's world. Granted, Muir often demonstrated fearlessness: He once scaled to the top of a 100-foot Douglas fir tree to rock back and forth in a windstorm. He once slept six nights in a Savannah graveyard, broke, hiding from prowlers, waiting for a packet of money to arrive in the mail. He once lived for three full years in the wilds of Yosemite, spending most of his time on solo journeys through the mountains. But fearlessness in nature doesn't necessarily lead to fearlessness in high society.

The four-story Italianate house near 21st and Lexington was part of America's highest society. It featured a redbrick facade punctuated by floor-to-ceiling parlor windows with elegant cast-iron balconies. The windows looked out on a two-acre park, its trees, shrubs, and flowers now exploding in springtime glory. Unlike most city parks, Gramercy Park was encircled by an eight-foot iron fence. It was private property. Only residents could unlock its gates, using keys of gold.

Even 120 years later, an aficionado defended Gramercy Park's fence as defining "a Ralph Waldo Emerson sort of world."[6] Emerson believed that nature was a philosophical ideal, a contrast to human society, deserving of protection and study. Thus Gramercy Park residents saw their park as the equivalent of an estate's garden—nature as an idealized sanctuary, controlled and protected from the degraded humanity that might walk by. This definition of nature differed greatly from that of John Muir. In the vast Sierra Nevada mountains around Yosemite, Muir's nature was a place of frontier adventure, vast geological forces, and webs of wildlife and habitat.

However, one of Muir's most underappreciated skills was his ability to transcend class differences. During his years of wandering, he'd developed a sort of patronage network across California. Although technically homeless, he never lacked for a place to stay because wealthy people were always inviting him home. They admired his intellect and spirit.

They wanted him to write. Indeed in his forties he married into one such family, gaining a permanent home. Now in his fifties he was in charge of their orchard estate. To feed his soul, he returned as often as possible to Yosemite and other places where nature's presence was overwhelming. Although he often did so alone, he was happy to share those experiences with anybody, of any class.

In 1893, Muir was visiting New York on his way to Scotland, his first trip to his birthplace since he'd left more than forty-four years previously. During a lengthy East Coast stopover, the editor who was publishing his best essays, Robert Underwood Johnson of *The Century* magazine, was parading him around like a VIP. In Boston, Johnson took Muir to visit Emerson's grave and meet Emerson's family, to visit sites of cultural history such as Harvard University and Walden Pond, and to stay at the mansion and gardens of the brilliant horticulturalist Charles Sargent. In New York, Johnson introduced Muir to scientists, writers, other intellectuals, and wealthy patrons. Everywhere Muir was treated as an honored guest.

The treatment surprised Muir, who had not yet published any books, only magazine articles. He wrote to his wife, "Almost every day in town here I have been called out to lunch and dinner at the clubs and soon have a crowd of notables about me. I had no idea I was so well known, considering how little I have written."[7]

James Pinchot, Gifford's father, invited Muir to 2 Gramercy Park as part of this tour. After inheriting a fortune and marrying into a bigger one, James chose to center his identity around art, culture, and intellectual pursuits. He collected paintings, especially those of the Hudson River School, a group of painters who loved to depict the American countryside. James and his wife, Mary, named Gifford after the Hudson River painter Sanford Gifford, a family friend. The Pinchots participated in literary, scientific, and cultural clubs, and especially welcomed dinner guests who could discuss James's passions for forests, plants, and wildlife.[8]

James especially wanted to hear Muir's dog story. Everywhere Muir went on the East Coast, people asked him to tell it—even people who had heard it just a few minutes previously. Muir told stories magnificently. His

Scottish brogue gave his voice a musical lilt. As a child he had absorbed rich, churchy language from his father, and then rich, romantic language from authors such as Robert Burns. Now complex sentences cascaded out of him, one on top of another, filled with extraordinary vocabulary in perfectly elegant form. Muir had developed a rare gift for holding an audience in his hand, keeping them spellbound in his adventures and descriptions. Yet he was humble and curious enough that audiences would rarely find him domineering or tedious. Muir was fluid and charming, humorous and thoughtful, and utterly consumed with the story he was telling. He would forget to eat the food in front of him, and barely notice it being taken away. This sort of small dinner party was peak Muir—in more formal situations, such as delivering a lecture or writing an essay, his inhibitions rose, and he had to work to make his words not sound stilted. [9]

Muir's style offered a contrast with the era's other famous frontier story-teller, William F. "Buffalo Bill" Cody. Buffalo Bill was more performative, flashy, and vulgar; his tales of exploits in nature usually featured horses, Indians, and thundering gunfire—thus he spoke in theaters, to the masses. Muir's stories were more quiet and philosophical, with bigger themes, better suited to the intimacy of an exclusive setting. Which is not to say that lower-class people didn't find Muir's dog story fascinating. As he wrote to his wife, likely referring to the night at Gramercy Park, "When I am telling it at the dinner-tables, it is curious to see how eagerly the liveried servants listen from behind screens, half-closed doors, etc." [10]

The story had a vivid, remote setting: a glacier on the Alaska panhandle, in what is now Glacier Bay National Park. It had a quirky protagonist: Muir himself, setting off to hike the glacier, alone, with no trail and little food or equipment, in the middle of a wild storm. It led to an insight, a firm philosophical conclusion about how the world worked, presented through an exciting narrative with an undeniable moral. And best of all, its true hero was a dog.

Stickeen was a two-year-old mutt with short legs, a huge tail, thin ears, and sharp eyes. His long, silky hair had the black, white, and tan markings of a shepherd dog, though he was only half that size. Muir's friend S. Hall

Young, a Presbyterian missionary stationed on the Stikine River, brought Stickeen on their boat trip north. Muir told Young it was a terrible idea: "This trip is not likely to be good for toy-dogs. The poor silly thing will be in rain and snow for weeks or months, and will require care like a baby." Instead, Stickeen turned out to be a dog version of Muir: independent and contrary. Stickeen wasn't a hunting dog nor one that enjoyed affection; the dog didn't even seem to express much joy, only stubborn determination. For example, Stickeen hated to return to the ship after a land exploration. "When we were ready to start he could never be found, and refused to come to our call," Muir wrote in a version of the tale that he eventually published. Then "as soon as we were fairly off he came trotting down the beach, plunged into the surf, and swam after us, knowing well that we would cease rowing and take him in. . . . We tried to cure him of this trick by compelling him to swim a long way, as if we had a mind to abandon him; but this did no good; the longer the swim the better he seemed to like it."[11]

One day, amid a terrible storm, Muir tried to sneak away before breakfast. To his dismay, Stickeen followed. They hiked three miles upstream along the glacier's edge, then seven miles across the glacier's surface. They continued another few miles uphill along the far edge, then followed a side-glacier to an iceberg-filled lake. It was gorgeous and fascinating and Muir wanted to keep going. But by now the day was waning, the storm was threatening to kick up again, and given the danger of falling into a deep crevasse on top of the ice, he faced an imperative to get back across the main glacier before dark.

Telling the story, Muir took his time to insert plenty of scientific details. In his wanderings through the mountains above Yosemite, he'd studied glaciers and their effects. He came to know more about that science than anyone in the country, and conveyed it in this story. As naturalist John Burroughs later commented, "You ought to hear him tell his dog story. It is one of the few really good dog stories. But you don't want to ask him to tell it unless you have plenty of time. He takes an hour to go through it, and you get the whole theory of glaciation thrown in."[12] Muir was not merely a storyteller, and not merely a scientist, but that rare person who could seamlessly and joyfully merge the two. The written version of the Stickeen story is also full of religious imagery and phrasings that recall the King James Bible. Muir's audiences would expect stories told in that style to have a deep philosophical point, so he was setting them up for his message.

The story then followed Muir and Stickeen on their return journey. Re-crossing the glacier at a different location, they encountered crevasses. At first the gaps were about a foot wide, jumpable. Then the gaps got bigger, requiring a search for a narrow place to cross. Then Muir lost sight of the forests on either side of the glacier. Then it started snowing. He was hungry, his clothes were soaking wet, and each crevasse proved more trying than the last. As a storyteller, Muir ramped up the suspense. Nevertheless, this was not a story about *conquering* nature. Muir did not see natural conditions as a challenge that could prove his worth. Instead nature could offer spiritual insights.

After jumping his biggest crevasse yet—slightly downhill, making it hard to backtrack—Muir realized that he was on an island. The only way off was across a seventy-foot sliver of an ice bridge. The middle of the bridge's span drooped about fifteen feet below its ends, and those ends were secured to the walls about ten feet below the surface. Muir pulled out his ice-axe and leaned over the cliff-edge to build stairs. Then he edged down those stairs and inched across the bridge. As he went, he smoothed its knife-edged top to a flatter surface for foot- and paw-holds. He believed that he got across thanks not to skill or strength but a "power beyond our call or knowledge." He could never recall how exactly he got up the cliff on the other side. "The thing seemed to have been done by somebody else."

For once, Stickeen did not follow. As Muir embarked on the crossing, the dog "looked me in the face with a startled air of surprise and concern." Stickeen seemed to recognize danger. "His looks and tones of voice when he began to complain and speak his fears were so human that I unconsciously talked to him in sympathy as I would to a frightened boy, and in trying to calm his fears perhaps in some measure moderated my own," Muir said. Finally, when Muir reached the other side, the once "silent, philosophic Stickeen" was "moaning and wailing as if in the bitterness of death. . . .

His natural composure and courage had vanished utterly in a tumultuous storm of fear." Finally, breathless with despair, Stickeen edged down the steps. Slowly, steadying against the wind, the dog moved across the bridge. Then in a brave rush, he tore up the cliff to join Muir.

As Stickeen reached safety, Muir said, "Never before or since have I seen anything like so passionate a revulsion from the depths of despair to exultant, triumphant, uncontrollable joy. He flashed and darted hither and thither as if fairly demented, screaming and shouting, swirling round and round in giddy loops and circles like a leaf in a whirlwind." Stickeen still didn't want to be petted or held, but would run from 200 yards away and launch himself at Muir's face. Finally they walked onwards, fortunately encountering no more large crevasses. They made it back to camp before midnight, and Muir silently consumed several bowls of chowder before telling the story for the first time. "Yon's a brave doggie," he began. [13]

Stickeen, lying exhausted on a blanket, wagged his tail.

To Muir, the story disproved mainstream Christians' claims that animals lacked souls or emotions. Although Stickeen was only a dog—and an aloof one at that—in the moment before crossing the bridge, "His voice and gestures, hopes and fears, were so perfectly human that none could mistake them." If animals had emotions, maybe they too were moral beings. Maybe every element of nature was not simply placed there as a resource for people to take advantage of, planted either by a human gardener or a heavenly one. Maybe all elements of nature—even the apparently random and useless elements—were expressions of God. In Muir's Christianity, nature *was* God, and God was nature. To the extent that people were abusing nature, we were abusing God. And to the extent that we alienated ourselves from nature, we alienated ourselves from God.

It was a message after James Pinchot's own heart. James had grown up in Milford, Pennsylvania, on the Delaware River at the New York–New Jersey border. His family fortune had come from cutting down all the forests in the area. James's father would buy a virgin woodland, clear-cut it, float the logs downstream to market, and then dispose of the useless, denuded acreage of stumps. As a child, James joined the logging crews. Since then, he'd come to feel terrible about it, as if he'd murdered these living, wondrous forests. James wanted to use some of the family money to assuage that guilt. He built a mansion in Milford, called Grey Towers, and used it as a philanthropic base. He joined the American Forestry Association, among other groups promoting science and rational politics. And like an overzealous sports dad, James hoped to fully realize his forestry dreams through his oldest son, Gifford.

Gifford was present at the dinner table that night in June 1893, listening to Muir's story. And a normal man in Gifford's position might have been nervous. Yes, Gifford was in his native milieu, at his parents' home. Yes, they were talking about his favorite subjects, outdoor life and natural science. Yes, Gifford often approached knowledgeable older men as potential mentors. But John Muir was beyond the webs of obligation in Pinchot's social circle. He arrived from California like Superman arriving from the Fortress of Solitude.

Furthermore, Gifford was at a difficult point in his relationship with his parents. They had funded him at Exeter and Yale. Then they funded his postgraduate study in Europe. When Gifford returned stateside in 1890, they funded further travel and study. The following year, Gifford landed a good job, preparing a forestry management plan for millionaire George Vanderbilt's grand Biltmore estate in the mountains of North Carolina. It should have been a short gig, a stepping-stone to something greater—but Gifford wasn't making that next step. Indeed, when Muir summarized the dinner for his wife, he didn't mention Biltmore, which was arguably the largest, most ambitious formal forestry project in the nation's history to that date. He said only that the Pinchots' "son is studying forestry."[14] Why didn't James brag about Gifford to the visiting naturalist? Perhaps because he was disappointed in Gifford. James could be as exacting a taskmaster as Daniel Muir was for John—and he always told Gifford that their interests were identical. If Gifford was quiet or sullen during the meal, the pressure of James's expectations may have explained why.[15]

Indeed, the tension between Gifford and his parents that night was heightened by a secret. Gifford was in love—and sure that his parents would not approve. Although his girlfriend Laura Houghteling was beautiful and kind, with an impeccable family background, she was suffering from tuberculosis. The disease had no cure. Once they learned of his love, his parents would naturally be concerned: even if being in her presence didn't infect Gifford, the relationship was likely doomed to an early, unpleasant death. Three months previously, he'd written a letter to his mother that described Laura as a friend: "I have seldom met so sane and straightforward a girl or one with so little foolishness about her."[16] But it would be another four months before he formally revealed the depths of his emotions.

It's hard to know exactly how Gifford acted at the dinner, because his diaries for 1893 later vanished, along with letters to and from Laura.[17] Presumably he didn't say much, or Muir would have remembered him as more than a student. But after the dinner, it was Gifford, not James, who became the main point of contact between Muir and the Pinchots. A few days later, Gifford supplied Muir with letters of introduction to his European friends, for Muir to use in his post-Scotland tour of continental glaciers. And a lengthier letter in September indicates how much the dinner affected Gifford, how much he liked the older man and hoped to learn from him. "Your advice has never gone out of my mind," Gifford wrote.[18]

Muir often advised young men to "get rich"—by which he meant the opposite of accumulating money. Rather, he preached filling the mind and spirit with observations of nature. Gifford told Muir he intended to follow this advice. "This coming winter I hope to do much more 'getting rich' than I have done for several winters past. Especially I want to get into the lumber camps in the Adirondacks and in Michigan."[19]

A lumber camp doesn't quite sound like Muir's natural ideal. Then again, Gifford Pinchot always took his own road. For example, even though he'd been offered a position two years previously in the tiny federal forestry office, he was instead hanging up a shingle as a "Consulting Forester" to private landowners. In Europe, even though everyone had advised him to enroll in a formal two- to five-year graduate program, he had instead dabbled in some courses and interned with leading foresters. Even though the Europeans taught a discipline of *scientific forestry* that created a highly controlled tree plantation, Pinchot instead believed in a yet-to-be-invented American *practical forestry* that wouldn't have so much sterile landscape or top-down structure. So if Pinchot wanted to "get rich" by observing nature in a lumber camp, this was not a rejection of Muir's ideas but an expansion of them. In remixing Muir's advice, he was honoring the original.

Clearly that's how Muir saw it. Upon returning to New York in September, he responded to Pinchot's lumber camp letter with another story, his version of additional advice. Although he enjoyed Europe, Muir reported, it was "so unlike the calm solitudes of nature however that I became very nervous and tired . . . London seemed a desperately lonely and dangerous wilderness to me. The only kind of wilderness I ever feared." Although Pinchot's letter offered him an opportunity to rail against lumber camps, Muir instead railed against a city. His fight was not so much against lumberjacks as against soul-deadening urban life. Nature provided a counterpoint, Muir believed, which was why it needed to be saved. He believed that Pinchot could be an ally in that battle. Pinchot too felt at home in forests and wanted to save them. The following spring, after Pinchot summarized some of his lumber camp experiences as helping him get rich, Muir commended him. "You are choosing the right way into the woods . . . I only regret I cannot join you in your walks."[20]

What made Muir so open to this relationship, so tolerant of Pinchot's alternate view of nature? Why did Muir hate cities more than lumber camps? What did he want from Pinchot? To answer these questions, one must dig more deeply into Muir's life.

2

"Radiate Radiate Radiate"

G iven his talent and complexity, given his remarkable effects on so many aspects of society, John Muir's story can be told in many ways. Politically, one might focus on Yosemite and the principles of national parks, plus his founding of the Sierra Club. Science buffs might prefer details on how his observations overturned geologists' theories about the formation of mountain valleys. In literature, his enthusiastic landscape descriptions and unadorned style of conveying science and emotion shaped the very genre of nature writing. His overall biography—the poor immigrant child of a cruel, distant father who grows into a much-loved leader with a successful family and a rich emotional life characterized primarily by joy—suggests a template for everyone to emulate.

But to a biographer the key question about any individual is: *What did he or she want?* And with Muir the evidence shows that he wanted to bring people to a richer spiritual life through appreciation of the natural world.

Activist, scientist, writer, and wanderer were all offshoots. At his core, he aspired to be a prophet.

In autumn of 1860, aged twenty-two, Muir lived for a few months in Prairie du Chien, Wisconsin, a tiny town on the Mississippi River. He found it pretty, with woods and prairies and limestone hills. He came for an internship with an acclaimed inventor who was about to debut a steam-powered vehicle that ran atop the river's winter ice. But the device quickly proved mechanically faulty, the inventor perhaps a fraud. Meanwhile, in exchange for rent, Muir did chores at a boardinghouse. This was the first time he was living away from home, and he struggled emotionally. He thought a lot about death, and about the dreariness of the career he expected: inventing mechanical devices on factory floors, "in a great smoky shop among devilish men." Muir was moving slowly away from his evangelical upbringing. He had rejected his family's farm as the source of salvation through backbreaking misery—but he still expected misery; he had not yet shed his father's dour judgmentalism.[1]

With irrepressible mechanical genius, Muir spent a lot of time inventing things, including an alarm clock that would automatically light a candle and woodstove before tipping him out of his cot. He felt homesick and lonely, "adrift on this big sinning world," he wrote. Socially, a friend called him "clumsy looking." Although Prairie du Chien was a small town that had failed to boom as expected after the railroad arrived, it felt almost urban compared to the remote Muir family homestead. The boardinghouse residents included several schoolteachers and a lawyer, as well as the innkeeper's orphaned niece, Emily Pelton, who was about Muir's age and single. Every week they gathered in the parlor for an intellectual discussion; although Muir occasionally attended, he almost never spoke. He went on long walks with Emily, but was painfully shy. He felt more comfortable interacting with the innkeeper's wife and her infant. He did find himself whistling while doing chores and tried to figure that must mean he was happy.[2]

At the boardinghouse's 1860 Thanksgiving celebration, the rich meal centered on turkey, which Muir ate only reluctantly. (Throughout his life, he had a famously small appetite—he could hike for days on a few crusts of bread.) After dinner, almost everyone played parlor games, such as blindman's buff. These were not risqué games, merely frivolous, although there may also have been dancing, kissing, or other public displays of relatively chaste affection. Prudish Muir refused to participate in any of them. Indeed, he expressed disappointment that a normally dignified Bible salesman joined in the silliness. When others tried to get Muir to lighten up, he quoted Proverbs 1:10 to them: "If sinners entice thee, consent thou not." He later reported to his sister and brother-in-law, "It was taken very gravely and caused an apology next day. I have a great character here for sobriety."[3]

He made that claim with some pride, as if he saw his presence in Prairie du Chien as bearing witness to right living. He was demonstrating the power of spiritual discipline to the folks of this small village with its reputation for feverish swamps and lousy churches. In other words, he was offering unsolicited spiritual advice—preaching. And like his uncompromising father, who gloried in misery more than love or forgiveness, Muir would happily scold those around him when they didn't live up to God's standards. A few years later, chastened, he wrote to Emily about the days "when I used to hurl very orthodox denunciations at all things morally or religiously amiss in old or young. It appears strange to me that you should all have been so patient with me."[4]

They likely saw a gentle soul making his first forays into the wider world, learning the hard way about the folly of his father's grim approach. Responding to Muir's letter describing Thanksgiving, his brother-in-law encouraged him to relax into the realization that he would someday grow and love. "I guess you have not yet felt that inexpressible something, or you would never call those sinners who play at blind man's buff, or who so far cast off all natural coldness and sullenness to kiss each other promiscuously," he wrote—and then showed Muir how to turn Christian principles into real-life forgiveness. "I will not at this time censure you for your stiffness for I know you are bashful and I spare you."[5]

In the coming years Muir became less sullen and judgmental. He rejected the joyless faith of his father, with its insistence that the only rewarding life was one of unrewarded toil. He became far better at expressing ideas in his own words, rather than those of the Old Testament—and he learned to express those ideas as stories, rather than slinging quotes like daggers. But he never lost a core insistence that spiritual quests were more worthy than flirty games. He eventually reached a key insight about himself—that he would be most fulfilled when he could appreciate God through the wonders of nature—and so he lived to bear witness about that insight to the rest of the world. He may have replaced his father's brutal dogma with a gentler, more modern one, but he retained the evangelical attitude. An individual's purpose here on earth, he believed, was to show other individuals how to rise to a higher spiritual plane.

Over the next six years Muir rejected a great deal. He enrolled at the University of Wisconsin, denying his father's creed that farm toil was more worthy than education. Soon he departed for Canada, refusing to enroll in the Union Army for the Civil War, rejecting war itself. In a remote Ontario village, he invented a machine to make broom handles, turning away from the university-based life of the mind to instead favor the hands-on engineering of a millwright. Although he lived in a small cabin with four young adults, including a single female, he found his most rewarding experiences walking alone in the woods—you might say that he rebuffed the possibility of romantic love, substituting nature for sex. And he was still trying to reject the formal structures of his religious upbringing, substituting nature for church.

In 1866 the broom-handle factory burned down, and Muir moved back to the United States. He eventually found a job at an Indianapolis wagon-wheel factory, where he vowed to make his mark as an inventor—but refused to patent his inventions, believing they should be given freely to mankind. He boarded with devout Christian families and befriended children. He was gentle and trustworthy and inspired people's generosity, but even at age twenty-eight he seemed lost, adrift in the world. Then came the blindness.

In March 1867, while Muir was engaged in routine belt maintenance on one of the factory's circular saws, a file slipped and flew into his right eye. When he opened his eyelid, goop dripped into his hand. Soon the eye went blind. Then, in sympathy, so did the other one. For a man who had received so much joy from looking at flowers and plants, from reading, from sketching, and from inventions whose design required visual acuity, blindness was devastating. It turned out to be temporary—after a few weeks his sight was restored. But the incident caused Muir to forsake his career in industry, to reject living in cities and accepting societal expectations. He vowed to instead devote himself fully to the study of nature.

Why so many rejections? Muir's personality involved polarities, and constant switching between them: from bashful to gregarious, from industrial inventor to nature-lover, from solitary wanderer to child-loving family man, from forgiving soul to opinionated rabble-rouser, from scientist to mystic. Thus he continually made wholesale rejections and then walked them back. He gave up on organized religion but later tried to attend church. He moved away from his family but throughout his life offered them profound support. He renounced farm life but would later own an orchard, derided cities but would almost always winter near them, frowned on book-learning but wrote books, didn't care for politics but would become an activist. Biographer Stephen Fox says that although Muir, especially late in life, liked to portray himself as driven by an insatiable hunger for wilderness, in fact he "neither loved wilderness nor hated civilization as much as he claimed." Rather, he was driven by tensions in his personality, "between people and nature, civilized constraints and wild freedom, love and loneliness. . . . The recurrent alternation of freedom and restraint made each seem all the more vivid by contrast." And because American society as a whole mirrored these tensions, Muir's attempts to work them out for himself became his greatest form of bearing witness. [6]

"There is nothing more eloquent in Nature than a mountain stream," Muir wrote, "and this is the first I ever saw." It was September 12, 1867, and he was on the Emory River in east Tennessee. Muir eventually became so associated with California mountains that it's a bit surprising to realize he was a flatlander until age twenty-nine, when as an itinerant amateur botanist he first ascended Tennessee's Cumberland Plateau. He had committed to explore South America, emulating the explorer-naturalist Alexander von Humboldt, but for the first leg of his journey he decided to walk across the American South. It was a slightly crazy notion, for a Yankee to wander unarmed through defeated territory just two years after the end of the war. He may have been influenced by the experiences of Alexander Campbell, the Scottish-born American preacher who had converted Muir's father to his teachings. Campbell had found God in the sublime landscapes of the Appalachian uplands, and even as Muir rejected the Campbellites, he shadowed their geography. [7]

Especially early on his walk, Muir enjoyed arguing with people he encountered, mostly about religion. For example, a blacksmith who gave Muir lodging and food commented over dinner that hard times required hard work from everybody, and "picking up blossoms" didn't seem to qualify. Muir replied, "You are a believer in the Bible, are you not?" and then lectured him on King Solomon's passion for botanizing, and Jesus's instructions to "Consider the lilies how they grow"—that the spiritual grace of the lilies' beauty excused them from toil. He concluded, "Now, whose advice am I to take, yours or Christ's?" [8]

In that era, arguments about religion were common. In the Scotland of Muir's birth, various Protestant sects engaged in continuous verbal skirmishes about their rival Biblical interpretations. Because religion in Scotland was state-sponsored, the stakes were bigger there, but even after the Muir family emigrated to America in 1849, the belligerent tradition remained. Religion meant so much to the Muirs that John's rejection of his father's interpretations became his central preoccupation, applied in intense, searching quarrels with both himself and everyone he met. In his best moments, he could approach the issues playfully. And in this case, his host was not offended. It was one of many sharp but amiable disagreements that would characterize Muir's friendships throughout his life.

Through east Tennessee, as Muir gained elevation, he entered relatively undeveloped territory, a woodsy frontier. He also encountered new kinds of plants and became entranced by them. For example, on the Emory River near Wartburg, overhanging trees shaded a streambank decorated with wildflowers. On a hot midday in late summer, he found the spot "one of Nature's coolest and most hospitable places. Every tree, every flower, every ripple and eddy of this lovely stream seemed solemnly to feel the presence of the great Creator."[9]

Muir carried three books on his walk: Robert Burns's poetry, the New Testament, and John Milton's *Paradise Lost*. He was rebelling against society, but not rejecting the Christian God. Rather, unlike many of his contemporaries, he saw God in nature. Before he left on this walk, Muir's mother had made him promise that he would never sleep outside, because she shared a common view that untamed nature was dangerous. But Muir regularly violated this oath. Sometimes Southerners were too suspicious of his motives to offer lodging, and sometimes he simply found glory in "the one great bedroom of the open night."[10]

On the Emory, Muir studied two types of fern that he had never seen in the North. He described in his journal a species of magnolia tree and noted the presence of oaks, laurels, azaleas, and asters. He "spent some joyous time in a grand rock-dwelling full of mosses, birds, and flowers." This was what made him happy: observing and studying a glorious natural site. So he kept walking. He didn't linger in this grand natural setting, because he expected to find other lands equally enthralling. And although he wouldn't make it to South America until his old age, the following year he discovered his ideal natural spot: the California Sierra.

Muir is often classified with Transcendentalist philosophers like Ralph Waldo Emerson and Henry David Thoreau. Transcendentalists believed in the inherent goodness of people and nature, the corrupting influence of society, and thus the need for individuals to be self-reliant to achieve purity. Muir did share that general philosophy, but his curious encounter with Emerson demonstrates the fascinating route he took to get there.

Muir had heard of Emerson during his studies at the University of Wisconsin, but hadn't read much of the older man's work. In college, Muir was fascinated by science and technology, where the Transcendentalists were poets and theologians, romantics. Emerson defined the essential American conflict as between Nature—a word that he and Muir always capitalized, to suggest its divinity—and the city, between "forest and town, spontaneity and calculation, heart and head, the unconscious and the self-conscious, the innocent and the debauched."[11] Emerson looked down on people's materialistic behavior and also on brainy utilitarian systems to combat that behavior. Yet Nature to Emerson was more of a theological ideal than a place of rocks and trees. Emerson's disciple Thoreau had more resembled Muir, with his love of natural settings, solitude, and technology, and his desire to show by example that a life need not be full of quiet desperation. Thoreau—who died in 1862, before he and Muir could meet—differed from Muir in that he didn't really like people. Thoreau went to Walden Pond to get away from bourgeois society; Muir went to Yosemite to be inspired by geology and trees.

In spring 1871, Emerson took a vacation in California. After visiting San Francisco, the sixty-eight-year-old and his entourage detoured to a seven-year-old park in the mountains: Yosemite. By railroad, then stage-coach, then mule, they approached through a forest of huge sugar pines. "These trees," Emerson proclaimed, "have a monstrous talent for being tall." According to a companion, Emerson spent much of the trip issuing such epigrams. Emerson was likely suffering from aphasia that hampered his ability to formulate sentences. He thus rarely spoke, which gave his few utterances the feeling of summary pronouncements.[12]

The Emerson party entered Yosemite's broad valley floor and saw meadows of wildflowers fringed by oaks, maples, and pines, and backed by stunning cliffs. The setting likely felt familiar to Emerson: the Yosemite Valley looked like a scene from *Paradise Lost*. Although poet John Milton never saw Yosemite—he was an Englishman who died in 1674—his book painted a vivid image of Paradise, with waterfalls and a river meandering through flowery meadows below steep cliffs and thick forests, all shining in a magical light that symbolized God's presence. *Paradise Lost* remained popular in America two centuries after its publication in part because it so effectively summarized the Puritan world view—but in part because of its lush descriptions of scenery, flowers, colors, and smells. Emerson loved Milton, and once referred to *Paradise Lost*'s "lofty images." And those descriptions, made by a blind poet about a landscape so wonderful that humans did not deserve to live there, bore a remarkable resemblance to this remote California valley. Especially after the difficult approach, which resembled a pilgrimage, some people literally described Yosemite as "the original Garden of Eden."[13]

Emerson might also have felt comfortable in Yosemite because, in that pre-automobile era, the valley's meadows, lakes, and trails resembled the city parks of Boston's Emerald Necklace. No surprise: the designer of those parks, Frederick Law Olmsted, had also been deeply influenced by Milton. But where the boundaries of a city park marked an encroaching corrupt human society, beyond Yosemite's placid meadows and streams were rugged, wild cliffs and mountaintops. This was a paradise even beyond what Olmsted could create.[14]

Emerson's party checked into a hotel with a view of the great Yosemite waterfall, half a mile in height, mist sprinkling in the breeze. The next day they lazed on the shores of Mirror Lake, with its reflection of Half Dome ruffled by the wind. "This valley," Emerson pronounced, "is the only place that comes up to the brag about it, and exceeds it."

They spent two more days appreciating the valley. On their third day, Emerson received an admiring, enthusiastic letter at the hotel. "Dear Sir I rec'd to-day a letter from Mrs. Prof. E. Carr of Oakland Cal. stating that you were in the valley . . ." John Muir was introducing himself. One of Muir's Wisconsin mentors, Jeanne Carr, had known Emerson in her youth. She'd recently moved to California, and although she failed to connect with Emerson in San Francisco, she wrote to Muir tell him of Emerson's impending Yosemite visit. She wrote Emerson as well, to urge a meeting; she was sure they would get along. However, in introducing himself to Emerson, Muir couldn't resist the urge to preach. Having heard that the party would depart in a day or two, Muir wrote, "Do not thus drift away with the mob while the spirits of these rocks and waters hail you."[15]

Muir's walk across the South had ended with something of a whimper on the Florida coast, the naturalist bedridden for months with malaria-like symptoms. His body rejected the subtropical climate. Eventually finding a cheap boat fare to San Francisco, Muir quickly headed for mountain streams. Arrriving in Yosemite in 1868, he saw "noble walls . . . all a-tremble with the thunder tones of the falling water" and "sunny meadows here and there, and groves of pine and oak; the river of Mercy sweeping in majesty through the midst of them and flashing back the sunbeams." [16] He did some work as a sheepherder and millwright, but spent most of his time wandering the mountains, collecting botanical specimens, and observing the geology. The neighbors found him eccentric if harmless. They might listen to his odd scientific and religious theories, but had no idea what to do with them.

Emerson, Muir expected, would understand him. Emerson was widely known as not only America's greatest intellect but also a kind-hearted man. Now that Muir had become more fascinated by philosophy than technology, Emerson might well match his spiritual-intellectual passions. "I invite you to join me in a month[']s worship with Nature in the high temples of the great Sierra crown," Muir wrote. [17]

The next day Emerson stopped by Muir's bird's-nest apartment above the sawmill. Muir called their meeting one of the supreme moments of his life. He felt Emerson radiating a shining presence, an Olympian composure, and a sense of inhabiting eternity. Muir's shyness fell away. He laid all of his treasures at Emerson's feet: his plant collections, pencil sketches, and rocks. [18]

Of course Emerson didn't want any of that stuff. He sidestepped the offer by claiming he'd rather bring his friends to see it all onsite. Nor did Emerson have any intention of spending a month sleeping on the hard Sierra ground—although blame ended up falling on the others in Emerson's party, whom Muir forever saw as "full of indoor philosophy, fail[ing] to see the natural beauty and fullness of promise of my wild plan." But Emerson did repeatedly return to Muir's apartment to listen to Muir talk. He invited Muir to accompany his party for part of their journey back to

San Francisco. On the way, they detoured south of Yosemite Valley to visit the Mariposa Grove of five hundred giant sequoias, many of them more than twenty feet in diameter. Amid the trees' mind-blowing immensity, Emerson pronounced, "The wonder is that we can see these trees and not wonder more."[19]

Although disappointed that Emerson didn't stay longer, Muir appreciated the great gift he'd been given. Emerson did understand. Emerson gave tacit blessing to Muir's entire philosophical outlook. During the eleven years before Emerson's death, the two men corresponded periodically. Emerson advised that once Muir was ready to end his solitary sojourn, he should come to Concord, where Emerson vaguely promised that Muir would be able to follow in his footsteps. Of course Muir didn't want any of that—a settled, Eastern, university life. Rather than try to politely sidestep the invitation, he argued strenuously about it.

Muir also started the catching-up process of reading Emerson's essays. Based on the comments Muir wrote in the books' margins, it was clear that he was going to take his own path rather than simply accept the master's teachings. For example, alongside Emerson's sentence, "The squirrel hoards nuts, and the bee gathers honey, without knowing what they do," Muir wrote, "How do we know this?" And alongside Emerson's declaration that a "disappointment is felt in every landscape" Muir wrote, "No—always we find more than we expect."[20]

In autumn of 1877, the thirty-nine-year-old Muir made one of his typically epic solo journeys, full of polarized swings between sociability and solitude. In September, he spent five weeks in a twenty-six-room Italianate mansion owned by his friends John and Annie Bidwell in the Northern California city of Chico. The Bidwells wanted him to stay all winter, toiling quietly on essays about his experiences in nature. For six years now, he'd published in magazines and newspapers, with enough success to pay his expenses—which were minimal because he had no home. Between excursions he typically boarded with well-to-do families like the Bidwells.[21]

For some people, wilderness appreciation is a phase of youth, followed by a settling-down. But Muir didn't go through phases, he bounced between the polar opposites of his personality. He loved nature, but he also loved people, whom he saw as separate from nature. Ideally he could unite them—"I care to live only to entice people to look at Nature's loveliness," he wrote Jeanne Carr in 1874—but even that would require him to alternate between looking at nature and looking at the people he hoped to convert to admiring it. [22]

Torn between writing and adventure, Muir looked from the Bidwells' mansion to the Sacramento River a few miles west. He wanted to escape, to float this long river southward through California's central valley. So the Bidwells' carpenter built him a wooden, flat-bottomed skiff, which they loaded with provisions. After launching into a river clogged with sandbars and snags (stuck logs), Muir christened the boat *Snagjumper*. He floated past 100 miles of farmland that he later remembered as once resembling a "bed of golden and purple flowers. Now it is ploughed and pastured out of existence."[23] Then at Sacramento he abandoned the skiff to head for the mountains. He took a train 200 miles south to Visalia, then hiked the Middle Fork of the Kings River, full of furious whitewater and steep granite cliffs. The landscape was so intimidating and impenetrable that it was previously believed to be utterly inaccessible. In twelve days of rock-hopping and swimming, the last four days without food, Muir proved that belief wrong. Then he built another raft himself, out of old twisted fence rails. The *Snagjumper II* floated him 250 miles down the Merced and San Joaquin Rivers to Martinez. Here, the water eased into a series of tidal estuaries on the northeast edge of San Francisco Bay. Discarding the raft, Muir walked through a mixture of pines, palms, live oaks, and brown grassy foothills up the valley of Alhambra Creek.

Poised between the fog of the coast and the heat of the central valley, the Martinez area had served as a way station for Gold Rush miners and perhaps as the birthplace of the martini. Today it's known for its oil refineries. In 1877, with less than 875 residents, it was still remarkably undeveloped. Rail access to Berkeley and Oakland had been slowed by rugged hills. The Spanish called it *Arroyo del Hambre*, valley of hunger, because they found little game. The first prominent white settlers, John and Louisiana Strentzel, renamed it the Alhambra Valley after the romantic castle in southern Spain.

The Strentzels were part of Muir's patronage network. Their Dutch Colonial mansion was Muir's destination that November day. John Strentzel, born into wealth in Poland and trained as a doctor, had curly white hair and a long, sculpted beard. He and his wife arrived in Martinez in 1853 and developed a notable fruit-growing operation, featuring Muscat grapes, quinces, walnuts, peaches, pears, plums, oranges, lemons, and apricots. Strentzel won accolades for his wines and helped pioneer the California raisin industry. As railroads finally hooked Martinez to the outside world, he was able to profitably ship his varied fruits nationwide. Although Strentzel's land was often referred to as a *ranch*, he himself was called a *fruit grower* rather than a rancher or farmer, to reflect the upper-class nature of his managerial toil. Constant experimentation with varieties was more horticulture than farming, more science than soil-work. He planted one thousand varieties of trees, and wrote and lectured on his research. Strentzel and Muir thus shared an appreciation for the intersection of science and nature, which meant that they could talk for hours on end.

On his arrival in November 1877, Muir wore a faded green coat tattered at the elbows and wrists. He likely hadn't washed after his long trip. His hair hung down to his shoulders. His long beard was likely matted. He looked like something of a mountain man, someone who never heeded civilized approaches to refinement.

This occasion certainly would have been an opportunity to present himself attractively, if he had known how to do so. The Strentzels had an eligible, unmarried daughter, as Muir well knew. His friend Jeanne Carr had already tried to set him up with her. Louisa "Louie" Strentzel was educated and well-read, Christian but liberal-minded, a concert pianist, a nature-lover, and a suffragist. She helped manage the orchard—including bookkeeping and finances—and was also its sole heir. Although sometimes referred to as plain-faced, she was not unattractive, with dark hair, dark eyes, and small, even features. The fact that she was still unmarried in her late twenties was usually attributed to her lack of interest in spending much time away from home; the isolation of the Alhambra Valley limited the available suitors of sufficient education and class.

Or was there something more? The relationship of John and Louie Muir is a great puzzle of history. Even on this visit, Muir presented little evidence of noticing her. After being invited to stay for a rich Thanksgiving meal—indeed, invited to stay as long as he wanted—he walked to Oakland and told a friend about the food and his discussions with Dr. Strentzel, and the friend finally had to ask him, "Did you by chance observe a young lady about the house?"

"Well, yes," he had to acknowledge, "there was a young lady there."[24]

Muir scholars have debated what the marriage meant to John: in one view, he was never much attracted to Louie, and when he finally married her in 1880, it was not for love but for money, security, some level of intellectual companionship, and children. "I was married last April," he wrote to one friend, neglecting to say anything about his bride, "and now I have a fixed camp where I can store [specimens]."[25] In another view, he started out bashful, but joyfully grew into the role of loving, devoted husband and father. And yet the question could be reversed as well: Was Louie ever really attracted to this wild-looking mountain man? Or did she marry a family friend for security, some level of intellectual companionship, and children?

Either way, what's equally interesting is Muir's reaction to the Strentzels and their home. He didn't demand, as he had with Emerson, that the family spend a month with him in the wild Sierra. He still loved Yosemite, but after three years living there fulltime, he had found that the other pole of his personality needed sociability and intellectual connection. For the rest of his life he would only visit Yosemite, always living closer to civilization. His marriage demonstrated a peace he made with human society: he acknowledged that access to unfettered nature, while essential, was just one component of a well-lived life.

In other words, he chose to segregate human society from wilderness, often-sinful people from a natural Garden of Eden. To Muir, connection with nature brought fulfillment. If you were unfulfilled, Muir unequivo-cally prescribed more nature. If you were fulfilled—as the Strentzels were, even though their forays into nature were largely limited to the Alhambra Valley—then no prescription was needed. Muir was fulfilled as well, and was open to having a rich relationship full of mutual respect.

By accepting that people didn't need 100 percent nature, Muir accepted that landscapes too did not need to be preserved everywhere in a natural state. Muir had no problem with the way the Strentzels, and before them the Spanish, had converted this dry valley of grasses and oaks to the pur-poses of commerce. Indeed in the 1880s, as Muir took over management from his father-in-law, he proved to be a prudent, canny, and successful fruit-grower.

Muir was not a solitary ascetic. He did always need wild places: he con-tinued to love Yosemite, and the rest of the California Sierra; he frequently visited Alaskan glaciers and made many trips to natural wonders around the world. But the image many people have today of Muir as someone who lived only in the wilderness is based primarily on a romantic vision he cultivated in his old age.[26] By contrast, most of his days were spent in everyday landscapes that he was content to see manipulated into farms, towns, reservoirs, and cities to fulfill obvious human needs. Living in civi-lization made him a better advocate for Yosemite, but it didn't make him a *local* activist. Today's question of how to live "sustainably" with nature didn't engage him. For example, on his excursions, he never collected pine nuts or berries; he simply lived off bread that he brought from home.

His choices implied a distinction: certain extraordinary landscapes pro-vided humans with deeper benefits of spiritual enlightenment, and thus deserved to be treated differently than everyday landscapes. What exactly made for an extraordinary landscape? Muir never published any inventories or definitions, because he wasn't interested in policy. He was interested in individual salvation. To him, the greater priority was telling stories about how those extraordinary places could make a person feel.

Standing on the summit of Washington's Mount Rainier, on August 14, 1888, fifty-year-old John Muir suggested that his enthusiasms for nature had run amok. "I didn't mean to climb it," he wrote Louie, "but got excited and soon was on top."[27]

That was his wry humor at work: climbing a 14,410-foot peak that had been summited only a few times previously required great planning. Comparing it to the other Northwest volcanoes—Mounts Baker, St. Helens, and Hood—Muir once wrote that Rainier "surpasses them all in height and massive grandeur—the most majestic solitary mountain I have ever yet beheld."[28]

Muir in 1888 had a contract with a publisher to compile a serialized, illustrated book on nature's beauty. It offered him an excuse to travel: from Martinez in the Alhambra Valley, he headed north with his closest friend, painter William Keith. Muir and Keith were both Scotsmen born in 1838, devoted to each other, and constantly sparring. "Those who know them best are convinced that the tie that binds their hearts together is the difference between their similarities," the *San Francisco Call* later wrote. "Mr. Muir is convinced in his heart of hearts that Mr. Keith cannot paint a true picture and Keith is sure Muir is all wrong in his glacial theories." The newspaper quoted Muir confronting Keith: "Why in the deuce don't you imitate nature? You'll never paint a decent picture till you can do that." On this trip, they visited California's Lake Tahoe and Mount Shasta, Oregon's Columbia River, and Washington's Puget Sound. In Seattle, Muir assembled a team of nine mountaineers and arranged for a guide who had ascended Rainier once before.[29]

Muir had a genius for combining recreation and work, spirituality and science. Clearly this trip was great fun, a vacation from his orchard and family obligations. Yet it was also work, research to be written up to fulfill a publishing contract. As always for Muir, his work proselytized for nature, encouraging people to gain a deeper, more spiritual relationship with the natural world. And yet his path to that spiritual fulfillment involved intense scientific observation of unusual snowfields and plants, both of which were abundant on Rainier's little-explored high slopes.

The plants led to a note in *Garden and Forest* magazine, which called Muir a "well-known student of the Cordilleran glaciers."[30] The magazine, which was founded in that same year of 1888, was the brainchild of eminent horticulturalist Charles Sprague Sargent, who knew so much about trees that he was compiling a fourteen-volume encyclopedia, *Silva of North America.*

Sargent directed Harvard University's Arnold Arboretum, an outdoor museum of plantings designed for botanical research. Although Sargent's interest was strictly scientific, the Arboretum, in the Jamaica Plain neighborhood of Boston, was also part of Olmsted's Emerald Necklace of Boston city parks. As a human-designed space, with plants manipulated to serve human needs, an arboretum resembled a private garden. However, Sargent also wanted to learn about plants in their natural settings. That's why he used part of his family fortune to start *Garden and Forest*: to contextualize the Arboretum's botanical research with field reports.

Sargent was a chilly man, heavyset and imperious, bearded, with a strong chin and nose. As a Harvard student he'd been undistinguished—eighty-eighth in a class of ninety, and without any study of botany—but when he got the opportunity to run the Arboretum, he succeeded through single-minded determination. Sargent spent most of his waking hours either studying plants or reading and writing about them. He was the sort of long-term strategist who negotiated a thousand-year lease between Harvard and the city—with an option to renew for another thousand years. He was well-bred, with a quiet charm, but his Boston Brahmin reserve meant that he preferred scholarship to people. As an heir to a banking fortune, he was economically conservative, generally opposed to government overextension. But he saw forests in crisis. He worried that as America eradicated its forests, it was dooming unusual plants to extinction. Thus Sargent and his magazine advocated for strict restrictions on forest development. Without government interference, he once wrote, "I don't see how our mountain forests can be saved from entire extermination." For five years now he had been urging the federal government to establish "forest reserves" in ecologically valuable places such as Mount Rainier. At the moment, Rainier was still open to homesteading; Muir encountered settlers cutting and burning the forest to provide meadows for their cows. [31]

Muir and Sargent were natural allies, given their formidable intellects and shared passion for plants. Indeed, after they met in person in 1893, they proved to be good friends, even traveling together for large parts of a round-the-world tour in 1903–04. But their outlooks and temperaments differed violently: Muir tattered and unpretentious, Sargent ponderous and formal; Muir enthusiastic and spiritual, Sargent reserved and pedantic. From Sargent's wealthy youth overseeing luxurious gardens, he had learned that people could improve on the randomness of nature; Muir's poor youth toiling on a homestead caused him to revere nature without man's input. When traveling, Sargent marched, seeing only trees and plants; Muir wandered, investigated, and lingered, seeing God. Approaching nature, Sargent the scholar sought knowledge, classification, and control; Muir the prophet sought opportunities for spiritual wonder. They personified societal rivalries in approaches to nature—although theirs was not the only rivalry in the small community of nature lovers.

In sum, this was the John Muir who encountered Pinchot in 1893: one whose remarkable journey was about finding the right way into the woods—his own right way. Muir rejected his obligations to family and society because he needed to find a path that led to his own fulfillment rather than somebody else's.

In his letter to Pinchot in June 1894, when Muir said, "You are choosing the right way into the woods," he added, "Happy man. Never will you regret a single day spent thus. . . . You have a grand future before you, and a grand present." In the rest of the letter, Muir implied that Pinchot needed to expand his horizons: less ambition, more spirituality; less Pennsylvania ravine, more expansive forest; fewer textbooks, more travel; less politics, more literature. [32]

Likewise, in another letter that spring, Muir wrote, "Yours must be not merely a successful but a glorious life." Pinchot had invited him to come to Grey Towers and stay as long as he wanted, and even to use Pinchot's stenographer to help with his writing. Muir's response playfully called Grey Towers a "cottage in the hills." He said Pinchot was fortunate to have the Biltmore estate in North Carolina as a center. But he didn't want those mansions to limit Pinchot. Muir may have been reading Walt Whitman, or maybe his exuberance that day just happened to match that of the famous poet, for he wrote, "Radiate radiate radiate far and wide as the lines of latitude and longitude on the globe."[33]

In some ways Muir too had a grand, radiating future ahead of him: in 1894, he assembled his first monograph, *The Mountains of California*, from previously published essays. His tally later grew to more than a dozen books, plus congressional legislation, Sierra Club lobbying, and a national monument named in his honor while he was still alive.[34] Yet in other ways, over those last twenty years of his life, Muir's horizons were shrinking. His ambition led him to politics, and politics led him to betrayal. Although his battle over Yosemite's Hetch Hetchy dam blazed a path into the woods that would be followed by generations of environmentalists, it would lead the man himself away from fulfillment.

3

The Tragedy of John Muir

In June 1889, the fifty-one-year-old John Muir camped at his favorite spot in the Tuolumne Meadows of California's High Sierra. The site was called Soda Springs because carbonated mineral water bubbled out of the ground. Nearby, a granite dome caught the early sunrise. At 8,600 feet, far above Yosemite Valley, the gentle Tuolumne Meadows nurtured meandering creeks under views of evergreen hillsides and distant snowy peaks. In spring, some of the grassy meadows were boggy with snowmelt, others exploding with wildflowers. Muir later wrote that the meadows made for "charming sauntering-grounds from which the glorious mountains may be enjoyed as they look down in divine serenity over the dark forests that clothe their bases."[1]

On this trip, Muir was accompanied by magazine editor Robert Underwood Johnson, who had come to California in search of stories. Johnson was a large, imposing man with a full brown beard and pince-nez glasses. Then thirty-six years old, the well-mannered but exacting Indiana native was second-in-command at *The Century* magazine. It was a *New Yorker* of its day, which paid top rates to well-known writers such as Mark Twain and Henry James. It endorsed Progressive causes, highlighting the changes that industrialization had brought to society and the need for the government to respond to those changes in the public interest. Johnson, who greatly appreciated parks and other outdoor attractions, drove the magazine's Progressive stance on nature, including an endorsement of botanist Charles Sargent's call for a commission to draw up a national forestry plan. On causes he supported, Johnson often augmented his editorial efforts with lobbying in Washington, D.C.

Johnson was visiting California because he wanted to publish a history of the gold rush. Meanwhile, he could finally meet in person with his regular correspondent Muir. That meeting came when Johnson was dressing for dinner in his room at San Francisco's Palace Hotel. The front desk announced that Muir had arrived, and Johnson suggested he come up to the room. Johnson wrote, "After an unusually long wait, when I was about to inquire what was the matter, I heard a voice away down the corridor calling out, 'Johnson, Johnson! where are you?'" Muir complained about "these confounded artificial canyons," implying that he was easily lost in palace corridors. [2]

They talked for three hours that night, and made arrangements to meet again. At the orchard in Martinez, Muir's wife Louie encouraged Johnson to get Muir to write more. Then the two men left on a two-week-long trip to Yosemite. When they arrived at the main valley, Johnson found it thrilling. The experience put him "continually in a state between awe and rapture," rendering this man of words nearly speechless. Muir pointed out that in the past decade, the once-bucolic Yosemite Valley had become increasingly overrun by development: saloons, lumberyards, butcher shops, a pigsty, ramshackle hotels, acres of tree stumps and weeds, and piles of tin cans. The valley had been set aside as a state park, but the parklike atmosphere that had entranced Emerson was now degraded, because the state governed too loosely. Johnson was soon convinced that "the treatment of the floor of the valley should have been put in the hands of the very best experts" in making attractive places, rather than be subjected to the lazy oversight of the state's political appointees. Progressivism stood for not merely government control, but control by scientists and managers insulated from tawdry day-to-day politics. [3]

Muir and Johnson hurried to hire mules and a cook and get out of the valley and into the high country. The mountains weren't protected as part of the state park—they were *public domain* lands administered by the federal government because they had not yet been claimed by homesteaders. But between their remote location and harsh weather, the mountains were so little used that Muir and Johnson could perceive them as being closer to wild, untouched nature than the state park was.

At the Soda Springs site, Muir and Johnson settled into beds of spruce boughs around a campfire. Alpenglow lit the peaks around them. Every night Muir would arrange Johnson's blankets, as if tucking a child into bed. Muir continually told stories: his arduous boyhood, his pleasure at discovering the world of plants and trees, his walk across the South, and his years of living in Yosemite Valley before it was much developed. "Muir loved this region as a mother loved a child," Johnson wrote, and he could see why. Falling asleep by the campfire, the city-dwelling Johnson felt like he was "on top of the world under the biggest stars I have ever seen." Waking to a sunrise that felt like a "revelation of glory," he was getting rich. [4]

One day they hiked down the Tuolumne River as it dropped out of the meadows northwest into a canyon. Johnson thought Muir resembled the Donatello sculpture of John the Baptist, raggedy-haired, clothed in a shaggy hide, with a fiercely admonishing expression. Muir leaped from rock to rock like a mountain goat, teasing his younger companion as a tenderfoot. But Muir later rewarded Johnson with the revelation that few others had made it so far down the gorge, had seen these splendid rock contours.

Far below them, the river cascaded into a peaceful valley floor, a heavenly setting similar to that of the main Yosemite Valley. This valley was isolated and remote, twenty miles northwest of the original. Most people called it "Hetch Hetchy," a mispronunciation of a Central Miwok word for a plant that indigenous people were harvesting there when the first white man came along. Muir instead often called it the "Tuolumne Yosemite."[5]

One night at the Soda Springs campfire, Johnson asked about one of Muir's previous *Century* articles, which had described Sierra meadows twenty years previously, when wildflowers grew tall and untouched to the breast of one's horse.

"We do not see any more of those now," Muir responded. "Their extinction is due to the hoofed locusts."[6]

It was the first time, Johnson later recalled, that he'd heard Muir use this biting nickname for sheep. That recollection was not really correct: Muir had used the phrase in a *Century* article ten years prior. However, on that occasion the magazine misprinted it as "hooped locusts," so Johnson had presumably seen it but failed to grasp its meaning.[7] Locusts were then the most-feared insect in the world; their massive swarms—one of which covered 198,000 square miles of the Great Plains—ate everything in their path. Just the previous decade, locusts had caused $200 million in crop damages ($442 billion in 2018 dollars). And Muir argued that sheep hoofs in vast numbers had similar effects. Muir knew because he himself had worked as a sheepherder when he first arrived in the Yosemite area. His job was to direct sheep to a delightful meadow and watch them tear through it, eating everything—grasses, ferns, and flowers—down to bare ground. Most sheepherders then simply moved on to another meadow. Muir, the amateur scientist and Yosemite-lover, paid attention to what happened to those meadows the following spring. As snow melted without the underbrush that once held it in place so that it could percolate into the earth, water descended the mountainsides in surface torrents. It eroded away topsoil while leaving too little moisture for summer. Yet the summer moisture, Muir explained to Johnson, was what fed the valley waterfalls that tourists so treasured. Sheep on these uplands were destroying the wonder of the state park in the valley.

"Obviously the thing to do is to make a Yosemite National Park around the Valley on the plan of the Yellowstone," Johnson responded, referring to the idea of a national park. Yellowstone, created in 1872, was at this point run by an incorruptible military. If the mountains around Yosemite became a national park, the military could enforce a sheep ban. Ideally such a park would also encompass the state park in the valley, eliminating the pigsties. However, even a donut-shaped national park would be valuable protection for the waterfalls tumbling into the donut's hole.

Muir at first expressed skepticism; a similar proposal had failed previously. But Johnson "was much impressed with both the necessity and the practicality of such a park and urged it strongly."[8]

They forged a deal. Muir would write two articles for *The Century,* one on the treasures of the Yosemite area and a second on the benefits of a proposed national park. Meanwhile Johnson would pull strings in Washington. The plan combined their strengths: Muir the lyrical populist with on-the-ground knowledge: Johnson the well-connected insider who could tie vision to policy. That combination would get the right ideas in front of the right people to protect nature. It was a remarkably ambitious goal, given that they were just two men. And although Muir found writing such difficult work that he took almost a year to finish his articles, the public turned out to be eager for their message.

Johnson deserves much credit. He began editorializing in January 1890. He solicited articles from other Yosemite fans. He networked with park designer Frederick Law Olmsted, who had been on the first state commission overseeing the Yosemite Valley in 1864; Olmsted responded to Johnson's request with a pamphlet.[9] But other developments fell into place, perhaps without Johnson's assistance. For example, nationwide newspapers published favorable editorials. Swayed by state-level scientists, a Los Angeles congressman introduced a bill to withdraw from homesteading a small portion of the lands that Johnson and Muir had highlighted. A parallel move to protect what is now Sequoia National Park, 100 miles south, gained its own momentum. And the powerful Southern Pacific railroad apparently lobbied behind the scenes. By September 1890, when Muir's second article was published with maps showing the full scope of his proposed donut-shaped park, Congress felt comfortable embracing most of it. On October 1, President Benjamin Harrison signed the national park into law.

The creation of Yosemite National Park was a great success, rapidly achieved. Muir and Johnson's genius came in recognizing that greater Yosemite needed protection, understanding that such protection needed to come from Congress rather than the state of California, and orchestrating the crusade to spur congressional action. They gained immediate, positive results: the military kept out loggers and sheep, preserving the natural wonders.

However, in some ways the hurried innovation wasn't fully worked out. To take a specific example, the beautiful Soda Springs campsite was not in fact available to be consecrated as a national park. Four years previously, a part-time goatherd and entomologist named John Baptiste Lembert had filed a 160-acre homestead claim there. In a sense, Lembert's claim demonstrated the urgency of creating a park quickly, before any other lands were homesteaded. And Lembert had only yet made a claim; it could always be denied, especially since the Homestead Act required you to live year-round on-site and Lembert, sanely, wintered at lower elevations. Or even if the claim was granted—as indeed it was in 1895, because the General Land Office rarely denied even blatantly fraudulent claims—it could simply become an inholding surrounded by a national park. In short, the Lembert claim wasn't a showstopper, but it did demonstrate the tricky practicalities of implementing this fragile idea of national parks. [10]

It also pointed to a more general problem. Muir and Johnson had settled on the national park idea as an alternative to what they *didn't* want: the lax, corrupt, state-level administration. They hadn't spent as much time defining what they *did* want. What sorts of developments would be allowed in the new national park? Would its natural conditions be actively managed—and if so, toward what goals? Olmsted's pamphlet contained considerable detail on how forestry principles could be deployed to improve scenery—but forestry implied selective logging, where Muir had railed against all logging. In applying his experience with city parks to the rural park in Yosemite, Olmsted was recommending the design of a human-manipulated recreational destination, where Muir typically spoke of nature in Yosemite as a spiritual destination in contrast to human society. Yet Muir at one point told Johnson of "its value as our grand 'Central Park' in the Sierra." Would Yosemite follow the model of a city park, or did Muir have more ambitious, as-yet-unarticulated goals?[11]

Twelve years later, in July 1901, the sixty-three-year-old Muir returned to the Soda Springs campsite, again with valued collaborators, again launching a new venture. This time he was accompanied not only by his daughters Wanda, aged twenty, and Helen, fifteen, but also by members of the Sierra Club on their first-ever summer outing.

The club was another outgrowth of Muir's alliance with Johnson. As Muir struggled to write the articles that would fulfill his end of the Yosemite park bargain, Johnson told him, "Why don't you start an association for preserving California's monuments and natural wonders—or at least Yosemite?" Then a few months later: "I should think with little effort you could interest some influential people to organize quietly so as to make themselves felt."[12]

Muir tried to duck the responsibility. Organizing a lobbying group didn't feel like his personality. Muir told Johnson, "I would gladly do anything in my power to preserve nature's sayings and doings here or elsewhere, but have no genius for managing societies." But a couple of years later, some of his friends from the University of California planned a social hiking organization, modeled on Boston's Appalachian Mountain Club. Muir agreed to preside over their first meeting because he believed that the club's goals—mixing recreation with scientific education and facility development—could also include political defense of natural wonders. He was unanimously elected president, and he agreed to serve because he expected to be mostly a figurehead.[13]

Based in San Francisco, the Sierra Club attracted middle-class city professionals and academics from both Berkeley and Stanford. Members generally liked recreating outdoors and supported Progressive causes in which well-functioning governments would help solve social problems.

Sierra Club members made their livings in urban settings, and appreciated urban culture, but also valued the recreational and spiritual benefits of the country—which they saw not as potential farms, orchards, timberlands, or mining claims, but as sublime sylvan beauty. They gathered for meetings, lectures, and advocacy on behalf of political efforts, especially in Yosemite. Muir saw them as a set of moral disciples. "The battle we have fought," he said to an 1895 meeting, "and are still fighting, for the forests is a part of the eternal conflict between right and wrong, and we cannot expect to see the end of it."[14]

The annual summer outing was conceived as a way to give that eternal fight a solid foundation. It was healthy: outdoor living. It was social: young romances bloomed. And it was enlightening: Muir told his stories, complete with science and spirituality. The outings were phenomenally popular from the start.

It wasn't exactly solitude. Even on this first outing, more than one hundred people gathered around the campfire. It was like a dude ranch or church camp, with folks of similar class background and beliefs gathered for an active outdoor group vacation. The outings' popularity relied especially on their charismatic leader—Muir offered not only entertaining stories but also a sense of moral authority. And Muir himself appreciated the trips because he styled himself as a latter-day John the Baptist, whose duty was to immerse in "mountain baptism" everyone he could.[15] The summer outing, more than the Sierra Club's political activities, fulfilled his prophet ambitions.

But as Johnson kept reminding Muir, if protecting the sense of spiritual wonder provided by these lands was a moral issue, then by necessity it was also a political issue. Johnson demanded that advocacy—more than recreation or education—be the Sierra Club's purpose. He was constantly alerting Muir and the club to political threats to Yosemite's integrity. For example, in 1896 he told Muir that "The moment the railroad gets into the Park, good-by to the peace, wildness and security of the reservation." Noting that the Boone and Crockett Club, a New York hunters' organization founded by Theodore Roosevelt and George Bird Grinnell, was already fighting against rail incursions in Yellowstone, Johnson urged that "this is a thing for the Sierra Club to take up and discuss."[16] Similarly, numerous congressional bills sought to reduce Yosemite's boundaries, sometimes to exclude legitimate inholdings like Lembert's, but other times to return timber or grazing lands to the public domain, where they could be privatized. Usually prodded by Johnson, the club continually protested, often successfully.

The efforts could feel piecemeal, because no standards yet existed for how a national park should be treated, nor for how an advocacy group should defend it. Indeed in 1901, just a few months before the first club summer outing, Congress passed a law allowing national parks to be breached by rights-of-way for electricity, telephone/telegraph, and irrigation/water supply. The Sierra Club did not protest. Why? Later, club members cited various reasons—they hadn't known about the bill, hadn't grasped its implications, or had been assured that those implications were minimal. Sadly, the implications turned out to be profound: under the clause allowing breaches for water supply, later that fall, San Francisco Mayor James Phelan would file for the rights to build a reservoir in the Hetch Hetchy Valley.

Despite these developments, up at Soda Springs, Muir deemed the first-ever Sierra Club outing a success. Of course he had no crystal ball. Maybe he was focused on the social and recreational, rather than the political, purposes of the club. Maybe he knew that the best way to unite people against a coming political challenge was to build camaraderie. Or maybe he was taking joy in the moment, as any satisfied person must. "God's ozone sparkles in every eye," he wrote. "I never before saw so big & merry a camp circle, a huge fire blazing in the centre."[17]

Muir's trip to Yosemite in May 1903 may be the most mythologized camping trip in American history. That's because his companion was President Theodore Roosevelt. It would be nice to believe that Roosevelt's vaunted environmental policies resulted from this trip with Muir, that the activist was able to show the president the value of nature by camping together. In truth, Roosevelt's commitment to the environment far predated this trip.

Roosevelt had cofounded the Boone and Crockett Club in 1887. He endorsed large-scale forest reserves as early as 1897. And just one month after his inauguration as president in 1901, Roosevelt wrote Muir to solicit his views on forests and sheep. Muir's response to that initial letter endorsed the idea of creating a Bureau of Forestry, which was the primary objective of Gifford Pinchot, who was one of Roosevelt's closest advisors. Eighteen months later, Roosevelt's Yosemite trip also took him to many other Western wonders. Indeed, in Yellowstone he camped with John Burroughs, whose nature writing Roosevelt actually preferred to Muir's because of Burroughs's relentless devotion to science. [18]

So Roosevelt's time with Muir was not a turning point. It was nevertheless an experience the president eagerly planned. Arranging the trip, Roosevelt requested that he get to spend time alone with Muir, away from photographers and dignitaries. Roosevelt wanted to be the sole audience for Muir's passionate storytelling in this enchanting setting. Upon learning of the request, Muir told Johnson, "Should the President invite me[,] I'll go and preach recession & forestry like—like a *Century* editor." [19]

Muir used *forestry* to stand for nature, for saving trees. *Recession* stood for the controversial idea that the California state government should now re-cede the 1864 grant of the central Yosemite Valley back to the federal government to include in the national park. Johnson and Muir continued to believe that state mismanagement tarnished the Yosemite experience. They were disappointed in the type of development in the valley. They wanted more urban-park aesthetics and more roads, trails, bridges, and hotels. Muir wasn't asking for unstructured wilderness, rather, he wanted the Yosemite Valley be a place to inspire certain emotional and spiritual reactions. That required a manmade visual experience of the kind that Frederick Law Olmsted had created for places like Central Park and Biltmore. For example, in 1895 Muir called for the state to employ a "skilled landscape gardener" in the valley to help create the desired experience. [20]

Powerful Californians opposed recession because it would be an insult to "take Yosemite away from California."[21] Indeed one commissioner accused Johnson of treating "my state as a cuspidor in which to eject his intellectual phlegm."[22] Debates about recession caused serious divides in the early Sierra Club. Some of the club's leaders who participated in the Bay Area political establishment didn't want to upset fellow Californians. Others worried that behind the scenes, the Southern Pacific railroad might, for some reason, be pulling strings for recession, and they hesitated to endorse a position that would benefit a big corporate monopoly. Meanwhile, club membership included both Southern Pacific executives and at least one of the state park commissioners.[23] Muir had limited interest in or talent for overseeing ongoing political discussions, so instead he went camping with the president.

Muir and Roosevelt met in Oakland in mid-May, and traveled by train and stagecoach to the Mariposa grove of giant sequoias. There they took leave of their companions, including the governor and the president of the University at Berkeley. Rangers prepared their camp and cooked their supper, but then kept out of sight. The next day they took stagecoaches to Glacier Point, 3,200 feet above the Yosemite Valley floor, where they posed for a famous photograph. In the photo, two warriors for nature stand on Overhanging Rock, a knob of granite with a compelling view of Yosemite Falls in the distance. Roosevelt marks his territory, barrel chest aggressively forward and one hand in a pocket. He wears high boots and a Stetson, a heavy sweater and a jaunty bandana. He confronts the camera with a square jaw and serious eyes, a leader soaking in his own power. Beside him, Muir almost cedes the spotlight. His gaze and feet both point to his right, toward Roosevelt. His arms are pulled behind his back. His clothes aren't stylish, nor his hat. His jacket is closed, his eyes and mid-torso shaded by the sun. Yet he looks no less satisfied, no less confident—a prophet soaking in his own spell.

That night they camped nearby without tents, and awoke to snow atop their blankets. The next day they went down into the valley, where Roosevelt spurned the formal arrangements of the state park commissioners in favor of a final night of camping and intimate conversation with Muir in a meadow near Bridalveil Fall.

Beguiling legends have become associated with the trip. Did the joyful Muir, after dark one night, set fire to a tall dead pine in a meadow, and then dance a Scottish jig around it? Did the pampered Roosevelt ask a ranger to lay out forty thick wool blankets for his bed? Did Roosevelt—after exclaiming over a campfire "Now this is bully!"—wake up to four inches of snow and say, "This is bullier yet!"? Did the two notorious conversation hogs fight over who could talk the most? Did Muir at one point slip a wildflower into Roosevelt's lapel, without permission, causing the hyper-masculine president to fume? Did Muir scold the Hunter-in-Chief to "get beyond the boyishness of killing things" and receive the chastened response, "I guess you are right"? The best stories are always told by those who weren't actually there. Muir's own most comprehensive account has been lost, and Roosevelt was too busy to write it up at the time. Clearly, they did feel a brotherhood. They shared a love for living strenuously and witnessing the evidence of God in nature. Muir told a friend that "Camping with the President was a memorable experience. I fairly fell in love with him." And Roosevelt did later note that Muir's "deep solicitude over the destruction of our great forests and scenery" impressed upon him the urgency of taking action before it was too late. [24]

It took another two years for Muir and the Sierra Club, aided by the Southern Pacific, to convince the California legislature to agree to recession. Then it took another year to get Congress to agree to accept it. In each battle, advocates successfully fought economic interests that tried to take the opportunity to change Yosemite's boundaries to exclude acreage useful for cattle grazing, timber cutting, railroad building, or reservoir construction. After Roosevelt finally signed the recession bill in June 1906, Muir wrote to Johnson, "The fight you planned by that famous Tuolumne camp-fire . . . is at last fairly, gloriously won." A unified Yosemite National Park was widely seen as a victory for the Sierra Club, although Muir grumbled to Johnson that club secretary William Colby was "the only one of all the Club who stood by me." [25] But recession meant only that the entire park would be managed from Washington. It said nothing about *how* these lands should be managed, as Muir would, to his sorrow, soon learn.

On Friday, August 30, 1907, a typically cool and cloudy summer morning in San Francisco, ten men gathered in the law offices of William Colby in a four-story building on the corner of Golden Gate and Fillmore Streets in San Francisco. The previous year's earthquake and fires had destroyed the city's downtown, including the Sierra Club's headquarters and many professionals' offices. While the downtown was being rebuilt, the unaffected Fillmore district served as a major commercial center.

The governing body for the club's nine hundred members included two scientists, two professors, two lawyers, a paint salesman, and the now-sixty-nine-year-old Muir. Among the four honorary vice presidents were the editor Robert Underwood Johnson and the forester Gifford Pinchot, now heading the U.S. Forest Service in Washington, D.C.[26] Although aftereffects of the earthquake had dented memberships and dues, and necessitated funds to replace circulars and other printed items, the club's outlook was positive. Membership was now rebounding. Seeking to encourage mountain travel, the club had recently planted rainbow and brook trout in previously fishless Sierra streams, and constructed and helped staff the LeConte Memorial Lodge as a visitor center in the Yosemite Valley. The board heard reports on issues like these and approved sponsorship of some lectures in Berkeley. Colby's minutes of the meeting then note, "The President was authorized to appoint a committee with full power to act in the matter of preparing a report on the Welfare and Improvement of the Yosemite National Park." After naming the committee's four members, the minutes continue, "Mr. Gifford Pinchot and Mr. Olmstead [Fritz Olmsted, one of Pinchot's lieutenants] of the Forest Service were both present and discussed matters pertaining to the Service." In the classic style of meeting minutes—especially those taken by an attorney—all of the drama is withheld.[27]

The meeting had been called to discuss the Hetch Hetchy Valley, which now seemed under threat. The city of San Francisco, in need of water sources beyond its lowland peninsula, had long eyed damming the valley.

In 1901 and 1903, Mayor James Phelan made various federal filings toward that aim, working as quietly as possible to avoid alerting his competitor, the Spring Valley Water Company. The private Spring Valley company possessed the existing contract to supply the city with drinking water. At the height of Progressivism, Phelan and other good-government types believed that the city should administer its own utilities. To do so, it would either have to buy out the private monopoly at an exorbitant price, or outmaneuver or outbid Spring Valley for a potential new reservoir.

Because Hetch Hetchy was located inside a national park, a dam required Interior Department permission. In 1903, the interior secretary twice denied the city's request. However, three years later, the earthquake and associated fires highlighted the need for robust municipal water systems, and city engineer Marsden Manson reinvigorated the Hetch Hetchy proposal. Hot-tempered and caustic, Manson was the kind of engineer who believed there was no problem that technology couldn't solve. Damming Hetch Hetchy was a brilliant technological solution—and the need for a water supply for San Francisco might now present a sufficient problem to require it. Manson solicited advice from Pinchot, who as Forest Service chief was also President Roosevelt's chief environmental advisor. In late 1906, Pinchot told Manson that new Interior Secretary James Garfield, son of the former president, might find the project more attractive than his predecessor had.[28] The next July, Garfield came to San Francisco for public hearings, which put the dam in a positive light.

In retrospect, it's easy to criticize the Sierra Club for not staying on top of this issue. Most embarrassingly, nobody testified against the project in those July 1907 hearings, which took place during the club's seventh annual summer outing in Yosemite. But the club did have a representative at those hearings: engineer Manson himself. As a young urban professional with training in science, a politically Progressive outlook, and appreciation for outdoor activities, Manson had joined the club and even written for its newsletter. When his newsletter articles spoke about preserving forests, however, he was an engineer referring to efficiency and control of timber and water resources rather than a prophet speaking of spiritual wonders.[29]

Returning from the summer outing, club leaders heard that they had missed important hearings and swung into action. In that board meeting in Colby's office one month later, Muir put four of his strongest allies on a new committee. Within three weeks they developed a sharply worded resolution. Hetch Hetchy, they wrote, was a major feature of the national park; damming it would damage the park profoundly and could set a precedent for eventually damming the main valley; drinking water for San Francisco could be acquired elsewhere, although it might cost a bit more money; and "we do not believe that the vital interests of the nation at large should be sacrificed and so important a part of its National Park destroyed to save a few dollars for local interests." They sent this letter to the Interior Department, and two months later requested that all club members send similar letters individually. [30]

But as with recession of the Yosemite Valley, the dam exposed splits in club membership. For example, engineer Manson obviously wasn't going to oppose it. Neither was Warren Olney, a cofounder of the club and a board member. As a former mayor of Oakland, Olney knew firsthand the dangers of private monopolies controlling city utilities. This was the era of trust-busting, when governments were finally standing up to the trusts that had made fortunes by gouging the powerless. From Olney's perspective, Hetch Hetchy would give the people of San Francisco the means to stand up to Spring Valley.

Olney attended that August board meeting. Did he argue for the vocal minority of club membership that agreed with him? And what about Pinchot? He continued to hold the vice president position even though two years previously he had articulated his attitude toward Hetch Hetchy in a letter to Secretary Colby. "I feel very strongly that San Francisco must have an adequate water supply," Pinchot had written. But "I agree with you fully as to the extreme desirability of preserving the Hetch Hetchy in its original beauty." To split the difference, Pinchot made a proposal, which he believed the club would support. Downstream from Hetch Hetchy, the Tuolumne River flowed into Lake Eleanor, a spot that was still inside the national park but not as scenic as the Hetch Hetchy Valley. A reservoir here would be smaller and might meet the city's needs for only fifty years. Kicking the problem forward fifty years was a compromise that Pinchot could heartily endorse—in fact, he had continually endorsed it since the earliest discussions of the dam in 1903. In doing so, Pinchot was certainly not placing the sanctity of national-park boundaries above the needs of a half-million San Franciscans. But neither was he yet proposing to sacrifice the Hetch Hetchy Valley.[31]

In that August 1907 meeting, did Pinchot remind the others of the potential Lake Eleanor compromise, and if so did Muir reject it? Months later, Muir implied that he might endorse it, but in 1908 the city rejected it. Both Muir and Pinchot failed to pursue what should have been a perfect compromise for them to broker.[32] More broadly, did the meeting's collection of learned individuals get at the deeper questions the proposal implied: How to weigh different benefits for different groups, and who gets to do that weighing; how to know what role nature should serve in people's lives, or what role public lands should serve for nature? The evidence suggests that no such discussions took place. Maybe the time wasn't yet right, or participants were not yet capable of effectively articulating their positions.

One specific hint we have of their interactions comes from a letter that Muir wrote to Interior Secretary Garfield the following week providing his personal protest against the dam. He mentioned speaking about Hetch Hetchy with Pinchot at the meeting, and Pinchot, *"never having seen it, seemed surprised to learn how important a part of the Yosemite Park the Hetch Hetchy really is."*[33]

The notion that you should never sacrifice a place you haven't seen has played a big role in the history of the Sierra Club. In the 1950s, club executive director David Brower and other opponents of a dam inside Dinosaur National Park agreed to a compromise in which they sacrificed Utah's Glen Canyon to a dam—a decision Brower often said he regretted, because if he had seen Glen Canyon in person, he would have understood that its wonders, although not part of a national park, were equally worthy of protection. Brower's attitude dates back to Muir's passion: when Muir was able to get decision-makers to see natural wonders in person, he usually convinced them to protect the wonders. For example, seeing other features of Yosemite had persuaded Johnson and Roosevelt to act on their behalf. In person, on site, Muir could explain the science, the emotion, and the spiritual connection of the place. He always believed that if he could get Pinchot to go with him to Hetch Hetchy, he would turn his old compatriot into a key ally.

In their discussion at the board meeting, Muir apparently proposed to Pinchot that the two of them head out to the valley as soon as possible. Muir was already envisioning a trip with his friend William Keith later that autumn. Pinchot had a busy schedule culminating in a speech to the International Irrigation Congress in Sacramento the following week. So Muir apparently asked if Pinchot could give his speech and then sneak away from that conference. That door was left ajar until Pinchot cabled Muir from Sacramento on Thursday, September 5: "Regret exceedingly pressing work keeps me here[,] must start east Saturday."[34]

As the rest of this book will explore, at that point Muir and Pinchot had benefitted from years of collaboration and friendship, whether it was fishing in Montana's Lake McDonald and camping at Arizona's Grand Canyon, fighting together to establish a government forestry program and debating how it should regulate sheep grazing, or comparing notes on the most fulfilling aspects of nature and politics. They generally enjoyed the time they spent together, but long distances and busy schedules meant that they often declined each other's invitations. They likely saw this as yet another in a series of missed connections. However, it turned out to be a lost last opportunity. They never again met in person.

It wasn't just San Francisco. The 1906 earthquake and fire highlighted a need for reservoirs throughout California. Another potential dam site was a valley on the southwest slope of Mount Tamalpais in Marin County, north of San Francisco. The land was owned by a man named William Kent, who had grown up in the area, graduated from Yale two years ahead of Pinchot, and worked in the family real estate business in Chicago before returning to California. Kent purchased the Redwood Creek valley because it was the last unlogged coastal redwood forest on the peninsula and he wanted to save the groves of magnificently tall trees.[35]

So when the private North Coast Water Company asked Kent to sell the land for a reservoir, he declined. He was a Progressive and an anti-monopolist; he believed that cities should administer their own water supplies and private for-profit water companies should not exist. The reservoir proposal also struck him as a potential ruse to cut down his beloved trees for valuable timber. Nevertheless, the post-earthquake Bay Area was obsessed with expanding infrastructure. When in 1907 North Coast sued to have Kent's land condemned, it pitted Kent against the public interest—which it defined in terms of municipal water supplies. Kent feared that local governments would intervene in support of North Coast for the opportunity to purchase additional private water. Opposition attorneys would portray him as an elitist locking up resources, a feudal lord denying basic needs of the nearby peasants. A judge might well take away his land.

Kent wanted to save the redwoods. As a savvy political operator, he realized that he didn't need to own the land to achieve his goal. The very same day that he heard about the lawsuit, he wired his friend and fellow Yale Skull and Bones alumnus Gifford Pinchot. To save the woods, he wanted to donate the land to the government, but "Must have it accepted as National forest at once." Kent was even willing to provide twenty years' worth of police protection as part of the deal. But the transfer needed to happen fast—within weeks—before he was served with court documents in the condemnation lawsuit.[36]

It was a desperate ploy, a last chance. Kent couldn't give the land to the state because that wouldn't save it from the possibility of condemnation. He couldn't wait for the lengthy, public process of declaring a national park—and besides, at 295 acres, the parcel might be too small for that purpose. Even the initial reaction from his friend Pinchot was troubling: Pinchot's California right-hand man, Fritz Olmsted, told Kent that national forests were all about multiple use, and the uses included logging and reservoirs—so making the land a national forest wouldn't necessarily preserve the trees. But, Olmsted explained, there was new tool that might work better. The land might qualify as a national monument under the recently passed Antiquities Act of 1906.

The suggestion pushed the limits of that law. The Antiquities Act allowed the president to withdraw from homesteading public domain lands that contained "historic landmarks, historic and prehistoric structures, and other objects of historic or scientific interest." It was primarily intended to protect prehistoric artifacts and geological phenomena from plunder by private "pot hunters" and other vandals. [37] It said nothing about preserving trees. Olmsted, Kent, and Pinchot argued that the trees had "scientific interest," but that novel interpretation would have run into trouble if anyone disagreed with it. Fortunately, the North Coast Water Company had a lousy local reputation, and most advocates of parklands were thrilled about preserving a glorious redwood stand in a spot so close to a big city. No government could ever afford to *buy* such land—the donation was a rare opportunity.

Pinchot and Olmsted worked hard and quickly. Even though their Forest Service was part of the Department of Agriculture, and national monuments were governed under the Department of Interior, Pinchot and Olmsted served as Kent's main contacts and advocates. They convinced Roosevelt and Interior Secretary James Garfield of the project's value, and processed all the necessary paperwork. Roosevelt signed a proclamation just twelve days after receiving Kent's formal request. Roosevelt and Pinchot wanted to call it Kent Woods National Monument, but Kent declined. He insisted that it be named after John Muir.

The Muir Woods story is often seen as a prelude to Hetch Hetchy, a further demonstration of the preservation-versus-conservation divide, in which the need for drinking water, supported by Progressives and conservationists, conflicted with the need for wondrously special natural places, supported by preservationists. But it's funny how in this episode so many players switched sides. Pinchot here was a preservationist, rewarded in 1910 with a plaque and a named tree in Muir Woods. Kent here was a preservationist, so much so that he named his gift after Muir—but was soon elected to Congress, where he advocated for damming the

Hetch Hetchy Valley.[38] Meanwhile, federal ownership of land, seen in Hetch Hetchy as a weakness that dam advocates took advantage of, was a strength at Muir Woods. Where North Coast's condemnation lawsuit might have succeeded against a single wealthy individual, it floundered once the federal government was already using the land for a different public purpose.

Muir was incredibly touched by the dedication, but he had never advocated for it. He was never involved in its politics. He was on the sidelines of this particular story; he and Kent had never even met. His only role was as a prophet whose essays and books had inspired Kent to express his love for nature. It was a role well-suited to his talents and ambitions. But only when his perspectives became allied with the efforts of statesmen such as Pinchot and Kent—his later rivals at Hetch Hetchy—did this beautiful place get preserved.

The Hetch Hetchy debate coincided with John Muir becoming an old man. His wife Louie died of pneumonia in August 1905. Close friends later passed as well: painter William Keith in 1911, neighbor John Swett in 1913, Sierra Club ally Edward Parsons in early 1914. Muir's daughters both married men he didn't like. With few responsibilities in Martinez, he returned to his patronage network, escaping rainy winters by making lengthy visits to wealthy friends in greater Los Angeles. Feeling weak and often suffering respiratory ailments, he tried to pour his passion and energy into his writing. Associates wanted him to instead focus on Yosemite politics.

Even the Sierra Club threatened to spiral away from him. The vocal minority of members who favored the dam feared that the club was being used as a pawn by the Spring Valley Water Company. If San Francisco couldn't develop Hetch Hetchy, the private monopoly would maintain its hold over the city, and it might even put its own dam in Hetch Hetchy. The argument depressed Muir, who believed simply that the valley was a special place that shouldn't be ruined. At one point he threatened to resign from the club entirely.

Nevertheless, Muir became a political organizer. Immediately after that August 1907 board meeting, Muir wrote to Roosevelt, asking the president to oppose the dam. Roosevelt responded that he would do "everything in my power to protect" scenic wonders, but he needed evidence of public support. With so much testimony already in favor of the dam, "I have been in the disagreeable position of seeming to interfere with the development of the State for the sake of keeping a valley, which apparently hardly anyone wanted to have kept, under national control."[39]

So Muir wrote to friends and acquaintances on the East Coast to urge them to lodge protests with the Interior Department. He and William Colby set up a shadow organization, the Society for the Preservation of National Parks, which shared offices and board members with the Sierra Club, but excluded dam proponents from its membership so as to make anti-dam politics its chief fight. It distributed pamphlets urging people who had never seen the valley to advocate for its preservation—initiating one of the first grassroots environmental campaigns in American history.[40]

In May 1908, Interior Secretary Garfield formally granted the city a permit to build the dam. The next step was a land swap, which would need congressional approval. In Congress, dam opponents were able to gum up the works. The politics dragged on endlessly: hearings, debates, committee meetings, and rulings. For years no decision quite gave the dam a full go-ahead, but neither did the door ever shut entirely.

Living in California and easily lost in palace corridors, Muir rarely lobbied or testified in person in Washington. He and allies did persuade a new president, William Taft, and two successive interior secretaries, Richard Ballinger and Walter Fisher, to visit Yosemite. Having seen the Hetch Hetchy Valley, all expressed skepticism about the dam. But none would quite kill it, with Fisher finally declaring in 1913 that Congress should rule on not only the land swap but also the dam permit itself. During that summer's House hearings, Robert Underwood Johnson grumbled at how few Californians made the trip to testify against the dam. Testifying for it were scientists, mutinous Sierra Club members, and Washington insiders, including Gifford Pinchot, who at that point had left the Forest Service but was still volunteering for conservation causes. Proponents argued that a Hetch Hetchy lake would be scenic. They—and even some of Muir's allies—hinted that Muir was exaggerating its scenic beauty.[41] They also pointed out that the dam would generate electric power, gaining the city victory over both water and power monopolies, two for the price of one. The 1913 Hetch Hetchy dam bill passed the House fairly easily, and several months later the Senate as well. In December, President Woodrow Wilson signed it, sealing the valley's fate.

In defense of Hetch Hetchy, Muir crafted some of his most famous prose. Denouncing dam proponents as greedy, he wrote, "These temple destroyers, devotees of ravaging commercialism, seem to have a perfect contempt for Nature, and instead of lifting their eyes to the God of the Mountains, lift them to the Almighty Dollar. Dam the Hetch Hetchy! As well dam for water tanks the people's cathedrals and churches, for no holier temple has ever been consecrated by the heart of man." He originally wrote those words for a Sierra Club newsletter, and later included them in a book published by Robert Underwood Johnson's Century company. They mark a departure from his previous writing style: less memoir, observation, natural history, or Emersonian uplift; more angry political rhetoric.[42]

As rhetoric it's brilliant, confirming Muir's mastery of language, his ability to express his thoughts in compelling, beautiful words. It mixes fiercely Biblical phrasings with vivid images from *Paradise Lost* to call on a deep moral authority. But if you try to translate it to policy, it's troubling. How does he define this *nature* that he's defending from contempt? The Sierra Club's vision for an undammed Hetch Hetchy Valley included roads, hotels, and other large-scale tourist facilities, which means that his definition of *nature* wasn't undeveloped.[43] Ecological theories of intact ecosystems had not yet been discovered, which means that his *nature* wasn't about science. Muir eventually agreed to sacrifice Lake Eleanor, which means that his *nature* wasn't defined by national park boundaries. His *nature* was instead about his idea of God. Yosemite was Muir's temple, and he wanted it saved. When faced with the theological question, *Do we save the world or just our own faith community?*, Muir revealed his evangelical upbringing.

He was like a modern-day preacher whose faith impels political action only on zoning laws that affect the church building.

Preservationists are often accused of being elitists who want to keep people out of nature. But Muir wasn't looking to save this Garden of Eden from the temple destroyers—rather, he wanted to use it to save the temple destroyers from themselves. He wanted to convert them to use this place the way he himself did, as a sanctuary.[44] He was a prophet calling people to fulfill their spiritual needs at his church. The problem was that his sanctuary was on public land with potentially competing uses, and Muir's rhetoric treated those uses with the same scorn that his father had used on competing religious sects.

Furthermore, Muir was scorning some of his oldest and closest friends. Some were members of the small Bay Area intellectual community who believed in Progressive ideals, such as Sierra Club cofounder Warren Olney, Stanford President David Starr Jordan, and University of California President Benjamin Ide Wheeler. Others were millionaires in his patronage network who never gave money to the Hetch Hetchy cause, including railroad tycoon Edward Harriman and industrialist-philanthropist Andrew Carnegie. There was William Kent, the donor of Muir Woods, who told fellow congressmen not to take Muir seriously on the Hetch Hetchy issue, because "with him it is me and God and the rock where God put it, and that is the end of the story." And there was the naturalist John Burroughs, who became so aggravated by Muir's argumentativeness on Hetch Hetchy that he told Muir, "I love you, though at times I want to punch you or thrash the ground with you."[45]

It's possible to perceive these as all run-of-the-mill intellectual disagreements, of the sort that characterized so much of Muir's life. But Muir's disciples, moved by this grand rhetoric, often depict Hetch Hetchy as deeper than other arguments, full of more moral clarity. If so, then it's an argument that utterly isolates Muir from his world.

In some ways these final years of Muir's life were productive. He took a nearly yearlong trip around the world, finally fulfilling his youthful ambition of following Alexander von Humboldt and Charles Darwin to

South America. He published the memoirs *My First Summer in the Sierra* (1911) and *The Story of My Boyhood and Youth* (1913), and the guidebook-cum-defense-of-Hetch-Hetchy *The Yosemite* (1912); he also labored on the posthumously published *Travels in Alaska* (1915).[46] But in the public imagination, he became increasingly associated with the Hetch Hetchy fight, as if it was his personal quest, as if stopping the dam was everything that he wanted.

And he lost. He lost in part because not enough people understood or appreciated his point of view. They didn't put enough value on Hetch Hetchy as a special place in nature, or on special places as essential to a fulfilling spiritual life, or on a spiritual life as being more important than the establishment of publicly owned utilities. If at his core, Muir was a prophet—if being an activist, scientist, writer, and wanderer were all off-shoots of this core desire—then the last years of his life play like a tragedy. He didn't make enough conversions. Like his father, Muir became an old man preaching a solitary gospel. Compared to his father's stern dogma, Muir's God-in-Nature was a kinder theology, which would eventually sway millions. But when Muir looked back at his father, he saw an uncompro-mising firebrand whose radicalization estranged him from society and left him to die alone. Muir wondered if his own life path wasn't sadly similar.[47]

When the Hetch Hetchy battle was complete, Muir expressed both sorrow and relief. To daughter Helen, he wrote, "I've done my best and am now free to go on with my own work." He refused to believe he'd fought in vain. Something might yet come of this moral battle. At the same time, there was a sense that Muir the political activist had been playing a role. He wasn't necessarily acting, but like a reality-TV star, he was improvising around an exaggerated element of his personality. Now that the effort was over he could throw off that cloak, return to his true self, turn from "faith-less politics to crystal ice and snow" and write about Alaska.[48]

In the fall of 1914, at the age of seventy-six, Muir developed pneumonia. In hopes of alleviating it, he visited his daughter Helen in Southern Cali-fornia. With a ne'er-do-well husband and two infants to care for, she bustled him off to a Los Angeles hospital. Describing his love of the mountains, he'd once said, "It would be awful to die down here on the level. I'm not thinking of dying yet, but when I do leave here it must be from the peaks."[49] However, it was in the Los Angeles hospital room that he died, on the day before Christmas, alone.

Part of the tragedy of John Muir is the way his story is equated with a political tragedy for Hetch Hetchy. As if Muir were merely an activist. He wasn't; for Muir, politics was a tangent. And in the long run, Hetch Hetchy wasn't a political tragedy. It would prove to be a useful defeat for the environmental movement—and given what we now know about the environmental impacts of hotels and roads, the opposite outcome might have been a useless victory. Rather, we should see Hetch Hetchy as a *demonstration* of the tragedy Muir perceived for himself: his feeling that he failed to achieve his evangelical objectives, that he didn't bring enough people to the spirituality of nature's divinity.

Meanwhile, it's interesting to track the blame for the loss of Hetch Hetchy's natural splendor. Blame might have settled on the Sierra Club, for its understandable failures in early political activism. It might have settled on the club's antagonists: San Francisco mayor Phelan, engineer Manson, or the city's paid lobbyists. It might have settled on the ultimate deciders: Congress, President Wilson, or Wilson's Interior Secretary Franklin K. Lane. It might have settled on the powerful politicians who expressed support for the valley but failed to act: Presidents Roosevelt or Taft or Secretaries Ballinger or Fisher. It might have settled on the voters of San Francisco, who endorsed Hetch Hetchy by a six-to-one margin, and who later voted for a bond to start building the dam while rejecting a smaller bond to buy the Spring Valley Water Company. It might have settled on Californians caught in the middle, such as William Kent or Warren Olney. But it didn't. It instead settled on one of the project's mildest proponents, a man who had never sponsored the dam, gained no benefit from it, and at the time of its passage was at a nadir of his political power: Gifford Pinchot.[50] Even more sadly, Pinchot was a person for whom politics wasn't a tangent. Perhaps even more than Muir's, Pinchot's was the tragedy of the era.

4

"Sufficient Confidence in His Own Wisdom"

ifford Pinchot wanted to be a statesman. He grew up with a rare opportunity to do so: he had money, connections, and the right family background. But Pinchot was born in 1865, and thus matured in a Gilded Age society of carpetbaggers and industrialists. Even the relatively minor statesmanship of someone like Henry Clay, the pre–Civil War senator known as "The Great Compromiser," seemed out of reach in an era so full of greed.[1] Was it still possible to dedicate your life to the public good?

Pinchot and his father had a vision of a very specific type of statesman: one who would pursue the public good in the woods. Pinchot's life journey sought to fulfill his teenaged ambition to become *America's first forester*. In retrospect, that sounds egotistical: Pinchot was, at best, the first *American-born person to receive formal education in forest management and then practice it*. Others before him—from the landscape architect Frederick Law Olmsted to uncounted numbers of indigenous people—had long practiced some form of forestry without formal education or official title; meanwhile, Pinchot's older rival Bernhard Fernow had far more formal forestry education than Pinchot did, but arrived in America after being born and educated in Europe. Nevertheless, Pinchot's claim demonstrated a serious, unusual, and admirable ambition. From an early age, he intended to use his family's fortune for the good of society and the environment. Indeed he hoped to specifically right some of his grandfather's wrongs—to treat forests with respect.[2]

The quest was personal, not merely generational. Gifford's most treasured childhood memory was of receiving his first fly-fishing rod as a gift from his father during a camping trip to Upper Ausable Lake in the Adirondacks. They hiked up a rocky road through mossy woodlands and meadows infested with black flies and mosquitoes. At the lake, they made beds out of balsam boughs, and Gifford awakened to flapjacks with maple syrup by a campfire. He described a "steep dark mountain slope across from the lake," a woodsy wonder that offered up the sounds of bears and panthers. At a big pool by the lake's inlet, the boy caught his first trout on a fly. His second-most treasured memory came from a few days later, when while casting his treasured new fly rod he overheard his father say to a friend, "That boy doesn't fish as if he were only thirteen."[3]

Gifford's mother exerted influence as well. With her Connecticut Puritan background, Mary Eno Pinchot believed in subordinating the individual to God and community. She encouraged Gifford to study Paul, the saint who had devoted his life to institutionalizing Jesus's teachings. "The closer you can get in knowledge of him and in following him—the nobler and broader your life will be," she wrote to her son while he was at Exeter, the New Hampshire prep school.[4] In other words, Mary Pinchot saw spirituality as tied to the nobility of service. She believed Gifford would feel fulfilled if he devoted his life to a cause bigger than himself, one that could enrich the lives of millions. Gifford thus received messages of selfless obligation from both parents, but his father, James, was particularly stern. For example, after receiving a letter without a date, he scolded his son: "Your carelessness and inattention to our wishes is painful." James also complained that at Exeter, Gifford's affection for activities and clubs, such as lacrosse and literary societies, were detracting from future success, which would come solely from his studies. [5]

At Exeter, Gifford played not only lacrosse but also football and tennis. He often wandered the surrounding forests to collect butterflies and bugs. Although he was a devout and dutiful student, fascinated by science, he longed to get out into the woods where his webs of obligation eased. Indeed, during his senior year, Gifford withdrew from school to instead study with a private tutor while vigorously hiking the Adirondacks. It was labeled a "rest cure" but involved little physical rest and instead plenty of hunting and boxing. Gifford's teenaged rebellion embraced physicality.

Then at Yale, where Gifford played backup quarterback, he discovered the Young Men's Christian Association. The YMCA combined his rebellious sporting interests with the outdoor and religious interests of his father and mother. Expressing a passion for religion, Gifford taught Sunday School, and when he started an eating club, he wrote his parents that he was making sure to include several evangelical Christians. He toyed with a career as a missionary, and just before graduation almost accepted a job with the YMCA. In the end, he concluded that the day-to-day life of a missionary or YMCA administrator would require sacrificing his love of science and forests while providing only a vague, long-term sense of improving the lives of the less fortunate. Being out in the forest felt like his true calling; what if it too could improve people's lives? Thus the forestry that he would come to preach was highly Puritan. It rejected individualism and mysticism in favor of working toward a just and sustainable society. He pursued this calling with the zeal of Paul, as he sought to institutionalize principles he found both scientific and Godly. [6]

Although Gifford's journey to see forestry as a synthesis of science and do-gooding was internally driven, it was a common type of journey for his generation. The turn of the twentiethth century saw the rise of American *professions*, in which educated young people dedicated themselves to medicine or engineering or law or social work not merely because it was an interesting topic or a way to make money, but because it had evolved into a discipline to be served. For example, the rise of complex industrial corporations created a need for accountants with an overwhelming obligation to the principles of accounting rather than the interests of a single party to a transaction. Governed by an accepted body of expertise and moral standards, professions filled a societal need to transfer increased knowledge. Because science could articulate, for example, how much load a bridge design could bear, both individual bridge-builders and society at large gained from the existence of civil engineers who were devoted more to transferring that knowledge than to building a cheap bridge. Meanwhile, an engineer might identify more with other engineers than with coworkers who served other functions—and young people were drawn to that sense of tribal community as advances in transportation and communication reduced the primacy of local neighborhood communities. [7]

Yet professions weren't born fully formed. A profession existed only with institutions: universities to impart knowledge, professional societies to maintain it, and employers to demand it. At Yale, Gifford discovered that American forestry involved no such institutions—indeed, in the United States the discipline of forestry wasn't even defined enough to *be* a profession. Forestry was more than logging, more than botany, more than natural history or economics or landscape architecture. Gifford saw it as a profession that used such diverse expertise to put tree-cutting into a larger, rational perspective. But if it was going to be a profession as meaningful as engineering or medicine, it needed an institutional base to define, and then compel obligation to, a body of expertise and standards. Pinchot's claim to be America's first professional forester was wrapped up in his quest to be forestry's statesman. He would build these institutions—schools, professional societies, and forward-thinking employers—for the forestry profession and thus the nation.

In Paris, in the fall of 1889, twenty-four-year-old Pinchot climbed the Eiffel Tower to look down on some neighborhoods that he had lived in as a boy. His grandfather was French, and he'd been raised in bicontinental luxury. Now he revisited the Jardin des Plantes, where he remembered a childhood fascination with insects and snakes. He took his girlfriend for a ride in a hot-air balloon. He attended Buffalo Bill's Wild West show, and remembered how a family friend, former Civil War General William T. Sherman, had once introduced him to the showman. He met with the U.S. ambassador to France, and remembered him as another old family friend.

Pinchot came to Paris to visit a World's Fair–style forestry exhibition. Through his network, he soon met eminent German forester Dietrich Brandis, who insisted that he enroll in a graduate school and learn the discipline. Pinchot chose the French National Forestry School in Nancy, in the northeastern province of Lorraine. He roomed with a family just outside the school's elaborate gate, on a narrow treeless street lined with dull gray three-story buildings. Lectures covered silviculture (how trees grow in relation to light, heat, moisture, soil, and each other), economics, and French law.

Pinchot was not impressed with his fellow students, whom he said had "no more moral sense than a bull frog." Like John Muir at the same age, he was a teetotaling prude who was often tempted to preach—indeed he'd even contemplated serving as a missionary in France, as if France was a backward society that could be improved by someone bearing witness to Christianity.[8] He did, however, love tramping through the French woods. Like Muir, Pinchot felt that he learned more from being out in forests than from reading about them in books. The province of Lorraine was filled with intensively managed hardwood forests, where trees were cut every 150 years. Compared to his grandfather's cut-and-run philosophy, this was sustainability. The forests were also neat and orderly: perhaps reflecting the influence of nearby Germany, they were divided by roads and paths at perfect 90-degree angles. They were clean, with peasants carrying away scrap wood. They were safe, lacking entirely in forest fires. And their limited resources were economically productive: woodsmen, supported by the regulated annual supply of lumber, passed jobs from father to son.

Taking charge of his own education, Pinchot departed Nancy in the spring. He arranged a six-week independent study at the city forest in Zürich, Switzerland. He was greatly impressed with its forest-master, "a stumpy little man in rotten jeans" named Ulrich Meister, whom he called Forstmeister Meister. Meister wore many hats. He presided over the Swiss Liberal Party, a large newspaper, a railroad, a fishing club, and a fishing magazine; he served in the legislature and army; "and in his spare time he was writing a book," Gifford later recalled.[9] Most impressively, the Sihlwald—Forstmeister Meister's government-owned forest of beech, ash, spruce, and maple—made money. Every year trees were removed so that younger ones could thrive. The timber sales from those removed trees brought the city a net annual revenue of $20,000 USD ($550,000 USD in 2018 dollars), or more than eight dollars per acre. This, to Pinchot, was the essence of forestry: effective management by a true statesman leading to both sustainability and profit.

Returning to school in time for late-spring field trips to the Vosges and Alps mountains, Pinchot then joined with some British students to follow Dietrich Brandis on a summer tour of German forests. The other students, who spoke little German, were bored and rowdy. Pinchot gained plenty of time to form a tight, lasting mentor-student relationship with Brandis.

Pinchot asked every expert he encountered for advice. His first question addressed how he should structure his career path. Many people suggested that he work with states to identify and protect valuable forests, as New York was doing in the Adirondacks. Brandis, who was familiar with Americans' vast undeveloped terrain and dislike of big government, went a step further. He suggested that Pinchot might best spread forestry in America by working for millionaires and large corporations rather than going into government service. After all, the purpose of most American government-owned land was to be given away to homesteaders. If you wanted opportunities for large-scale forest management, you had to find clients who not only owned large-scale forests but also intended to keep them. Brandis even suggested that Pinchot's wealthy relatives might spot him half a million dollars to buy such a forest, a proposal they declined.[10]

Pinchot's second question was how long he needed to study before he embarked on that career. Almost every expert—including Brandis, the

Harvard horticulturalist Charles Sargent, and the German-American forester Bernhard Fernow—said at least two years. Some recommended four to six. Pinchot didn't want such lengthy study. "When I get along a certain way in the study of anything, I seem to stick," he wrote in his diary, meaning that he felt stuck.[11] He was grasping the principles of how things were done, but learning more details would make him a sort of engineer of the forest. Instead, he wanted to know just enough to become an overseer of the forest and its engineers. Later, he decided that his impatience with this education arose because natural conditions in America were different, and European remedies wouldn't address America's needs. You couldn't transform an untamed, democratic American wilderness into a sterile, autocratic German tree plantation; indeed, you shouldn't. This sentiment of American exceptionalism proved an incredibly popular talking point for Pinchot's crusade. But even he eventually admitted that he probably should have studied more; for example, in developing American forestry law, it might have been nice to know more about French forestry law.

At its heart, however, his decision to abandon his education was more personal: he was feeling pressure from his father, who was impatient for Gifford to come home and start making his mark—the way James phrased it was that conditions in the United States were now ripe for Gifford to thrive. Finally, Gifford decided to listen to the one mentor who felt the same way. Forstmeister Meister, the Swiss statesman, "paid me the compliment of saying he thought me fit now to organize an administration in the United States. He said I must not lose any chance to get a good chance at home by staying here to study."[12]

Although James Pinchot exaggerated the favorability of conditions, in the big picture he did have a point. In 1890 the American frontier "closed," with census results highlighting a new scarcity of undeveloped land. Experts believed that a timber famine loomed. In recent decades loggers had exhausted the old-growth forests of the upper Midwest, and they now threatened those of the Pacific Northwest, the last available in the continental United States. An American society once based on limitless natural resources was bumping up against limits. Forestry ideals were gaining new importance.

In 1864, Vermont's George Perkins Marsh had launched the argument about diminishing resources, pointing out that advanced civilizations always stewarded the Earth's resources rather than destroying them. In 1873, New York's Franklin Hough called on states and Congress to protect America's surviving forests. In 1874, Ezra Carr—one of John Muir's mentors at the University of Wisconsin, now living in California—likewise warned of deforestation and urged people to see forests as a renewable, profitable crop. In short, scientists, and the people who believed them, had been saying for almost three decades that some form of forestry offered the only way out of a looming environmental crisis.

But on the ground, Americans consumed wood at five times the rate of Europeans. Wood built and heated homes. Wood fenced corrals and fields. Wood buttressed mine tunnels and tied rail lines. Tannin from tree bark turned hides into leather. Wood pulp fed the newspaper boom. Charcoal (derived from wood) fired forges, and charcoal by-products yielded industrial chemicals.[13] In short, cutting down trees undergirded the entire American economy, the amazing system that offered opportunities for immigrant and poor farmer alike.

The problem with wood was that compared to other economic bastions such as wheat, corn, or tobacco, trees took decades to replenish. A denuded forest couldn't contribute very well to the economy. In fact a *thriving* forest didn't really contribute, either—the real economic incentive was the harvest. If you logged all your land today, you could reinvest those revenues in something like railroads or steel factories—almost any enterprise offered a higher rate of return than waiting for trees to grow a little taller.

Many sectors of the nineteenth-century economy suffered from similarly mismatched incentives, including, most famously, drilling for oil. During Pennsylvania's first oil boom, in the 1860s and '70s, anyone who discovered oil needed to start producing it quickly, before a neighbor tapped into the same pool. Massive simultaneous drilling produced a widely fluctuating supply against a growing but still small demand. Gluts drove down prices such that Pennsylvania oil was at one point literally cheaper than drinking water. The system involved profound waste: much oil was sold at prices far less than a stable market would have supported, and some oil proved so unprofitable that it was simply dumped on the countryside. When John D. Rockefeller organized this chaos into a monopoly, he not only made a fortune for himself, he also conquered those mismatched incentives, creating stability that aided development of the sector and the economy at large. Rockefeller eliminated waste—which meant that his actions felt religiously appropriate. To the Christianity of Rockefeller and Pinchot, waste was a failure of not only efficiency but also morality.[14]

Could something similar happen in forests? If they had a single owner, could incentives be aligned, supply stabilized, and waste eliminated? Certainly plenty of timber companies were willing to make a fortune in the process of trying. Taking advantage of poorly written, barely enforced laws, they arranged for individuals to cheaply acquire government land and pass it along to corporate hands. Monopolies reduced waste of collectively owned resources but increased inequality in the process.

Meanwhile, scientists were starting to understand interconnections—for example, between forests and water supplies. In Yosemite, John Muir could show you how overgrazing by sheep caused spring snow to melt more quickly and deplete waterfalls. A similar principle held for forests and streams: if you clear-cut too many trees, meltwater would flood downstream rivers instead of percolating into groundwater that would mitigate summer droughts. Waterborne shippers in the East thus joined with agricultural irrigators in the arid West as fans of forests that *conserved* water by holding it through the spring as snow under their canopies. Charles Sargent wrote that a mountainous forest, "absolutely unfit for agriculture or grazing, [was] only valuable as a reservoir of moisture."[15]

At the same time, hunters were coming to appreciate how forests conserved their game by providing habitat. Aristocratic hunter-explorers like George Bird Grinnell were dismayed at the dwindling herds of bison and other creatures. It was easy to blame the appalling overkill of commercial hunting, but they also saw a deeper problem: homesteads crowded out habitat for bison, elk, deer, and other wildlife. The Boone and Crockett Club—the elite hunters' group founded by Grinnell and Theodore Roosevelt—thus urged preservation of habitat in large, undeveloped forests.

In sum, James Pinchot could see a long-term societal interest in forestry and conservation. He could see support for these ideals, especially in his educated circle. But in the short term, as Gifford looked at how to make a living, the situation proved far more difficult. Plenty of people warned Gifford about it, upon his arrival back home. In Boston, Charles Sargent told him about political obstacles and personality conflicts in the small world of American tree-lovers. In New York, the secretary of the state forest commission told Gifford that politics would preclude the state from hiring a forester for the Adirondacks any time soon. In separate meetings, General Sherman and former Interior Secretary Carl Schurz reported similarly dismal prospects in federal agencies.

Bernhard Fernow, who headed the federal government's tiny forestry advisory service from an attic in Washington, D.C., did want Pinchot to come work as his assistant. They would spread the gospel of forestry through persuasion. However, Pinchot wasn't sure Fernow was the best leader for such a crusade. Fernow was "not a man to make a cause popular," Pinchot wrote in his diary, in part because Fernow was "unhealthily apt to take up any real or imaginary slight or offense."[16] Furthermore, Brandis had cautioned Pinchot against the approach of giving advice without taking responsibility for its implementation. Mere rhetoric wouldn't work. America needed to see forestry in action.

On October 14, 1891, Pinchot's train pulled into Swannanoa Bridge, also known as Best or Asheville Junction, two miles south of the courthouse in Asheville, North Carolina. The station was just a platform, and the village surrounding it a confusing mess.[17] Two years prior, George Vanderbilt, the dashing young scion of one of America's wealthiest dynasties, had bought the entire community and relocated its residents.

Vanderbilt spoke eight languages, and as a twenty-nine-year-old bachelor was much gossiped about in New York society. He devoted himself to culture—including architecture, books, and art—with the same brilliance and fervor that his grandfather, father, and brothers applied to business. At the confluence of the Swannanoa and French Broad Rivers a few miles west of the train station, Vanderbilt intended to build the Biltmore castle, a gigantic residence in the French Château style. Famed architect Richard Morris Hunt designed the 178,926-square-foot building—still today the largest privately owned house in the country. Its construction required one thousand workers and a private brick kiln, woodworking factory, and three-mile rail spur. To assemble the grounds, Vanderbilt bought out nearly seven hundred small landholders, many of whom had struggled to make a living off timber-cutting and cattle-grazing. Then he hired the landscape architect Frederick Law Olmsted to make the land, which eventually totaled 125,000 acres, or 195 square miles, as luxurious as the house.

Any château needed an adjacent village to serve as an aesthetically pleasing entrance and to house supporting businesses, château workers, and other residents. Thus Vanderbilt's plans also included transforming Swannanoa Bridge into a picturesque new European-style town called Biltmore Village. But in autumn of 1891, just two years into the project, most of the village's buildings were temporary. When Pinchot arrived, even the rail station, planned to replace the current freight platform as the village's focal point, was still four years away from completion. [18]

Having received a telegram from Vanderbilt, Pinchot was arriving from Grey Towers, his family's own Hunt-designed mansion, which in its entirety was only slightly bigger than Biltmore's planned banquet hall. He was in his element: all of Biltmore's major players—owner Vanderbilt, architect Hunt, and landscaper Olmsted—were friends of the Pinchot family. They were all part of the Gilded Age American aristocracy, a remarkably small and rigid community that was perhaps best brought to life by Edith Wharton in novels such as *The Age of Innocence*. Indeed, after ending an engagement to Hunt's daughter, Pinchot had recently dated both Vanderbilt's future sister-in-law and Wharton's niece. [19]

Pinchot had spent much of the year on a lengthy trip around the country. He saw hardwood forests in Arkansas, on a tour sponsored by the federal forester Fernow. He detoured for a quick stop at Biltmore, seeing its possibilities for forestry. He then saw Arizona lands owned by the Phelps Dodge company, which had asked him to evaluate the possibility of planting trees there.[20] He saw the Grand Canyon, which prompted in him such a deep spiritual reaction that he bowed his head and sang the doxology. He saw Yosemite, which at first paled by comparison, although its subtler wonders gradually won him over. He saw the vast forests of the Pacific Northwest. He returned East with greater knowledge but no job. He was plenty available when the telegram summoned him to North Carolina.

When Pinchot got off the train at Swannanoa Bridge, Olmsted was waiting to greet him. With a bald pate, full white beard, and slender frame, Olmsted was slightly aloof but kind, even lovable. Then sixty-nine years old, Olmsted was capping off a profound career, with accomplishments that made him a particularly valuable mentor to Pinchot. He was generally seen as an artist—Harvard's Charles Sargent called him the "greatest of all American artists"—even though his canvas was landscapes. Olmsted's legacy included the design of New York's Central Park, Boston's Emerald Necklace park system, Brooklyn's Prospect Park, and the grounds of the U.S. Capitol. On a deeper level, Olmsted also professionalized a new American discipline: landscape architecture, which mixed art, horticulture, and engineering with an element of political science. Olmsted had a particular genius for making man-made landscapes look natural, a quality that Americans loved—but Olmsted used that genius to create spaces with political dimensions as well. Olmsted rarely worked for private individuals like Vanderbilt; he was more interested in civic interactions, in public parks as places to foster democratic values. For example, his taxonomy of park usage contrasted the exertive recreation of a baseball game with the gregarious crowds at a parade grounds and the soul-restoring tranquility of woods and pastures. Olmsted applied rules noting that each use had a different distribution across a city or estate, and required a different type of public space, with a different design, which would inherently train the public to use the space as intended.[21]

Olmsted had already been working at Biltmore for two years. He had designed its stunning three-mile approach road, which now shaped his encounter with Pinchot. The road proceeded alongside a stream, engineered to alternate between a near presence and a distant glint, between still pools and babbling falls. Then the road entered dark, dense foliage, remote and closed-in. Then it topped out to reveal the château site, with wide lawns and commanding views of the French Broad River Valley backed by the magnificent Blue Ridge Mountains. Olmsted had designed the road to evoke an emotional climax at this moment, an awe at the sudden explosion of beauty. Someday the vision's centerpiece would be the Biltmore château itself. Even at this moment, with the future four-story mansion not yet one story tall and its future lawns and gardens covered with construction materials, Olmsted and Pinchot arrived to breathtaking vistas. [22]

In Vanderbilt's original vision, every inch of land he owned would be meadows and parks. It would be Central Park, but bigger and private. However, Olmsted was disappointed to learn that the area's trees were mostly runts and saplings, struggling to survive in soils exhausted by decades of subsistence farming. Olmsted suggested that if lands more distant from the house were made into European-style forests instead of parks, they could serve as game habitat and a future source of revenue from timber. Even before Pinchot arrived, Olmsted and Vanderbilt had committed to heal Biltmore's lands and make it a poster child for American forestry. They'd developed an operational plan for improving forest quality. They'd submitted that plan to Charles Sargent for his approval and on Sargent's recommendation hired an Illinois nurseryman to begin implementing it. However, the complexity of implementation suggested the need for an overseer more broadly trained in forestry. Eager young Pinchot was the obvious choice. [23]

"Had delightful talk with [Olmsted] on the way up the Approach Road," Pinchot recorded in his diary. "Found he had advised [forest management]. And it was decided on. Was much delighted, naturally." [24] Later Pinchot would learn that things weren't quite decided. Olmsted insisted that Pinchot spend a few days touring the estate and then come to his office with a detailed management plan. In that meeting about a month later, Pinchot later told friends, "after delays which nearly drove me wild[,] we had our talk." Olmsted coached and prodded, dramatically improving the content of Pinchot's proposal and conforming it to Olmsted's vision. Finally, Pinchot recalled, Olmsted "said he would advise that the forest at Biltmore be put in my hands."[25]

Olmsted served as a valuable mentor, one of many for Pinchot. Where John Muir learned best in solitary contemplation of nature, and neither man claimed to learn much from books, Pinchot learned best from older, accomplished practitioners. He had left school in France to study under Meister and Brandis, and then left Europe to eventually work under Olmsted. Meanwhile he built relationships with Fernow, Sargent, and Muir, among others. The mentorship approach offered advantages including personal attention, opportunities for hands-on experience, and ways to capitalize on Pinchot's strengths in networking. The disadvantage: long-term relationships can fray. Pinchot and Olmsted always got along well, although Olmsted was a hands-off manager who completely retired by 1895. Pinchot and Brandis always corresponded warmly, although they were separated by an ocean. Pinchot interacted more frequently with Sargent and Fernow—and in those cases, sparks flew.

Pinchot had an ambition to change the world. That ambition drove him to soak up as much as possible from older experts, and then diverge from those perspectives. For example, Olmsted was never terribly interested in plants themselves, as plants. Instead, he saw them primarily as elements that could provide form, color, and texture to his landscape compositions—like paint to Monet. Sargent, by contrast, loved plants only as wonderful individual creatures—he literally didn't see the forest for the trees. And Muir loved plants mostly as a springboard to spiritual contemplation. Pinchot incorporated elements from all three into his unique vision of seeing plants and forests as elements of systems that provided not only beauty but also other benefits to society.

As Pinchot developed that vision, egos and hurt feelings sometimes got in the way. Where Muir could argue with a light touch, with humor and detachment, young Pinchot often stewed over arguments, turning them into dramas. Pinchot's Biltmore work proved a great example. When it started, the forest advisor Fernow told Pinchot that although his forestry operations might improve Biltmore's environmental conditions, he would never turn a profit. Pinchot disagreed. He then put a good deal of spin on the first year's results to show them as profitable. When Fernow saw through the spin, Pinchot accused him of needless disparagement. Fernow responded that he was merely agreeing with Pinchot's mentor Brandis "when he called the experiment 'verfehlt' [failed, unsuccessful], from that point of view [profitableness] only!"[26] Pinchot, unappeased, came to see Fernow as a rival, even an enemy. He came to hold Fernow in increasing contempt—upon Fernow's retirement decades later, Pinchot said, "I believe Fernow did more to retard American forestry than any other man that ever lived."[27] From Biltmore on, one of Pinchot's primary ambitions became to replace Fernow as the leading voice in American forestry.

Another example arose after Pinchot left Biltmore in 1895. Vanderbilt replaced him with a respected young German forester, Carl Schenck. Pinchot became frustrated with Schenck's focus on economics and efficiency over silviculture, while Schenck believed that Pinchot opposed big timber companies too aggressively. In their heated arguments, Pinchot once called Schenck the Antichrist.[28] In the late 1890s, Schenck and Fernow established America's first forestry schools, at Biltmore and Cornell respectively; when Pinchot responded by establishing a school at Yale, he made sure it had a bigger endowment to out-compete his enemies.

Maybe nothing could have stopped these men from bitter opposition. Founding a new profession required big egos, and big egos can clash easily. In young Pinchot's case, the spectacle was exaggerated because he often clashed with powerful older men, as if betraying their mentorship. Would his future relationship with Muir follow the same pattern?

Pinchot saw Biltmore as a one-year stepping-stone; he kept returning for another three years only because he wasn't yet getting the call-up to the major leagues. "What I want most is charge of the Adirondacks," he had written in his diary in 1890. "To manage a forest area is the right way to begin."[29]

The Adirondack region of far northern New York boasted one hundred peaks and thirteen hundred lakes. Its thin soils had long discouraged permanent settlement by Mohawk or Algonquian tribes or by early European colonizers. Eventually its thick forests did attract loggers, especially in the timber-hungry years after the Civil War. Those were the same years when its proximity to New York City attracted wealthy, influential families who enjoyed relaxing amid natural beauty.

The Adirondacks became an early battleground: Would they be completely logged over, or could some forests be saved for other purposes? In 1873, activist Verplanck Colvin recommended that the entire Adirondack region, including lands that were then privately owned, be set aside as a state forest preserve. In some ways this marked the beginning of the nature preservation movement: although Yellowstone National Park had been established the previous year, and in 1841 painter George Catlin had proposed a "Nations Park" that would preserve the bison herds and indigenous tribes of the Great Plains, those proposals had addressed remote places with few competing demands and no private ownership. In the Adirondacks, for the first time a U.S. state government was asked to stand against private ownership and development in service of nature. As an 1884 commission chaired by Harvard's Charles Sargent phrased it, the Adirondacks should be "forever kept as wild forest lands."[30]

Although one might see the Adirondack argument as extraction-versus-recreation, it was expressed as science. In stressing the need for the preserve, Sargent didn't talk about scenery or even wildlife habitat, but instead about keeping a steady year-round volume of navigable water in the Hudson River and Erie Canal, and preventing forest fires caused by loggers' waste piles. Many people could agree with Sargent's description of the crisis, but his government-based solution was more controversial. People weren't sure that a government could be trusted to administer natural systems. Indeed, Sargent himself was horrified by graft and patronage in the era when "Tammany Hall" served as shorthand for New York's deeply corrupt politics. To keep machine insiders from ruining the public's desires, Sargent wanted the Adirondacks to be controlled by an unpaid, permanent, unpolitical three-man commission.

Instead, when the state legislature implemented Sargent's recommendations, it tweaked the commission to be paid and politically appointed—and the governor soon chose unqualified hacks who ignored Sargent's plans. Sargent was devastated: "The whole matter is simply disgusting from beginning to end," he wrote. [31] He felt like he couldn't trust policymakers with his science. Indeed the Adirondack issue exposed deeper rifts in trust across society. As wealthy people bought up lands to prevent development—or urged the state to do so—the rural poor resented the loss of job opportunities and access to land. They didn't feel they could trust the elites. New laws restricted everybody's hunting and fishing, and a new forest police force was created to enforce those limits—suggesting that preservationists might secretly want to replicate Europe's rigid hereditary class system, saving the forests at the expense of the peasants. [32]

Problems of trust were even greater for the timber industry. Although Sargent recommended that regulated logging be part of the wild preserve, such a solution would require loggers with ethics and state regulators with integrity. Given the history of catastrophic, corruptly regulated logging practices—and given the uncurbed abuses perpetrated by monopolists in other Gilded Age industries as well—that seemed too much to ask. Instead, in a new state constitution in 1895, New York voters enshrined the Adirondacks as "forever wild," interpreting that phrase as never permitting any destruction of timber except to create campsites.

This was the preservation impulse, a deeply rooted backlash against industrialization. A majority of New York voters didn't want to cut down trees in the Adirondacks, ever. Neither John Muir nor the newly formed, California-focused Sierra Club played any political role in sparking New York preservation. A preservation-versus-conservation divide arose from the deeper societal breakdown of trust.

Pinchot returned from Europe in late 1890, amid this breakdown. That's why Sargent and the New York state forest commission secretary were so pessimistic about Pinchot's job prospects. Political discourse was so caught up in extremes that there was no room for the compromise of scientific forestry.

Pinchot nevertheless tried. For example, at a forestry conference in March 1894, he laid out the desired forestry principles to support Adirondack logging. Behind his technical discussions of trunk diameter and overmature stands was a basic philosophy: that selectively removing trees would improve long-term forest health while providing a regional economic base. Few of the conference attendees embraced his ideas. Then the following year, any opportunity to implement forestry policy on the Adirondack forest died with the voters' decision to ban the good logging with the bad. [33]

Pinchot always believed that forestry could work in the Adirondacks. He believed that humans could coexist with scenic wild places, that ethical logging could sustain nature *and* maintain scenery *and* provide jobs *and* make money for landowners, all at once. What the Adirondacks needed, he believed, was for somebody to convince loggers to reform their practices, and then convince the rest of society to trust that process. The New York voters didn't even let him try. He was baffled. He wrote, "It is as though a man were to let his valuable farm lie fallow because he had not sufficient confidence in his own wisdom, ability, and honesty to do anything else." [34]

Aside from his frustrations regarding the Adirondacks, Pinchot had rich, varied experiences in the mid-1890s. He started dating Laura Houghteling while living at Biltmore in early 1893; that December, they got engaged. Three months later, she died. Pouring the energy of grief into his work, Pinchot earned several forestry consulting contracts, gave speeches, published books, and got involved in forestry politics at the federal level. Part II of this book will describe his role in a remarkable revolution in which the federal government, under the Forest Reserve Act of 1891, started setting aside vast forestlands under its permanent management. But for now, to highlight his rivalry with Muir, let's pick up the story a few years later.

In the summer of 1897, Pinchot had an ideal forester's job: he was wandering the West as a special agent for the Interior Department, examining forests to decide exactly where public land boundaries should be set. Many of these lands had been withdrawn from homesteading with little geographic knowledge, before their surroundings were even surveyed. Pinchot volunteered to make those surveys, tramping through unfamiliar forests in the Idaho panhandle and Washington State. He loved it. In his straightlaced, forest-surveying style, he was imitating his friend Muir's free-ranging soul.

Additionally, Pinchot was always something of a marketer. Thus while he was traveling, he networked with bigwigs to talk politics. For example, in late August, between his surveys of the Cascade and Olympic Mountains, he made a stopover in Seattle. On that single day he twice called on an influential lawyer named Thomas Burke, a friend of Pinchot's Yale friend Henry Stimson. Burke was a short, round man who fanned rumors that he was the one who had convinced railroad magnate James J. Hill to choose Seattle, rather than Tacoma, for the terminus of the Great Northern railroad—which was arguably the most momentous decision in the city's short history. Pinchot was now trying to win Burke over to forestry.

Burke's ideas, his biographer wrote, were generally "conventional and conservative." Between Burke's small-government ideals and the interests of his monopolist patron Hill, he was one of the least Progressive of the era's Republicans. However, Burke "had never been a particularly good judge of the views and motives of others" and never seemed to recognize even the most shameless flattery. [35] Furthermore, Burke had long been a member of the local Forestry Association, alongside men who owned extensive timberlands. If federal policies slowed the cutting of trees on public lands, the trees on these men's private lands would become more valuable, and their power would increase compared to their landless competitors. In short, as a representative of Seattle's wealthy timber interests, Burke did have some reasons to agree with Pinchot's forestry arguments.

Pinchot masterfully navigated these personal and policy characteristics. In their long conferences, he listened to Burke and learned about local public opinion. Then he laid out his case: forestry policy—including these new forest reserves—was about *using* resources, but using them with efficiency and coordination to support long-term, sustainable prosperity instead of boom-and-bust cycles.

Burke was swayed, at least enough to bring Pinchot to meet with the editor of the *Post-Intelligencer* newspaper. Newspapers were a particular target of Pinchot's outreach, because most of the era's journalism was slanted, and most Western newspapers decried federal land policy. After all, most frontier newspapers were fragile institutions, dependent on local merchants, likely to thrive only if the city grew exponentially. Seattle's railroad had arrived just a few years previously, amid an economic downturn, and only now was the city poised for a boom. Yet that boom might be slowed by restrictions on logging, mining, or other activities that extracted resources from the land. Indeed the *Post-Intelligencer* had previously labeled the forest reserves "an intolerable blunder." [36]

In their meeting that evening, the editor "came to the right view," Pinchot wrote in his diary. It was an amazing turnaround: the voice of a depressed, resource-dependent city would immediately cease editorials that criticized conservation of those resources. It would turn from a virulent opponent of forest reserves to a favorable or at least neutral position. And indeed, the editor even offered to publish a gentle, flattering "interview" that Pinchot himself could dictate. They would plan it for early September, after Pinchot returned from his work on the Olympic Peninsula. [37]

In Pinchot's diary for September 5, 1897, he recorded that it was "not a clear day," but he wasn't talking about the weather. For the three years since the death of his fiancée Laura Houghteling, Pinchot had believed that he and Laura were spiritually united. In his diary he recorded each day as "blind" or "not so clear" or "good"—with *good* or *clear* indicating that he felt Laura was present with him or even speaking to him. The best days followed nights when he dreamed of her. Many days he described as "good and hard," as if Laura were the new agent of his Calvinist workaholism. Laura merged with God to provide the reason to withstand toil or misery, the inspiration to do God's work in the world. Pinchot's toil for September 5 included touring a sawmill, lunching with a friend, attending a church service, and dictating his interview to a *Post-Intelligencer* stenographer. [38]

His base for these activities was the Rainier Grand Hotel. Just two blocks from Seattle's downtown waterfront, the elegant, four-story, 225-room hotel was buzzing with excitement that summer, thanks to the flood of aspiring entrepreneurs departing for the Klondike Gold Rush. The Rainier Grand, then just four years old, served the upper-class traveler. It was the sort of place that published its register of new guests in local newspapers, and entertained those guests with a locally styled interior design indicating they were in a special place. For example, its spacious lobby, overlooked by a mezzanine, offered accents in local Douglas fir, left raw in the rustic Western style. [39]

That afternoon in the lobby, Pinchot met an old friend: John Muir. Muir was also staying at the Rainier Grand, on his return from one of his many trips to see Alaska glaciers. Muir found the gold rush a "wild, discouraging mess" and the miners "daft." Nevertheless he seemed amused by it all, in high spirits. [40] The two men spent part of the afternoon together, ate dinner together, and engaged in pleasant conversation into the evening. "Much delighted to see Mr. Muir again," Pinchot wrote in his diary that night. But a set of events that allegedly occurred the next morning came to define a devastating split in the environmental movement. [41]

Reading Pinchot's interview in the morning paper, Muir exploded in fury, according to William Colby, who heard the story from Muir several years later when they were working together at the Sierra Club. Pinchot had told the newspaper that sheep grazing did little harm to forests. *Hoofed locusts!* How dare he? According to the story that Colby related to Muir biographer Linnie Marsh Wolfe, Muir's eyes were "flashing blue flames." With newspaper reporters in earshot, Muir confronted Pinchot with the article: "Are you correctly quoted here?" When Pinchot agreed, Muir said, "Then . . . I don't want anything more to do with you. When we were in the Cascades last summer, you yourself stated that the sheep did a great deal of harm." [42]

This, biographer Wolfe announced, was the origin of the preservation-versus-conservation divide. This moment defined the apparent split between the Muir and Pinchot philosophies. Wolfe left to the reader the obvious implications: Pinchot's craven appeasement to politically powerful Northwest newspapers and sheep interests demonstrated his untrustworthiness. *Conservation* was nothing more than a giveaway to big business. Pinchot was a Judas who betrayed his mentor Muir. Preservation was nature's true salvation.

Wolfe's story was widely accepted until the 1990s, when historian Char Miller disproved it. Muir and Pinchot could not have had a confrontation in the hotel that morning, Miller said, because Muir's boat for California left the docks at 8:00 A.M. He had to have boarded a few hours earlier. When would he have had time to read a newspaper? And why didn't any of the journalists, allegedly hanging around this hotel lobby, write about such a dramatic incident? Perhaps, one could argue, Muir awoke incredibly early, or saw a prepublished version the previous evening. But when Miller looked up the article, its lone sentence on sheep grazing read, "Pasturage may also be permitted by the [interior] secretary under suitable rules and regulations."[43] Muir opposed most sheep pasturage, but this phrasing hardly declared a huge corporate giveaway or a rejection of Muir's concerns. Instead, what was most remarkable about the article and accompanying editorial was that Pinchot had indeed convinced the *Post-Intelligencer* to join Muir in supporting federal forest policy.

Furthermore, Miller argued, if there was a dispute, why didn't either Muir or Pinchot give any evidence of it in their actions of the coming days and months? Pinchot wrote nothing in his letters or diaries, contrary to the considerable angst generated by arguments with previous mentors. And Muir did not, as Wolfe claimed, break off relations with Pinchot: They continued to correspond for years, even about issues like sheep grazing. They continued to use the word "delight" about their encounters.

Nevertheless the story endured, and sometimes still holds sway today. It feels like it *should* be true. It captures the personalities we want our heroes to have, as opposed to their actual personalities. Muir: principled, passionate, and could he also please be hotheaded? Pinchot: too political, trying to make everyone happy, and could he also please be duplicitous?

Some subsequent historians have used the alleged incident to claim that Muir felt betrayed by Pinchot.[44] Certainly the two men had rivaling views of the value of allowing sheep onto public lands. Clearly Pinchot did not blindly accept Muir's ideas; he instead tried to alter those ideas to the constraints he felt, to the needs of the society he saw around him. And it's true that Charles Sargent felt that Pinchot's divergence from his own viewpoints amounted to treacherous disloyalty. But Muir—perhaps seeing in Pinchot some of his own contrarian individualism—gave no indication of feeling betrayed.[45]

In March 1898, six months after the alleged Rainier Grand Hotel confrontation, Muir wrote to his editor Robert Underwood Johnson of his disappointment in Pinchot's evolving sheep-grazing policy. He explained to Johnson that "he [Pinchot] told me last summer that in his opinion sheep in moderate numbers did no harm to Washington & Oregon forests." This account suggests a scenario more likely than the one painted by Wolfe: Muir learned of Pinchot's opinions in person, perhaps during that friendly post-dinner discussion, rather than through the next morning's newspaper. Muir's next sentence in the letter to Johnson—and presumably in his discussion with Pinchot—was: "But if any [sheep] are allowed[,] all will push in."[46]

In other words, Muir didn't necessarily dispute the detailed science that Pinchot commissioned, which showed moderate sheep grazing to have surprisingly limited effects, especially outside of California.[47] Muir and Pinchot disagreed here not on big philosophical issues—the preservation-versus-conservation divide that so fascinated future observers—but on tactics. When was the compromise of allowing a few regulated sheep acceptable, and when would it be taken advantage of? They disagreed on how optimistically to view their fellow humans. It may be ironic that Pinchot, with his reputation for pragmatism, was the idealistic one who believed that wool growers could follow societal rules, while the cheerful, forgiving Muir dared not begin to compromise with such sinners.

However their in-person conversation at the Rainier Grand Hotel played out, Pinchot didn't ponder it in his diary because it was the type of discussion he would expect to have, and enjoy having, with Muir. For Muir's part, the letter to Johnson demonstrated his belief that this was a small disagreement: "I still look for lots of good work from Pinchot."[48]

Muir was a prophet, free to preach bold moral declarations: *Trees are good. Sheep are bad. Nature is God.* He didn't have to worry about how to implement these principles in the real world. Pinchot, however, was a statesman. He was in the thick of implementation; he was the one who had to deal with real people struggling to match individual actions to philosophical theories. The theologian Reinhold Niebuhr once described *prophet–versus–statesman* as a central paradox of morality. One is committed to an individual interpretation of the voice of God, the other to obligations of community in a sinful world. Who was morally superior, Niebuhr asked, abolitionist-prophet William Lloyd Garrison or opportunist-statesman Abraham Lincoln? Neither—they were morally equivalent: "The moral achievement of statesmen must be judged in terms which take account of the limitations of human society which the statesman must, and the prophet need not, consider."[49]

Muir aspired to be nature's prophet. Pinchot aspired to be its statesman. Muir's assignment required one-in-a-million talent, but as demonstrated by the Northwest sheep issue, Pinchot's assignment was thornier.

5

The Tragedy of Gifford Pinchot

O n the afternoon of October 11, 1905, after a hard rainstorm in Washington, D.C., a message arrived at Gifford Pinchot's office. The president wanted to go for a walk.

In the eight years since Pinchot's encounter with Muir in Seattle, he had replaced Bernhard Fernow as chief federal forester, implemented management of the forest reserves, and used his friendship with now-President Theodore Roosevelt to influence conservation policy.

Roosevelt's message was not a surprise and portended nothing troubling. The president simply loved physical exertion, particularly with trusted associates. Rather than a "kitchen cabinet," Roosevelt's informal advisers were known as his "tennis cabinet." He regularly called on colleagues to get outside with him, Pinchot, perhaps, most of all. And Pinchot was always willing. His diary regularly recorded, "Tennis with T.R." The previous week, he'd noted, "I beat him 5-6, 6-2, 6-0, 6-3, I believe."[1]

Pinchot and Roosevelt were cut from the same cloth: wealthy, outdoorsy, Protestant, educated, immersed in masculine physicality, and appalled by America's destruction of forests, wildlife, and natural beauty. They first became friends in 1899 when Roosevelt was governor of New York State. When Pinchot visited the governor's mansion, Roosevelt challenged him to a wrestling match. Roosevelt, seven years older and six inches shorter but thirty-five pounds heavier, pinned Pinchot—and then they moved to the boxing ring, where Pinchot's longer arms proved superior. Athletics and outdoor adventure provided the continuing base for their frank, intimate, and incredibly productive relationship.

On this day they walked along the Potomac River, joined by Robert Bacon, a banker and old Harvard classmate of Roosevelt's who had just been appointed as an assistant secretary of state. Roosevelt walked briskly, and Pinchot, with his long legs, always matched his stride. But Bacon was not yet familiar with T.R.'s habits. Indeed, on this day, Bacon was wearing a derby hat, patent-leather shoes, and a cutaway coat, while carrying a beautifully rolled silk umbrella. In those years, the banks of the Potomac were quite swampy, not yet landscaped into parks, so within minutes the men were drenched to the knees. After about an hour, with darkness falling, they came across an inlet, about 200 feet wide, where Roosevelt expected to find a boat that they could paddle to the other side. The boat was tied up on the inlet's far shore. They stood momentarily silenced, defeated.

Clearly, Roosevelt announced, they would have to swim. He started handing his valuables to Bacon. As the newbie, Bacon would have to try to retrace his steps back home. Bacon protested. He didn't want to be left behind. So Roosevelt put his watch, wallet, and other valuables into his own hat and put his hat atop his head. Then he waded in. Pinchot and Bacon followed. Halfway across the inlet, Bacon lifted the fancy umbrella that he was still carrying in his left hand, and said, "A lot of good this is doing me now!"[2]

They loved the experience. "We walked back to the White House with much merriment," Pinchot recorded. After dropping off Roosevelt and Bacon, Pinchot walked home. Upon arriving, his wet sleeve brushed the hand of Mary McCadden, who had been his nurse as a child and was still employed as a family servant. "Drenched!" she scolded. "You've been out with the President."

Pinchot and Roosevelt were more than playmates. They had an intellectual bond. They were mutually fascinated by a variety of topics, especially politics and conservation. In the four years since Roosevelt had become president, he had continually elevated Pinchot's role. Most importantly, they engineered the transfer of 63 million acres of government-owned forestlands from the Department of Interior to the Department of Agriculture, where Pinchot ran the Division of Forestry. The transfer gave Pinchot the chance to administer land, thus taking full responsibility for forest policy. He and Roosevelt renamed the division the U.S. Forest Service, and Pinchot built it like an entrepreneur builds a startup. He hired young professionals, trusted them to do their jobs, and made them believe in their mission, giving the agency an esprit de corps resembling that of a Yale fraternity. One of Pinchot's early hires—himself a Yale grad, like many others—recalled in the 1950s, "He [Pinchot] personally planned much of the organization and administration that has stood the test of fifty years. He attracted to himself an exceptionally able, devoted, and zealous group of young men, who entered this new profession of forestry because of Pinchot's leadership . . . Pinchot was such an extraordinary organizer and executive that he got the Forest Service with its young crew started on ways that have been its strength ever since."[3] Meanwhile, Pinchot established the Society of American Foresters, which met first in his office and later in his home, with gingerbread and baked apples provided by his servants. And in 1900 his family established the Yale School of Forestry, America's first graduate forestry program.

Pinchot was both inspirational manager and policy wonk. Roosevelt sought his advice on a host of issues, especially in regards to natural resource policy. Roosevelt once told the magazine editor Robert Underwood Johnson that on forestry matters, Pinchot was the keeper of his conscience.[4] Pinchot wrote Roosevelt's speeches on conservation and later even ghostwrote the conservation chapter in Roosevelt's autobiography. In one of the few sentences of that chapter that Roosevelt wrote himself, he said, "Among the many, many public officials who under my administration rendered literally invaluable service to the people of the United States, he [Pinchot], on the whole, stood first."[5]

They could openly express anything to each other. For example, as they walked home from the Potomac on that October day in 1905, Roosevelt voiced a desire to serve as secretary of state under a president such as Elihu Root or William Taft—a curious ambition for the most powerful man in the country to say out loud. Likewise the following year, Pinchot suggested that Roosevelt appoint him as a Department of Interior assistant in charge of the General Land Office for a six-month temporary assignment in which he would clear the bureaucracy of its incompetent employees and corrupt practices, and then return to the Forest Service. Intrigued, Roosevelt admitted that if tradition didn't dictate that the interior secretary be a Westerner, he would unquestionably name Pinchot to that even higher-profile job.[6] Although nothing came of the exchange, it demonstrates their mutual transparency and respect.

Roosevelt served as the partnership's front man: extroverted, charming, forceful, decisive, larger than life, and eager for limelight. Pinchot was not exactly a wallflower, but he did prefer the contemplativeness of fly-fishing to the thrill of big-game hunting. His gaunt frame and hollow cheeks suggested a man more austere than jovial; his sociability could be interrupted by inexplicable periods of disconnectedness. He also had characteristics that benefitted a behind-the-scenes organizer, such as administrative efficiency—he insisted that Forest Service underlings answer all correspondence before 10:00 A.M.—and a bottomless capacity for hard work. He subsumed his private life to his public responsibilities. Family wealth provided his income. He lived with his parents in a mansion they bought near the White House. And he still showed no interest in romance beyond communing with the spirit of his late fiancée. He was able to devote all of his attention to governance.

The partnership with Roosevelt activated Pinchot's genius for politics. He could understand an issue and how to frame it, he could speak extemporaneously, and he liked people. Thanks to this genius, Roosevelt's conservation ambitions both succeeded and grew. One component of Pinchot's genius was that he never forgot that his actions always required public support, so he worked tirelessly to educate and arouse the public about conservation issues. Roosevelt coined the phrase "bully pulpit" to refer to his platform for public advocacy; Pinchot and his staff of press agents, headed by a Yale classmate, were the largest component of that pulpit. A contemporary muckraker called Roosevelt and Pinchot the two most talented publicity men in all of politics.[7]

Pinchot himself must have been surprised at the emergence of some of these talents. He began his career as a consulting forester, working alone, and ended up running a large federal agency.[8] In Europe, he'd asked lots of experts about how to make a career in forestry, and now he was giving answers to supplicants only a few years his junior. At the beginning of his career he felt unfairly boxed in by the anti-logging prejudices of New York State forestry policy, and now he controlled logging policy at the federal level. And he began with a thin skin, filled with emotion every time Dietrich Brandis, Bernhard Fernow, or Charles Sargent expressed disapproval, but with power he came to relish confrontations.

On the morning of June 20, 1907, Gifford Pinchot walked across the stage of the Broadway Theater in Denver, Colorado. Under a scalloped proscenium arch, he faced an orchestra pit, onion domes, balconies, and an ornate ceiling. The majestic theater occupied the ground floor of the Metropole Hotel, which along with the adjacent Brown Palace offered the finest accommodations in the city. On this day, the theater was filled with attendees at the Denver Public Lands Convention, a prestigious and politically charged event commissioned by the Colorado legislature. With his slim six-foot-two frame encased in an elegant tailored suit, the forty-one-year-old Pinchot exuded confidence as he approached the podium.

The crowd booed.

"If you fellows can stand me," Pinchot began his speech, "I can stand you."[9]

Pinchot was at the peak of his power. His Forest Service now controlled almost 175 million acres. He had helped Roosevelt double the number of national parks from five to ten, create the first eighteen national monuments, and create the first fifty-three national wildlife refuges.

Pinchot's speech at the Broadway Theater climaxed the convention, which had been spurred by opposition to one of Roosevelt and Pinchot's most blatant actions: the *midnight reserves*. In February 1907, congressmen, frustrated by Roosevelt usurping their policymaking power, passed a law prohibiting the president from unilaterally setting aside forest reserves. They attached it as a rider to a bill that Roosevelt couldn't veto. Indeed he signed the bill, but only because moments beforehand, he proclaimed 16 million acres of new reserves—basically all of the potentially reserve-able land in six Western states. Pinchot and his staff had worked day and night to prepare the paperwork that slipped in these reserves barely ahead of the deadline. [10] Opposition to this proclamation centered in Colorado. Indeed, many Coloradoans opposed the entire Roosevelt-Pinchot conservation platform, which saw forests and grazing lands as publicly owned resources, deserving of management rather than free-for-all giveaway. Thus Colorado was hosting this convention, which attracted participants from across the West. Historian Michael McCarthy, in a book about a decade of Colorado conservation politics, called the convention a watershed event.

The convention opened with a keynote from Montana senator Thomas Carter, who set an emotional tone: "If the people of this country are to be held in terror, now is the time to resent it." Later Colorado senator Henry Teller railed against the midnight reserves and indeed all public lands. "There is no glory in following the plow unless a man follows it upon his own land," Teller said, to cheers. "It is our duty to see that every man gets his land and that it is not tied up by the government." With a call for "freedom," a newspaper summarizing the first day demanded the right to "people our lands and use our waters and open our mineral fields *now!*" Through most of a second day, the only speakers supporting government policy were those sent by the government itself. They included the interior secretary and his deputy, because Roosevelt understood that a Western revolt could jeopardize his public lands legacy. Another newspaper claimed that "men of all parties" were "well-nigh unanimous in condemnation of the policies of Roosevelt and Pinchot." And then Pinchot opened the conference's third day. [11]

It would have been easy for him to get cynical or discouraged. His opponents' arguments were emotional and irrational, with their accusations of terrorism and references to the nostalgia of homesteaders plowing their own land. Pinchot, by contrast, could offer only a clear-eyed look at environmental limits. He could talk science and efficiency. Although he wasn't above associating his cause with its own hot-button issues, such as income disparity and fear of monopolies, he had to know that audiences in Colorado might resist such appeals from an educated Easterner, a member of the elite. With good reason, Westerners feared that increasing federal power would actually increase income and class disparity. They feared that wealthier stock growers, wool growers, miners, timber magnates, and railroad owners would gain outsized clout at an agency office. At a time of class warfare between labor and capital, farm and industry, West and East, country and city, commoner and robber baron, any policy's primary drawbacks were its class implications.

Here at the Broadway Theater, Pinchot marched into the heart of his opposition to deal with his adversaries openly and frankly. He had also done so on previous trips to Colorado. In December 1905, Pinchot's address to a cattlemen's rally in Glenwood Springs left the ballroom silent, the protesting stockgrowers disarmed and almost embarrassed at their previous vitriol. In January 1906, he met with a smaller group of cattlemen at Denver's Brown Palace, and again they found him suave and polished, a gentleman whose diplomacy chastened them. And now here in Denver in June 1907, he calmly and reasonably explained why forest reserves were valuable, why grazing fees were important, why the system helped the small operator fight monopolists, and why he personally resented charges that he was an arrogant demagogue. On this occasion, his opponents weren't entirely silenced—the afternoon continued with attacks on his positions—but when the convention voted on resolutions summarizing critiques of federal policies, the critiques proved milder than pre-convention speculation had predicted. Newspapers described the convention's abortive revolt with words like "fizzle" and "frizzle." Pinchot himself wrote to a friend, "We had a great time and we were by no means eaten up. The resolutions were absolutely harmless."[12]

In addition to his interpersonal skills, Pinchot's success drew on his media skills. With an aggressive outreach program, Pinchot declared the convention a victory, and so it became one. He told newspapers that the convention had "deliberately set out to break up the forestry work of the government. . . . They failed miserably." He dispelled rumors that the coming Irrigation Congress in Sacramento was also awash in anti-government sentiment. In the months between the Denver and Sacramento conventions, Pinchot went on a speaking tour of the West, using charm and logic to persuade audiences. He always received newspaper coverage summarizing his speeches, his victorious view of the Denver events, and often his remarkable personality. Articles called him straightforward, sincere, and plain spoken. Although argumentative, they said, he was affable and even-tempered. Several noted that he'd come from wealth but was selflessly dedicated to public service. Even if a newspaper held back from admiring his policies, it could admire him and trust him as a person.[13]

Pinchot's media strategy thus created a trusting space in which Westerners could move toward his positions. A small timber operator might appreciate Pinchot's anti-monopolist rhetoric; a big one might read profits into his push for stability or his support for standardizing sizes and grades of lumber. Most anyone could appreciate his efforts to reduce forest fires or his gallant personal commitment to his country's governance rather than capitalist excess. Capitalism was then so raw, unregulated, and vicious that many producers felt trapped by its unstable, hypercompetitive markets. Pinchot gave them a chance to escape the markets' Darwinian mechanisms by proclaiming that they too altruistically wanted to safeguard trees for future generations.

Pinchot still faced plenty of criticism from logging, grazing, and mining interests big and small. Even other foresters, especially native

Germans like Bernhard Fernow and Carl Schenck, complained that he placed too little emphasis on creating forests that were easy and efficient to log.[14] Pinchot's brand of forestry had too many other goals, such as anti-monopolism, wildlife habitat, and water resource protection. Trying to please too many people, Pinchot saw forests too holistically to profit from them.

Pinchot believed that with better scientific knowledge of trees, better analysis of markets and transportation networks, and better processes to extract one resource while protecting those that remained, forestry could use efficiency to improve forest conditions, scenery, profitability, and forestry jobs all at the same time. At Biltmore, it didn't: Pinchot had needed to jigger his ledgers to show his project breaking even. Yet even fourteen years later, Pinchot still trusted his base notion of profitable forestry. Every year, in his budgetary requests to Congress, he asserted that a self-sustaining national forest system was just around the corner.

In adapting Forstmeister Meister's Sihlwald to a nationwide scale, Pinchot's great innovation had been to expand German "scientific forestry" to "practical forestry." Rather than create a German tree plantation, he was adapting to forest conditions he encountered. Rather than merely organize the forest for economic gain, he was seeking environmental and social gains as well. Yet he never seemed to consider that these expanded ambitions would cost money. He always expected a sort of efficiency bonus, an ability to achieve all his ambitions solely by eliminating waste. Defensively, egotistically, he kept insisting that his unique brand of forestry would transform the nation for the better—a dangerous gambit, because if statesmanship was his primary aim, then egotism was its biggest roadblock. One great tragedy of Pinchot's life was that even as his 1907 victory in Denver demonstrated some mastery of the tools of statesmanship, it also exposed the limits of his vision of profitable forestry. Yet forestry was his very reason to pursue statesmanship.

On the evening of January 7, 1910, Pinchot and his widowed mother were getting ready for dinner in their mansion at 1615 Rhode Island Avenue, six blocks north of the White House. Roosevelt was no longer in the Oval Office. The Pinchots' grand home was built for entertaining—tonight's small dinner party was nothing compared to the thousand-guest reception that they had hosted for a 1908 conference. In the front hall, Pinchot chatted with one of the recently arrived guests, John Callan O'Laughlin, a journalist and close friend of the former president. The doorbell rang. Pinchot opened the door, and a messenger from the new Taft White House handed him an envelope. [15]

"I looked into the envelope, found the letter I half expected," Pinchot later wrote. He and O'Laughlin walked into the dining room to greet his mother. Pinchot waved the letter at her. "I'm fired," he said. Just five years after he founded the U.S. Forest Service, his career as the nation's chief forester was over.

Thus climaxed a complicated and deservedly obscure feud known as the "Pinchot-Ballinger affair." At its base was a disagreement between Pinchot and Interior Secretary Richard Ballinger on the acceptable scope of executive power. Ballinger was a Westerner, short and stocky, raised poor, and trained as a lawyer—all the opposite of Pinchot. Their temperaments differed as well: Pinchot, like Roosevelt, believed that to save nature and fight monopolies, you needed bold actions of questionable legality, such as creating the midnight forest reserves and Muir Woods National Monument. Ballinger, by contrast, wanted executive-branch actions to be more restrained, so as not to usurp the roles of Congress or the private sector. Furthermore, with Pinchot's rise in the Department of Agriculture's forestry division, he had gone beyond forestry to seek broad conservation outcomes on all public lands—but managing public lands was Interior's job, so Pinchot's aspirations and methods were robbing Ballinger's department of its functions. Ballinger did consider himself a Rooseveltian conservationist, but he wanted to accomplish the goals with less drama, fewer disruptive tactics—and William Taft, Roosevelt's handpicked successor to the presidency, largely agreed. To Pinchot, the goals couldn't be accomplished with the lesser methods. Conservation required unified planning, which required concentrated power.

When William Glavis, an ambitious lowly Interior employee, raised allegations that some Alaska coal patents might have been obtained fraudulently, and that Ballinger might have failed to stop it, Pinchot acquired a tool to use in criticizing Ballinger. Now older and more confident than the youth who feuded with Bernhard Fernow and Charles Sargent, Pinchot taunted Ballinger cagily. Disingenuously calling attention to how he never used the word "corruption," Pinchot instead claimed that Glavis's charges showed Ballinger to be "unfit for office." Pinchot did so publicly, leaking documents to the press, surely aware that a feeding frenzy would end up questioning Ballinger's integrity. Taft investigated, found Ballinger largely blameless, and tried to convince the men to play nice. He failed. Finally, when an investigating senator asked for information, Pinchot made an unnecessarily frank response that publicly questioned Taft's judgements and actions.

Taft was stuck. Pinchot's letter to the senator was clearly insubordinate, deserving of firing. Although Pinchot was a great Forest Service administrator, his desire to control all conservation policy made him a bad team player. Taft could not allow this insubordination to pass and still maintain his authority with the cabinet. But, on the other hand, Pinchot had a high, favorable public profile, both as an individual and as the personification of Roosevelt's legacy. Taft had been elected to continue Roosevelt's policies, and was already faltering in that promise, simply because his temperament differed from Roosevelt's. If Taft now fired the last prominent Roosevelt man left in his cabinet, Roosevelt and his fans would be furious.

The brouhaha titillated to no end—not because the issues had long-range importance, but because the press could frame all sorts of little items as hard-to-answer questions. Were the coal patents obtained fraudulently? (Retrospective judgment: yes, although "through routine, mild incompetence" was also a good answer.) Was Ballinger literally corrupt? (Almost certainly not, though people love to speculate.) Had Pinchot engineered the whole episode in a *House of Cards*–style ambition to bring down Taft and replace him as president? (Same answer.) Were Ballinger's other actions stymieing further progress on the Roosevelt-Pinchot conservation legacy? (Probably.) Was that why Taft supported Ballinger? (Taft couldn't say *no* unless he was ready to fire Ballinger for being legally prudent, but he couldn't say *yes* for fear of betraying Roosevelt. Which left only one available answer: he was a poor leader.) Had Ballinger, as his lawyer claimed, "committed the unpardonable sin of defeating the ambition of a self-exaggerated man [Pinchot]"?[16] (Ouch!) Pinchot stoked the intrigue while hiding his true motivations. His actions thus struck observers as mysterious and troubling, or even arrogant, power-thirsty, and reckless. He had built the Forest Service from nothing, loved it like a parent loved a child—couldn't he see that this path might blow it all up? Even in his late-life autobiography, when Pinchot expressed satisfaction with the way he'd handled these events, his intentions are still inscrutable.

In the end—after all the congressional investigations, the revelations of bureaucratic missteps, the well-timed leaks, and the behind-the-scenes requests for resignations—the affair accomplished nothing except to end the careers of nearly everyone involved. Pinchot was fired. Ballinger later resigned, exonerated but humiliated, his career as a public servant finished. The coal patents were cancelled. The whistleblower Glavis got a better job but soon lost it in his own corruption scandal. Roosevelt expressed his disappointment by challenging Taft in the 1912 election—on the independent Bull Moose platform, which split the Republican vote and delivered the presidency to Democrat Woodrow Wilson. Wilson, who didn't have strong personal opinions about conservation, named as interior secretary a Californian who had worked hard on his campaign, Franklin K. Lane. As a former San Francisco city attorney, Lane had attitudes that sealed the fate of the Hetch Hetchy Valley.

On the January night at the Pinchot mansion, however, all those events were in the future. Pinchot showed his mother the letter by which Taft fired him, and they both rejoiced. "As for me, here was the end of a chapter," he later wrote. "But not in the least the end of the book and most emphatically not the end of Conservation."[17] Entangled in his chess matches with Ballinger and Taft, Pinchot may have perceived his martyrdom as merely temporary. Still just forty-four years old, he did have bigger ambitions.

He worked on Roosevelt's 1912 campaign, and clearly would have enjoyed running for president himself.

But Pinchot was also becoming more well-rounded. Leaving the Forest Service gave him a chance to achieve more personal goals. In the next few years he would stop recording in his diaries the presence of his dead fiancée, get married, start a family, travel to the South Seas, lobby for forestry, informally mentor foresters and their Forest Service, and write the first of several rousing, if self-congratulatory, books on the history of conservation. In 1920, he took a far lesser job, as commissioner of forestry for the state of Pennsylvania. With his typical mix of moral instinct, political skill, and hard work, he parlayed that into two well-regarded terms as the state's governor. He never showed any suggestion of feeling unfulfilled.

Still, in retrospect, the grand arc plays like a Greek tragedy, with the great man's worthy ambitions undone in part by his own blindness, his foolish ego. His ego led him to pointlessly harsh disputes with Ballinger, Taft, Fernow, Sargent, Schenck, and others. His ego led him to write memoirs claiming immense individual credit for advances achieved by groups. His ego must have secretly enjoyed his opponents referring to conservation as Pinchotism. His conservation cause might have developed a better footing if his hubris could have set it free.

Like our image of John Muir, our image of Pinchot is largely based on memoirs he wrote in his old age. We expect people to mellow as they age: become less radical and less egotistical as they learn from life about the value and power of other people. Defying those expectations, Muir became less willing to compromise with society—and projected that back onto his memories of early Yosemite. Likewise, Pinchot became less willing to give others credit—and projected his self-inflated contributions back onto the history of the movement.[18]

For example, in one of his autobiography's most mocked episodes, Pinchot claimed to have invented conservation. It was late on a gloomy February day in 1907. He was riding his horse Jim on Ridge Road, above a precipitous gorge in Washington's Rock Creek Park. He was pondering the relationship between forestry and water—flood control, navigation, dams—as well as soils, coal and oil, fish and game. "Suddenly the idea flashed through my head that there was a unity in this complication." These rival issues were not enemies, separate and antagonistic, but "made up the one great central problem of the use of the earth for the good of man . . . it was like lifting the curtain on a great new stage."[19]

It's a great summary of the ideals of conservation in a memorable story format that puts the thunderstruck Pinchot as St. Paul on the road to Damascus: the character that his mother had always wanted him to be. And as with derision over his claim to have been the first forester—when presumably he was merely trying to claim that he'd professionalized forestry—he did have a wider point here. His horseback insight was that various federal and state agencies needed a unified *policy* on conservation. He realized that government would run most effectively if it had what amounted to a conservation czar. Pinchot was egotistical enough to believe that he should be that czar, but the story was intended to demonstrate his vision of how to implement the conservation idea, not his literal invention of that idea. He wanted to show that he could be conservation's St. Paul, not that he had been its Jesus.

Furthermore, it's interesting that Pinchot does not tell the story in his earlier work, *The Fight for Conservation*. That 1910 book, written immediately after Taft fired him, was criticized for self-centered preachiness: "Mr. Pinchot needs to learn that men may decline to be led by him and still be strongly attached to the great cause for which he is fighting, and to the success of which he has made contributions of incalculable value," said a *New York Times* review. Nevertheless, in that book Pinchot focused on "Roosevelt's ideas" and the greater cause.[20] Only later in life—perhaps motivated by the disappointment of his perception that he'd failed at statesmanship—did he feel the need to assert his own centrality to that cause.

What made Pinchot's relationship with Roosevelt extraordinary was that Pinchot subordinated his ego. For one of the few times in his life, Pinchot let someone else take most of the credit. As Pinchot's biographer M. Nelson

McGeary wrote, "No executive ever had a more loyal assistant than Roosevelt had in Pinchot. And no boy ever had a greater hero than Pinchot had in Roosevelt."[21]

Roosevelt labeled Pinchot among his "faithful bodyguard," presumably referring to an ability to take blows for the master.[22] With each blow Pinchot received from foes, you wonder: Why did he accept this criticism so much more easily than criticism from former mentors like Fernow and Sargent? Maybe because he wasn't taking them personally, but for the great Roosevelt. Why did he not complain when "Pinchotism" was used as a slur? Maybe so the great Roosevelt's name would remain unsullied. Why did he seem happy that Taft fired him from the job he was born for? Maybe because he cared more about the great Roosevelt's legacy than his own. When Pinchot made his ego subservient to Roosevelt's, he achieved his statesmanlike goals—at the cost of his own reputation.

Pinchot and Roosevelt combined to temporarily stitch together a grand coalition for nature. They aligned conservationists and preservationists, Sargent and Fernow, Muir and woolgrowers. They enlisted foresters, scientists, dam-builders, engineers, and other professionals; farmers and ranchers; big city mayors, planners, civic reformers, and electric-power developers; anti-monopolists, socialists, and big businesses; loggers, hunters, and bird lovers. When Roosevelt stepped away from the government in 1909, Pinchot volunteered to stay and try to hold the coalition together. But it scattered. Ballinger went his own way, Muir went his own way. The grazers wanted more and the loggers wanted more and the water developers wanted to dam every valley they saw. The coalition's mix of anti-monopolist rhetoric and business-friendly action finally wore thin on all sides.[23]

You might say that they had all come together to address a crisis of scarcity, the timber famine on the closing frontier. Then Pinchot's innovations in management efficiency barely averted the crisis and everybody lost interest. Or you might say that everyone jumped on what Pinchot thought was a bandwagon, until it turned out to be a pendulum that inevitably swung back toward growth and exploitation. Or you might say that the entire coalition had only ever been held together by Roosevelt's charisma. Nobody but Roosevelt could have grafted the conservationist Progressive agenda onto the pro-business Republican party. And when he departed, the grafted branch withered. Suddenly, the mission seemed poorly defined, the methods barely legal; a phrase such as "the greatest good for the greatest number in the long run" no longer roused millions, struck too many as vague and circular. The ideals of conservation now sounded dangerously at odds with fundamental components of the American character.

It's no small thing to have assisted a great and charismatic man in briefly assembling a coalition to protect—and set up attitudes and agencies to continue protecting—230 million acres of natural glory. Pinchot facilitated a lasting transformation in environmental governance. In fact, as the second half of this book will show, he did it twice: first partnered with Muir, and then here with Roosevelt. This second time, he also aspired to something greater. He hoped that after the leader departed, he himself would possess the skills, network, moral vision, and personal strength to continue to hold that coalition together. Instead, it fell apart.

The tragedy of John Muir was that he perceived his life as tragedy. If Gifford Pinchot had possessed a similar capacity for self-reflection, he too might have seen tragedy all over his biography. Pinchot's deepest ambition was to manage a profitable forest for the benefit of society. Although he set up magnificent management structures at the U.S. Forest Service, it never achieved the profitability he expected. He sought to combine European forestry science with American democratic principles. Although he quickly gained influence, each advance made him hungrier for consolidated power unconstrained by democratic processes. He wanted to practice a forestry akin to missionary work. Although he pursued that work for two decades, after he was forced out of the profession he felt that his successors too often lacked humanitarian impulses. He had dreamed of making a difference. In 1940 he was still trying, when he delivered a lecture arguing that a global expansion of forestry principles—"international cooperation in conserving, utilizing, and distributing natural resources to the mutual advantage of all nations"—could bring about world peace. "Good talk," he wrote in his diary, "but not especially well received."[24] As the world descended further into war, he became an old man preaching a solitary gospel.

Then, after Pinchot's death in 1946, Muir's disciples portrayed Pinchot as a greedy temple-destroyer, a sellout, a tool of monopolists. They saw him as an opponent of Muir and thus an enemy of the *land ethic* and *wilderness*—ideas that didn't launch until after Pinchot's power had waned, and that actually fit well into the management framework he devised.[25] Outside of the Forest Service, Pinchot's name became known primarily as a counterpoint to Muir's, as a person allegedly responsible for killing a beautiful valley and thus also killing a visionary prophet. The tragedy of Gifford Pinchot moves from the way he might have perceived it to the way the rest of us do.

We need not perceive it that way. After all, like Muir, Pinchot was on his own personal journey. Their lives weren't preordained by the divide they have come to represent. Each man had his own dreams, passions, faults, and rivalries. Each had his own relationship to the natural world and his own destiny in sharing that relationship with others. When those journeys intersected, it wasn't in the sense of a formalized championship showdown. Instead, they sometimes had opportunities to help each other, as when Pinchot wrote letters of introduction for Muir's 1893 trip to Europe. They had opportunities to work together, as they did in an 1899 tour of the imperiled Calaveras grove of redwoods in California—a trip that Pinchot said was one of the "brightest spots in my year."[26] And they had opportunities to express disagreements both mild and vehement, as they did over sheep grazing in forest reserves and over the fate of a little-known Yosemite valley, among other issues.

They had rivaling viewpoints, but weren't locked in opposition. They were yin and yang: rivals like night and day are rivals, or hot and cold. Although they embodied contrasts, they were complementary and interdependent. The world needed both of them.

It still does. The questions that Muir and Pinchot grappled with are still with us, perhaps even more intensively now. To take a specific example, is the Alaska National Wildlife Refuge more important as a remote redoubt of nature, or as harvestable natural resources? And at the broadest level, can we really preserve *any* "natural" retreat in an age of climate change, or should we focus on finding more sustainable approaches to slow or mitigate that changing climate?

Most people have instinctive responses to these preservation-versus-conservation questions. If you lean toward science, engineering, or management, you tend to respond as Pinchot did, and admire what he tried to accomplish. If you lean toward religion or poetry, you tend to respond as Muir did, and admire what he said and how he lived it. It'd be nice to admire them equally. But when politics is partisan, it's all too easy to declare your tribal membership by demonizing the other side. So we argue preservation versus conservation, which means that we end up arguing Muir versus Pinchot.

But notice the *settings* of those arguments, the locations of the natural resources we want to preserve and/or conserve. The arguments center on how to manage federal public lands: national parks, national monuments, national forests, national wildlife refuges, and lands of the Bureau of Land Management. In 1890, when Pinchot returned from Europe to embark on his career, he chose not to work on public lands, because they offered no management opportunities. In 1914, when Sierra Club member Stephen Mather signed up to do the work that would found the National Park Service, he chose specifically to work on public lands because by then they offered great management opportunities.[27] Somehow, in those years, American ideas changed. Somehow, the notion of *public lands* became an American hallmark.

How did that happen? And did it gain from the rivalry, the cooperative competition, of John Muir and Gifford Pinchot?

PART II

THE BIRTH OF PUBLIC LANDS

6

Bigger Stakes at Play

To this day, Yellowstone and Yosemite engage in an ongoing rivalry regarding which can claim to be the world's first national park. California's Yosemite was the earliest to gain special status, in 1864, soon after European Americans first stumbled across its magnificent scenery. Congress could easily agree that the valley, along with the Mariposa Grove of giant sequoias, should be withdrawn from homesteading and deeded to the state of California as a park. At that point it was a state park, not a national park—a distinction that fuels the friendly rivalry. In some ways it's a minor distinction, but in other ways it's central to the birth and growth of the national park idea, as this chapter will chart.[1]

In 1864, with New York City's Central Park under construction, the idea of parklands was gaining popularity. Urban populations were exploding, and so was demand for parklike, semirural reservations. Frederick Law Olmsted built a career on the idea that these public spaces could become neighborhood centerpieces, landscaped as attractively as a private English garden. Olmsted worked primarily for cities—small government, close to the people, genuine democracy. But expectations of tourism and population growth dictated the wisdom of setting aside even far-off places like Yosemite.

The purpose of such a park was public enjoyment. The public enjoyed natural features such as trees, streams, and pastoral vistas. Sometimes Olmsted even improved on what nature provided. The goal wasn't nature for nature's sake, but a collection of natural features that would enhance human enjoyment. For example, Yosemite's enabling legislation called for "public use, resort, and recreation." It did not use the words *preservation* or *wilderness* or even *nature*.[2] It might as well have described the place as a "city park (city not included)."

Indeed one of the first state commissioners overseeing Yosemite was Olmsted himself. The park designer, who briefly moved to California to manage a mining estate, couldn't help but take an interest in this scenic valley. To his great credit, Olmsted was capable of seeing Yosemite as something different than a city park. He wrote a report on Yosemite's ideal philosophy and management that brilliantly discussed how scenery affected human perception, why democratic governments had a moral responsibility to preserve natural beauty, and how people could use such a park without damaging the environment.[3] Sadly, however, the report was ignored. Olmsted soon returned to the East, and due to other demands for his services, he never again had much involvement with Yosemite. The California state commissioners ended up managing the park with scant attention to its uniqueness or natural splendor, indeed without much attention to any principles at all. Arguably, one reason for that failure was that the state government was too far removed from the local conditions at the park.

Then in 1872 a similar set of events played out in Yellowstone: White people discovered an extraordinary landscape (the Mountain Shoshone tribe had been living there for at least several hundred—perhaps several thousand—years). A movement arose to treat it differently than standard homestead-able farmland. The Yosemite template suggested that Congress should deed it to a state, but no state or municipality yet existed to accept and administer this remote land as a park. Neither Wyoming, where most of the features were located, nor Montana, with the only relatively nearby populations or available entrances at the time, had yet gained statehood. As mere territories, their bare-bones governments lacked the authority to own or control land. But waiting for statehood would allow the land to be homesteaded and kill the opportunity to reserve it for a park.

If Yellowstone was to be a park, it had to be held at the national level, and thus governed at an even farther remove from local conditions. Furthermore, the federal government would have to decide that it wanted to own this land forever, rather than holding it in trust for eventual privatization. These struck some people as new and dangerous concepts.

The U.S. government had first set aside a natural resource for federally owned permanent public use at Arkansas Hot Springs (now Hot Springs National Park) in 1832. As tourists sought medical treatment and personal renewal, cabins and hotels arose around these springs in Arkansas Territory. To secure fair, coordinated management of the hot water, the community needed some sort of joint ownership and administration. Thus the Hot Springs Reserve was established for an economic purpose: to ensure sound, sustainable exploitation of a shared natural resource. [4]

Little controversy accompanied the Hot Springs reserve. The Constitution clearly allowed the federal government to own land. [5] Ownership made sense for some government functions, such as military forts, post offices, lighthouses, and the Capitol building. Those economic missions even extended to federal ownership of certain southern forests of live oak, useful in ship construction, a practice that dated back to 1799. There was a national interest in those trees, because naval dominance contributed to national security—one factor in the Revolutionary War was that colonists cut off British access to American trees for ship masts, leading to more-frequent repairs that weakened the Royal Navy's ability to supply its troops. [6] So the shared resource at Hot Springs was another economic purpose for which the government should retain land. Nobody dug deep enough to ask why. What was the national interest that warranted government ownership of health-giving waters? Couldn't these goals be accomplished just as easily by transferring the land to a local or even private concern?

Such questions did arise when Congress debated Yellowstone. It was a debate about the scope of legal and economic power, not the meaning of nature. The request for Yellowstone's reservation came from scientists, not businesspeople. It reserved not an economic resource but rare geological phenomena. Yellowstone's waters weren't for bathing, just observing. The geysers and canyon were often compared to Niagara Falls, an attraction surrounded by tawdry private development that upper-class tourists felt detracted from the sublime wonder—Yellowstone's supporters wanted to avoid that fate. When they pushed to reserve the landscape from home-steading, however, they were implying that permanent government land ownership might preserve and show off the features better than the free market could. That idea met with philosophical resistance.

"The natural curiosities there cannot be interfered with by anything that man can do," said Cornelius Cole of California in the Senate's Yellowstone debate. "The geysers will remain, no matter where the ownership of the land may be, and I do not know why settlers should be excluded from a tract of land forty miles square. . . . I do not see the reason or propriety of setting apart a large tract of land . . . in the Territories of the United States for a public park."[7]

To get around such opposition, Yellowstone's supporters suggested that what they were doing was no big deal. They portrayed the establishment of the world's first national park as a reversible, trivial, cost-free experiment. They omitted a key word, *inalienable*, that had been used in the Yosemite act to make it last forever. Debating Yellowstone in the Senate, Lyman Trumbull of Illinois assured Cole that the law would simply be repealed, the park rescinded, "if it is in anybody's way." In the House, Henry Dawes of Massachusetts argued that because Yellowstone was not yet populated—the era's racism allowed him to ignore its long indigenous history—it "infringe[s] upon no vested rights . . . treads upon no rights of the settler." Finally, proponents agreed not to fund any *management* of Yellowstone. The total budgetary request for Yellowstone's first five years was zero dollars. As the old saying goes, if you want to know politicians' priorities, don't look at what they proclaim—look at what they fund. Congress funded zero priority for public land, even in the form of a wondrous national park.[8]

Meanwhile John Muir arrived on the scene. His first article about Yosemite, published in the *New York Daily Tribune* in 1871, described his discovery of a glacier at the head of the Merced River above the Yosemite Valley. Muir's report made news because he was speaking as an amateur scientist about a little-known area of the American West, much like John Wesley Powell had done two years previously with his boat trip through the Grand Canyon. It was a golden age of natural-science publishing, with men such as Powell, Clarence King, and Ferdinand Hayden gaining wide popularity and government sponsorship for their science-based explorations of Western landscapes. Muir's findings were particularly newsworthy because he was contradicting the expert Josiah Whitney by persuasively arguing that glaciers, not a single cataclysm, carved the Yosemite Valley. Glaciers had rarely yet been studied in the continental United States.

Muir augmented his scientific results with poetic descriptions of the glacial valley and a great sense of story, describing the valley's geology as a book whose pages revealed secrets. Furthermore, he took time to describe one of his campsites, in a small round meadow. "The meadow was velvet with grass, and circled with the most beautiful of all the *coniferae*, the Williamson spruce. I built a great fire, and the daisies of the sod rayed as if conscious of a sun." He described gleaming trees, gushing with life, seeming to come closer to him as the starry sky created a dome above them. It invoked an emotion: "Never was mountain mansion more beautiful, more spiritual; never was moral wanderer more blessedly homed."[9]

In his first published work, Muir laid out his spiritual quest for all to see. Yosemite's mountain landscape, he said, was the place to seek his own soul. Sure, that journey might uncover scientific theories, astounding scenes, mountain mansions—but at heart, he was a moral wanderer, and only in nature did he feel at home.

This was the quality that drove Muir's popularity then, and still resonates today. God is nature, nature is God; God is within us, nature is within us. As he declared in a letter to Jeanne Carr the previous year, "I'm in the woods, woods, woods, and they are in me-ee-ee."[10] In nature we find ourselves and God; to access ourselves and God, we must find pure nature.

For Muir, the purest nature was in the Sierra Nevada, among the glaciers, among the clear skies and velvet grasses and gleaming spruce. When he later took people to Yosemite—from editor Robert Underwood Johnson to President Theodore Roosevelt to his hundreds of acolytes in the Sierra Club summer outings—his ambitions were more spiritual than political. He was opening up for them his moral home, in hopes that it might be theirs as well. As he matured, he accepted that others might have other moral homes: his wife and in-laws in their Martinez orchard, Charles Sargent in his Boston gardens, the dog Stickeen on an Alaska glacier. Muir always described other natural places with as much gusto as he could, to try to connect with those whose moral homes were atop Mount Rainer or in the meadows below Mount Shasta or even in the treeless lava beds of Northern California's Tule Lake, "the grand Modoc landscape, which at once fills and takes possession of you."[11]

However, many readers saw Muir's journey as literal rather than metaphoric, a guidebook rather than an exemplar. If his truest moral home was in the Sierra, then the Sierra must be the most true, most moral home in America. Muir was speaking to a generation of nineteenth-century Americans who were becoming more urbanized and less in touch with nature—he was trying to show them what nature provided, what they were missing. Yet precisely because this sense of natural wonder was missing from their lives, they didn't know where to find it, or even that they should look for it. Muir gained authority by default. If he said the Sierra was a special, spiritual place, then the Sierra would become the nation's ultimate symbol of lands that provided people with the benefits of nature—and thus the Sierra should be uniquely deserving of honor, protection, and memorialization.

A month after his first *Tribune* article, Muir followed up with another Yosemite story. In this one he wrote primarily of the twenty-six people who overwintered in the valley and the "broad, loving harmonies of our whisky soirees of which about seven are held weekly." He concluded with a description of a picturesque snowstorm, the flakes "steady, exhaustless, innumerable. The trees, and bushes, and dead brown grass were flowered far beyond summer, bowed down in blossom. . . . From wall to wall of our beautiful temple, from meadow to sky was one finished unit of beauty, one star of equal ray, one glowing sun, weighed in the celestial balances and found perfect." What Muir cherished in the Sierra wasn't just glaciers, rocks, or bears—rather, it was a place where he experienced an event as simple and common as a snowstorm to be a magical, indescribably beautiful expression of God's joy. His next article, in the spring, expanded the message. After forty days of minor earthquakes, he wrote that Yosemite's inhabitants "have all become philosophers, deep thinkers." God used nature, Muir insisted, to give people rich spiritual benefits. If the public heard him saying that people got rich spiritual benefits from nature *in Yosemite*, then at least they were getting part of his message. [12]

That spiritual message was a new interpretation of Yosemite's meaning. Yosemite had become a park because this unusual place deserved to be held as a unified valley rather than carved into multiple homesteads. The lands were withdrawn from homesteading so that they could better serve tourism or other nonagricultural economic purposes—but now Muir was talking about spiritual purposes. Muir was helping to transform the way people saw these lands. Thanks partly to Muir, a visit to Yosemite was not simply about appreciating outdoor scenery. It was about appreciating how outdoor wonders could transform your internal self. But if Yosemite was an expression of the divine, then it needed to be preserved in this pristine and holy state—a need that had not yet been expressed for other American landscapes.

Muir departed from traditional ways of seeing landscapes, and also from traditional methods of controlling landscapes. Anyone else in his position might have placed a homestead claim just outside the state park. Granted, the law was written for farmers pursuing a Jeffersonian ideal, but in practice plenty of homesteaders used their land for grazing, logging, to establish a toll road, or for nothing at all. And granted, Muir was a wanderer, but homesteading didn't have to be about setting down roots. Again, that was the ideal, but plenty of people filed a claim and then continued wandering. If you didn't tie yourself to the homestead, you might not *prove up* on it, but why not try? There wasn't much penalty for failure, and the General Land Office might approve you anyway.

The General Land Office, a division of the federal Department of Interior, was in the business of giving away land. Like a subprime-mortgage lender before the 2008 crisis, it wasn't going to look too skeptically at its customers. The more customers it found, the better it accomplished its mission. It needed only to assure some level of fairness, such that fraudsters didn't beat legitimate entrants to desirable parcels.

The sooner the General Land Office could deed a parcel over to an individual owner—be that a legitimate farmer, a monopolistic railroad, or an amateur naturalist who didn't want to be tied down—the sooner that parcel could contribute to the economy through private enterprise. Even if someone like Muir obtained a homestead fraudulently and never did anything useful with it, he might eventually sell it to someone who would. If it stayed in the government's hands, capitalism could never take over.

In a nation based on property rights, land that had not yet been homesteaded had none. In a classic tragedy of the commons, anyone could graze cattle on this *public domain*, which meant that too many people did. Nobody was worried about the condition of the range next month or next year, everybody just tried to get as much grass as they could right now. Much of the West's cowboy mythology—in which cattlemen and sheepmen engage in pitched battles over the open range, unscrupulous operators fence off lands they don't own, and freelance cowpunchers drift off into the sunset—arose out of this abnormality that nobody owned that open range. Nobody took responsibility for it, or committed themselves to enforce rules on it, or would be rewarded for taking good care of it. It was literally a free-for-all, and the General Land Office was nominally supposed to keep some order. It didn't want to hire thousands of law enforcement officers, an expensive approach that smacked of Old World tyranny. The wiser approach was to let markets do the regulating: get the land into private hands as quickly as possible, so that individuals and their property rights would have the incentives to do society's work.

When Muir chose not to homestead in the Sierra, then, he was rejecting not just farming, but settled traditions in how to organize and govern the nation. It was like when he walked out of the Indianapolis wagon wheel factory, preferring instead to pick up blossoms. The rejection may have been a wise choice for him individually, but how do you organize a society around it?

Pity the poor visitor to the Old Faithful geyser, in Wyoming's Yellowstone National Park, who is suffering from stomach distress. The rumbling sounds, acrid smell, and burbling feeling of incipient explosion are mirrored outside and inside the body. In August 1885, a worst-case scenario played out: the geyser erupted, and, a visitor wrote, "my organ began spouting vast quantities of hot acid water in close accord."[13]

That visitor was John Muir. It was the first visit ever to a national park by this man who is sometimes called the Father of National Parks.[14] Muir, at the time, was unusually burdened with responsibilities. His wife, Louie, was pregnant with their second daughter. He had taken over daily supervision of the estate from his father-in-law just four years previously; Muir's biographers often describe him spending the entire decade of the 1880s fully absorbed as an orchardist. Yet this summer he felt compelled to travel back to Wisconsin to visit money-strapped siblings and his melancholy mother. He dreaded the three-month trip. He had not been back in almost twenty years, and worried that his parents were both on their deathbeds. Indeed Muir's father, the itinerant preacher now living in Kansas City, did pass away during his visit, although his mother would hold on for another eleven years.[15]

Muir's route took him first to Northern California's Mount Shasta, which had always drawn him with its green meadows, vast woods, deep streams, and icy mountain cone. "Never while I live will this mountain love die," he wrote Louie. "Though on the way to see my aged mother and father and sisters and brothers and old friends and neighbors, I still feel a strong draw to the wilderness impelling me to leave all and linger here. But *I will not*—putting away the temptation as a drunkard would whiskey."[16] He ventured north to Portland, Oregon, then east on the Northern Pacific railroad. Its line through the Montana and Dakota territories had been completed less than two years previously. A highlight was its branch from Livingston, Montana, fifty-one miles south to Cinnabar, near the northern edge of the nation's park.

Muir was tired. Descending from the railcar in Cinnabar, he was doubting his powers of endurance. He hadn't felt this weak since his bout with malaria in Florida seventeen years before. Even at the beginning of this trip he'd felt tired. Bad digestion and stomach pain complicated his entire journey; in Portland, he even went to a doctor for some pills.

He knew that a mere weeklong visit would not do Yellowstone justice, especially in his condition. "Afraid I will not learn much," he wrote Louie, "still I may get some good facts besides the mere pleasurable mass of wonderment from the spouting steam and muds and suds."

Yellowstone made a poor first impression. Muir found the treeless sagebrush hills between Cinnabar and Mammoth Hot Springs "gray and ashy and forbidding," nothing like Yosemite's leafy glory. At first glance, Mammoth's famed terraces struck him as "piles of salt" that "look like the refuse heaps about chemical and dye works."[17]

If the natural setting was uninspiring, the human culture was downright repulsive. At the Mammoth Hot Springs Hotel, Muir described one meal as a "hot soda biscuit and gray-looking lava-like puddings with blood-curdling sauce and slime, more wonderful in color, some of them, than the variegated geyser muds." In the morning, touring the oddly formed and brightly colored terraces, he found the sun's glare overwhelming. "I became thirsty and weary, and my old trouble began, and I was afraid I never would be able to do any more with my old battered body." He went back to the hotel to rest. "After lunch, which was as bad as possible though costing a dollar," he tried again to tour the terraces, and succeeded only after he vomited up the lunch. Supper too was "abominable," but he learned some facts and made some friends. Alfred and Fay Sellers, honeymooners from Chicago, joined him in hiring horses and a cook/ guide for a 150-mile tour.[18]

Yellowstone at the time was very poorly administered. Congress had started giving the Department of Interior a tiny management budget, but the arrival of the railroad and its patrons strained the park to bursting. Tourists regularly defaced formations, left campfires burning, and threw debris into geysers. Rail access made it easy for poachers and other criminals to use the park as a haven; park employees lacked authority to do effective policing. Administrators were at best incompetent, at worst corrupt. Their overseers were too far removed from local conditions—and furthermore, the federal government had little experience at *managing* anything. Few of today's big management agencies had yet been established; tasks of admin- istrative organization rarely extended beyond the post office and military; Reconstruction in the South had been a disaster. For this reason, the fol- lowing year, Yellowstone's administration was transferred to the army—a move that may have saved the national park cause.[19]

Muir and the Sellerses endured rain, hailstorms, bad roads, and poor food. "In galloping along a smooth piece of ground," Muir wrote Louie, "my horse[']s front feet broke into a hole[,] he fell head over heels pitching me ahead half a mile or so, whirling me over in somersaults." In the Hayden Valley, their progress was slowed by fallen and burned timber. The Grand Canyon of the Yellowstone disappointed Muir with treelessness, its walls "half ashes half stone . . . a land of desolation? [no,] only a cañon of deso- lation[:] green grassy woods atop[,] green glassy river below."[20] At Old Faithful, Muir brought back up his latest meal, timed in perfect sympathy with nature's geyser. He told Louie, "it was all very violent very painful very wonderful."[21]

Wonderful. There it was: Muir's passionate insistence that his innermost self was deeply connected to the natural world. He was Nature, Nature was his stomach. He would happily experience pain, from nausea to miserable weather to sleeping on the cold, hard ground, if the pain brought him into harmony with the rocks and trees and animals that he perceived as a spiritual presence, not only around him but also within him. If he and Old Faithful were retching at the same time, that was magnificent harmony.

However, Muir seemed to understand that not everyone shared his absurdly high tolerance for pain. When proselytizing for nature, he skipped over the complaints that he made in his private letters and diaries. He also skipped over his initial perceptions of Yellowstone as bizarre. The Yellowstone essay he published later that fall focused not on his experiences but on the scientific facts he had worked so hard to learn. The essay depicted Yellowstone as an educational place. Muir was most captivated by the notion that in this region were the headwaters of the Missouri, Snake, and Green Rivers, flowing to the Atlantic Ocean, Pacific Ocean, and Gulf of California, respectively. Being the fountain of such great and diverse rivers gave it a wholeness, a unity. As a place of origin for rivers, it was also one for the human spirit. [22]

"To everybody over all the world water is beautiful forever," Muir wrote, "whether falling upward into the sky in snowy geysers, or downward into deep resounding cañons, or gliding and resting in calm rivers and lakes." He portrayed Yellowstone as a "capital camping-ground" with lakes, parks, meadows, woods, streams, and waterfalls. The geysers, he wrote, "display an exuberance of strange motion and energy admirably calculated to shake up, and surprise, and frighten the dullest observer out of soul-wasting apathy, and make him begin to grow and live again." No longer described as chemical wastes, the Mammoth Hot Springs were "terraced hills of marble or silex, pearly white, tinged here and there with delicate pink . . . the glaciers building downward, volcanos building upward, grinding and laving and making beauty only." [23]

Muir had experienced Yellowstone the same way most people did at the time, and, aside from improvements in food and transportation, largely the way most people do today. He didn't backpack to hidden valleys or discover previously unknown geological features, as he had at Yosemite. A tourist, he visited the main wonders and spent far less time with them than he knew he should have. He battled disappointing weather, a wobbly gut, unappetizing food, and his own life-weariness. In many ways the trip's bright spot—certainly its most lasting effect—wasn't any of the natural features but the people he met: the Sellerses became lifelong friends. Yet in part by putting in the hard work to dig up facts, he was able to overcome the hardships and transform his initial impression of the park. He was able to deepen his aesthetic sense and develop his ability to capture that sense in language. Furthermore, because he could write so eloquently, his transformation also transformed the way others saw the park.

Muir saw beyond Yellowstone's wonderful strangeness. In his description, it was not merely a collection of weird smoky vents, surprising gushers, and odd white terraces. It was not merely a geology field trip. It was not merely a vast mountain lake flowing into a peaceful stream and then a stunning canyon. It was a place, he wrote, where "harmony rules supreme. *Linnaea* [twinflower] hangs her twin bells over the rugged edges of the cliffs, forests and gardens are spread in lavish beauty round about, the nuts and berries ripen well, making good pastures for the birds and bees, and the bears also, and elk, and deer, and buffalo—God's cattle—all find food and are at home in the strange wilderness and make part and parcel of the whole."[24]

The whole. Nature to Muir was holistic, a system—God's system. Part of the joy he felt in nature was an appreciation of his place in that system, in God's world. It wasn't easy for him to find his place in Yellowstone, because the human overlay on this natural setting was still so unrefined, thus making travel such hard work. But to Muir, the rewards for that work took him far beyond Yellowstone's curious spectacles. He constructed a holistic, aesthetic view of Yellowstone as the epitome of a society's relationship to nature—and then shared that view with others. He was relating a form of *conversion narrative*, the sense of religious rebirth that served a central feature of most American religious traditions: *this happened to me, it saved me, save yourselves by letting it happen to you.*

Given Muir's desire to share with others his mystical relationship with God as nature, he needed nature to thrive in special places such as the Sierra and northwest Wyoming. However, he didn't have strong opinions about how to achieve that goal. Yellowstone being a *national park* didn't neces-sarily mean much to him. He visited and wrote about the place because it was a celebrity among landscapes, a "strange region of fire and water" that would spark readers' curiosity.[25] He himself would have been happier at Mount Shasta, even though it wasn't a national park. Yet in Yellowstone, he applied his unique way of experiencing nature to the nation's park. That vision helped send Yellowstone on a journey: from a place of majestic curiosities to a place reflecting deep American values.

When Yellowstone was the equivalent of a city park, a detractor might wonder why it was needed in a rural area and why it should be held by a federal government. Muir helped Yellowstone become more: a vast haven, a symbol of nature as a holistic system, an embodiment of the divine, a physical representation of American ideals, and a fountain of the soul. Muir put bigger stakes at play. If you accepted Muir's view, collective national ownership of this park became transformed from an annoying necessity of its remote, territorial location to a feature essential to its meaning.

Muir's love for the California Sierra reached its most eloquent heights in the sublime setting of the Yosemite Valley. But a key to the politics of that valley's set-aside had been tying it to the Mariposa Grove of giant sequoias, 30 miles south. Muir did love sequoias, especially the soaring, cathedral-like verticality of a grove of giant trees. Muir was fortunate to also possess the rhetorical gifts to describe the ineffable wonder of the Yosemite Valley. For those who lacked those gifts—such as the congressman who introduced the 1864 Yosemite act—the Mariposa Grove was easier to talk about. After all, a tree was an obvious artifact, a measurable thing existing in the world. These foothill Sierra redwood trees, *Sequoiadendron giganteum*—shorter but more massive than their coastal relatives *Sequoiadendron semperverin*—were the largest living things on earth.[26]

In addition to the Mariposa, groves of sequoias dotted the western foothills of the entire Sierra range. Among the first to be discovered by white people had been the Calaveras Grove north of Yosemite, in 1852. The famed Calaveras Discovery Tree was cut down that very first year.

Wandering the Sierra, Muir visited and wrote about many of these groves. To him it seemed obvious that such astonishing trees had a higher and better use than being turned into lumber or firewood or a dance floor—which was the fate of the Calaveras Discovery Tree, now known as the Calaveras Big Stump. In Calaveras, Muir had no direct political impact, although his eloquence may have helped convince the grove's private owners to stop cutting trees and build a tourist hotel. Muir had a similarly indirect effect in Tulare County in the southern Sierra, which was blessed with the two largest trees in the world, named after Civil War generals Ulysses S. Grant and William T. Sherman.

In Visalia, the nearest city to the Sherman and Grant trees, the *Delta* newspaper eventually took up Muir's cause of saving giant sequoias. In 1878, five years after Muir's first visit there, it editorialized against cutting down any "Big Trees" for exhibitions in the East. The following year, the Tulare County groves came to the attention of Interior Secretary Carl Schurz, a liberal Republican. Born and raised in Germany, Schurz had German notions of forestry—he commissioned Charles Sargent to conduct a comprehensive census of American forests. Schurz called for the withdrawal from homesteading of four square miles around the General Grant tree.[27]

As long as it wasn't *inalienable*, such a withdrawal was an easy, temporary administrative action. Schurz' requested withdrawal of the Grant Grove was accomplished the following year. A similar withdrawal occurred three years later, high in the mountains to the east of the sequoia groves. The leader of a scientific expedition to Mount Whitney, the highest peak in California, recommended its use as a weather station by the United States Army Signal Corps, which was responsible for weather research. With approval of the National Academy of Sciences, in 1883, the army asked for 132 square miles to be withdrawn from homesteading as the Mount Whitney Military Reservation. In 1890, weather research was transferred to the Department of Agriculture, and everybody basically forgot about the remote, high-elevation reservation, useless for agriculture or logging or mining.[28]

A third withdrawal came in 1885 at the sequoia grove that boasted the General Sherman and several other massive trees, a grove that Muir had dubbed the Giant Forest. In an odd get-rich-quick scheme, fifty revolutionary socialists had filed for homesteads in the Giant Forest, intending to use the timber and/or land-sale proceeds to fund an imminent workers' revolution. Seeing that many of the applicants were recent immigrants, the General Land Office said it suspected fraud. It withdrew from homesteading four townships that contained the Giant Forest (a township is 36 square miles) and fourteen additional townships throughout the Sierra. The socialists, known as the Kaweah Colony, nevertheless filed their claims, settled the area, and began building a road, hoping that their path to gaining title to the land was only temporarily blocked.

The city of Visalia was split. Timber mills and the associated railroads would bring economic development. On the other hand, irrigation water for the farms of the San Joaquin Valley might be threatened by a loss of upstream forests. Upper-class Visalians also liked to escape summer heat in the peace of forests and mountains. Some newspapers stayed silent. The *Delta* and its editor George Stewart supported the Big Trees by focusing on less-controversial issues, such as eliminating forest fires and itinerant bands of sheep.

Because withdrawals were temporary, easily reversed by a future politician, the issue felt unresolved through the 1880s. Indeed, in 1889 a new interior secretary announced plans to put back on the market withdrawn lands including the Giant Forest and the Grant Grove. The *Delta*'s Stewart realized that they needed a permanent solution, a congressional law rather than an administrative decision. Stewart and other locals started arranging meetings, circulating petitions, and developing maps. They enlisted the support of their local congressman William Vandever. And they reached out to Eastern journalists, including George Bird Grinnell, the hunter-conservationist who edited *Forest and Stream*, and William Stiles, who edited Harvard horticulturalist Charles Sargent's *Garden and Forest*.

Stiles was particularly enthusiastic. To him, *conservation* was all about trees. At a time when Muir and the *Century* editor Robert Underwood

Johnson were promoting protection of Yosemite's high-altitude meadows, Stiles wrote Johnson, "Just now, I am more interested in rescuing that grove of Sequoias in Tulare County than in Yosemite or Yellowstone." Stiles didn't care about the spiritual aspects of a national park, he simply saw such designation as the best path to permanently saving the trees. Although it didn't stop his support, Stiles did grumble about the term *park*, which suggested "to most people some attempt at gardening or decoration." The sequoia groves were forests, and "should be so designated," he wrote in an editorial. To Stiles, a *forest* needed conservation to maintain its primeval character, whereas a *park* would be developed artificially, in ways that would detract from the preservation of wilderness qualities. [29]

In July 1890, Congressman Vandever introduced a bill to establish "a public park or pleasure ground" in the remote Garfield Grove, the last Tulare County sequoia grove that had not yet been claimed by any homesteaders. Vandever's bill was a first step toward a long-term goal of protecting sequoia groves all the way north to Yosemite—starting with a non-controversial action that wouldn't tread on any private claims. The bill gained support from the governor and many newspapers statewide; the only significant opposition came from sheepherders. After House and Senate passage, on September 25, 1890, President Benjamin Harrison signed it into law, making Sequoia the nation's second national park.

One week later, Harrison signed the Muir-Johnson Yosemite bill, which had been rewritten at the last moment. Now, in addition to creating the donut-shaped Yosemite National Park, this bill tripled the size of Sequoia National Park, adding the Giant Forest. And it created a new General Grant National Park for the Grant Grove. Today, most historians believe that the Southern Pacific railroad was behind the changes. Dispossessing the Kaweah colonists would enrich competing timberlands that the railroad owned. It would also safeguard irrigation for Southern Pacific lands downstream, and make the new national park more accessible to rail tourism. The socialist Kaweah Colony was deeply distrusted outside of Tulare County; rail executives may have also enjoyed the irony of confiscating socialists' land for a government scheme. In Visalia, however, locals generally liked the colonists and distrusted the powerful railroad monopoly. To some of the Big Trees' biggest advocates, the bill's alterations seemed mysterious and perhaps dangerous backroom maneuvers. Years later Muir and Stewart admitted to each other that neither had any idea how the bill got changed.

Establishing Sequoia and General Grant marked a shift in the park movement. In Yellowstone and Yosemite, the absence of any known economic value gave a non-controversial victory-by-default to science and the potential for tourism. By contrast, advocates for these southern Sierra parks argued that the trees had greater value in undisturbed form than in their competing use as timber. They convinced Congress to take away the rights of parties who had already made economic claims on that timber. The argument was successful, but just barely, on a small scale—and thanks in part to the Southern Pacific's subterfuge and in part to the nationwide mistrust of immigrant socialists. The dissonance nevertheless demonstrated how difficult the fight for public land would continue to be. [30]

In May 1891, about thirty miles upstream from the eight-month-old General Grant National Park, John Muir made camp with painter C. D. Robinson. They found an old log cabin at the edge of a meadow on the South Fork of the Kings River, at the foot of Grand Sentinel peak. The deep, scenic, U-shaped mountain valley—a "yosemite," as Muir liked to call them—was rimmed by rugged, purplish-gray granite peaks. Beyond the meadow lay the confluence of two rivers, the smaller one jammed by huge timbers, which created shady swirls and ripples ideal for trout. "This surely is the most romantic fishing-ground in the world," Muir wrote. He met a pair of fishermen who claimed that when conditions were right, it was easy to catch a hundred trout in a morning. Muir himself was more taken with the lupine; the birds, such as tanagers, grosbeaks, orioles, and finches; the squirrels; and a bear, "jet-black, sleek, and becomingly shaggy; with teeth, claws, and muscles admirably fitted for the rocky wilderness." [31]

It was Muir's fourth visit to an extraordinary landscape today enshrined in Kings Canyon National Park. His group saw just two other parties in the remote valley: the fishermen and a father-and-son hunting team that killed the bear Muir described. Despite the lack of crowds, Muir was dismayed at the changes that had come in the sixteen years since he had first visited this area. In a line that might have been aimed at Senator Cornelius Cole, who said that Yellowstone's natural wonders didn't need government protection, Muir wrote, "At first sight it would seem that these mighty granite temples could be injured but little by anything that man may do. But it is surprising to find how much our impressions in such cases depend upon the delicate bloom of the scenery, which in all the more accessible places is so easily rubbed off." [32]

Muir was coming to describe landscapes politically. Two years previously, he'd made his fateful Yosemite journey with editor Robert Underwood Johnson, as described in Chapter 3. The two *Century* articles he wrote from that experience helped expand and nationalize park protections in the greater Yosemite—now he wanted to do the same thing for the southern stretches of the Sierra. Muir was here to write what he called a "3rd Yosemite article." [33] Their plan was a carbon copy of the previous effort: Muir would write eloquent prose and draw maps with boundaries for a proposed national park; Johnson would publish the article and use it to lobby in-person in Washington. On this trip, Muir was accompanied by illustrator Charles D. Robinson, a muscular, strong-willed, and extremely outspoken man with glittering blue eyes. Robinson had painted more than ninety scenes of the Yosemite Valley, and contributed some of the illustrations to Muir's previous Yosemite articles; he was Johnson's choice to make the trip. Muir would have preferred to bring his friend William Keith, or to draw sketches himself for later reduplication by an artist. [34]

Johnson's original schedule called for publication in the fall of 1890, to coincide with Congress's work on Yosemite, Sequoia, and General Grant. However, Muir kept delaying his trip, as he had to attend to his dying father-in-law, who passed away in October. His trials continued: when he finally got to Kings Canyon, in May 1891, the three-week journey turned out to be "a little hard." [35] They arrived too early in the season, when snow and high water impeded travel. Robinson, Muir claimed, wouldn't help gather wood, cook, or wash dishes, so Muir decided to leave the camp dirty and let the dogs lick the dishes clean. Muir, Robinson claimed, wouldn't help pull the horses out of a snowbank they got stuck in, kept following incorrect trails, insisted on going everywhere with a favorite ten-inch wheel of cheese, and was too cheap with the *Century*'s expense account to have the guide cook and clean for them. Robinson infuriated Muir so much that later, when Muir received the published article and made notes on it for potential future reuse, he everywhere crossed out the name *Robinson* and replaced it with *an artist*.[36]

Then after returning to Martinez, Muir had his typical difficulties wrestling his thoughts into sentences, and condensing them sufficiently for magazine publication. As delays mounted, he complained to Johnson, "My stock of cliff & cascade adjectives are all used up, & I am too dull to invent new ones."[37]

Johnson had instructed Muir, "I think you might call the article 'A Rival of Yosemite.'"[38] Muir found the angle attractive for reasons that traced back to his debate with the geologist Josiah Whitney: multiple yosemites further proved that the original Yosemite was not unique, not caused by a cataclysm. So Muir allowed the "rival of Yosemite" metaphor to rule his prose. Muir continually compared this new place to the famous old one: this was a "yet grander valley of the same kind." He provided physical descriptions, and although they were beautifully-wrought portrayals of beautiful country, they too often relied on Yosemite-style language to describe a darker, more baroque landscape. Furthermore, the comparisons were at best mechanical—"This new Yosemite is longer and deeper, and lies embedded in grander mountains, than the well-known Yosemite of the Merced" and at worst unflattering—"[waterfalls] of the new valley are far less striking in general views, although the volume of falling water is nearly twice as great." Submitting the final version, Muir's cover letter expressed fear that it was "terribly dry & geographical." He may have realized that it lacked the resonance of his grander work.[39]

Muir's article also spoke of the endangered sequoia groves downstream from Kings Canyon. He described how the mills' activities had intensified in the past sixteen years. "As if fearing restriction of some kind, particular attention is being devoted to the destruction of the sequoia groves owned by the mill companies, with the view to get them made into lumber and money before steps can be taken to save them. Trees which compared with mature specimens are mere saplings are being cut down, as well as the giants, up to at least twelve to fifteen feet in diameter." But he also wanted wholeness. "Some of the sequoia groves were last year included in the national reservations of Sequoia and General Grant Parks," he wrote. "But all of this wonderful King's River region, together with the Kaweah and Tule sequoias, should be comprehended in one grand national park."[40]

Describing a grand regional mixture of sequoias, "yosemites," and high peaks met Johnson's requirement that Kings Canyon and Yosemite sound like rivals. Yet the article's greatest weakness was a flawed conception of rivalry. Rather than possessing different qualities equally worthy of admiration, the one was presented as a lame Hollywood sequel to the other. Kings Canyon did have unique features, but the rivalry angle failed to capture them. Worst of all, Muir did not learn from this strategic mistake. In retrospect, what's most striking about his Kings Canyon crusade is that a decade before Muir proclaimed that the nation should preserve forever the Hetch Hetchy Valley because it was a less-heralded twin to Yosemite, he had made the exact same argument for Kings Canyon.

The argument failed at Kings Canyon, just as it later would at Hetch Hetchy. Congress never acted. Indeed, Johnson couldn't even get a bill introduced, so we can't even know what arguments would have been made against it. In retrospect, the problems are clear. No legislators—and not even Johnson himself—visited the place in person. The Southern Pacific didn't get on board. Muir didn't coordinate much with local activists, who may have been jaded or exhausted by the years of inconclusive back-and-forth. And with Congress having just acted on Yosemite, Sequoia, and General Grant, "rival to Yosemite" wasn't inspiring enough to get people committed to the long, tedious work of legislation. It would take until 1940 for Kings Canyon to become a national park.

But Muir and Johnson were not daunted. They were making progress in changing public perceptions of parks and nature. To them, national parks started as a *vehicle* for enshrining human relationships to nature. Now that the *national parks* vehicle had four occupants, Congress hesitated to try squeezing any more in. So Muir and Johnson needed another vehicle. Another way to celebrate, enshrine, and redefine nature. Indeed, they would soon learn of a new strategy that might give protection to special natural places—without having to rely on Congress to declare them national parks.

7

Free Land for Many Uses

Mark Twain called the late 1800s the *Gilded Age* because materialistic excesses represented a thin gold gilding atop tremendous income inequality. Beneath the gilding, a nation recently wracked by civil war faced labor and environmental crises. As once-endless herds of bison thinned to the point of near-extinction, some people predicted that once-endless forests would be next. The market would not save them. Fueled by the innovations of the Industrial Revolution, the American economy was firing on all cylinders and consuming everything in sight. Yet for what? As common folk endured poor wages and horrific working conditions, too much of the great new wealth seemed to accrue to the *robber barons*, *tycoons*, and *moguls*—characters whose fortunes were so extraordinary that these terms that had to be borrowed from German, Japanese, and Persian, respectively, to describe them.

President Theodore Roosevelt often gets credit as the trust-buster who led an anti-monopolism crusade. This crusade demonstrated that the moguls' monopolies had broken the traditional model of capitalism across so many industries that the federal government needed to step in. Some historians debate Roosevelt's importance to the cause, in part because his successor, William Taft, did more, and in part because the cause had been growing for decades before Roosevelt took office in 1901.[1] Indeed, as this chapter chronicles, anti-monopolism grew in creative rivalry with a movement to alter America's relationship to the environment—resulting in a productive tension that started changing people's attitudes about land ownership.

Before Roosevelt, one of the great, underappreciated anti-monopolists was Congressman William S. Holman, Democrat of Indiana. Holman had graying blond hair, scraggly whiskers, a high forehead, and a fondness for chewing tobacco. He was raw-boned and nimble, courteous and humorous, not a great orator but an earnest speaker. He was honest, religious, and scandal-free. Considered provincial in his habits and tastes, he dressed carelessly, frequently forgetting to knot his black string tie, or tying it in a peculiar fashion. His long tenure in Congress earned him a reputation for "hay-seed statesmanship."[2]

Holman was known as the Great Objector. His tagline was: "Mr. Speaker, I object!" Most of his objections were to excessive or unnecessary government spending. Born in 1822 on a small Indiana farm near the Ohio River, Holman experienced a frontier boyhood that accentuated his remarkably thrifty character. For example, on a congressional trip to investigate appropriations to Indian reservations in 1885, Holman refused to ride in a sleeper car, or stay in a hotel room with a bath, because the extravagance would cost the government too much money. As committee chair, he reluctantly approved the expenses of other congressmen sleeping in Pullmans, but insisted they vacate those cars during non-sleeping hours. At one point on the tour, he arrived at a fort after the rest of the party, and the fort's officers wanted to fire a salute in his honor. "No, no, for God's sake, don't!" said Congressman Joe Cannon. "He will object to the useless waste of powder."[3]

As chair of the House Appropriations Committee in 1889, Holman reduced appropriations for nearly every bill, the chief exception being a bill for river and harbor improvements that would benefit his district on the Ohio River—which is to say that he was human, not a saint. Trying to evade Holman's axe, in one session some congressmen purposefully brought up their bill while he was strapped in the Capitol barber's chair—but to no avail, as he rushed into the House chambers with the barber's apron still wrapped around his neck, one side of his face shaved but the other full of lather, shouting, "Mr. Speaker, I object!"[4]

They're funny stories, but they also show how Holman stood up for traditional Jeffersonian values amid challenges from railroads, industrialism, and high finance. The *New York Sun* said of Holman that "frugality with accountability is the capital axiom in his system of legislation" and claimed that he had singlehandedly saved the country one hundred million dollars, which was one-sixth of the annual federal budget.[5] Holman himself explained that the nation's founders sought "a plain, frugal government that should treat its people with equal-handed fairness, opening up to all alike an equal chance in the struggle for life by protecting all, granting special favors to none."[6] In other words, Holman opposed spending not merely because he was cheap, but also because that spending would confer special benefits. Those benefits would likely accrue to some parties more than others, large corporations more than working-class voters. Keeping the government pie small would keep the greedy monopolists from growing fat on it.

One of Holman's best examples of wayward government practices contributing to income inequality was homesteading policy. In theory, homesteading represented a perfect small-frugal-government Holman ideal: transferring land from government to citizens through sale or give-away. This attitude was so ingrained in American political philosophy that it predated the Constitution. After the Revolutionary War, when Britain ceded lands west of the Appalachian divide, the country, under the Articles of Confederation, passed laws that provided ways for settlers to buy land from this *public domain*. Then, over the years, new laws actually reduced the price of land, to make sure that federal revenues remained small and land ownership remained widely dispersed.

The principle distinguished America from Europe, where governments evolved from ancient monarchies or feudal lordships. Regardless of how wisely it ruled, or how much democratic self-governance it granted to its subjects, an Old World government's power and legitimacy arose largely from land ownership. Even today, the world's twelve biggest private land-owners include only royals and the pope.[7]

Arriving in the New World, European colonists ignored or stole the rights of the continent's indigenous residents, and brought diseases that decimated indigenous populations. Those actions allowed them to perceive a clean slate. The kings, queens, and landlords listed on colonial charters were so distant from colonists' day-to-day lives as to be irrelevant. Land appeared to be free for the taking—if you could tame it through toil and determination. The promise that any man could apply his sweat to free land powered the ideal Jeffersonian society of entrepreneurial, middle-class, landowning farmers. That society shamefully excluded many people, most notably Native Americans, African Americans, and women. Nevertheless, it took a remarkable step forward from the previous feudal model. The colonists then built that ideal into their post-Revolutionary governments: the farmers, not the government, needed to own all the land. When the 1801 Louisiana Purchase resulted in a huge tract of "empty" land that had legal title residing with the federal government, everyone involved operated under the assumption that federal ownership should be a temporary condition. When governments owned land, tyranny resulted. Free your land, and your people will follow.[8]

Through the 1800s, land was given or sold to soldiers, then to squatters, homesteaders, and railroad companies. Most famously, the Homestead Act of 1862 offered 160 acres free to eligible farmers who could "prove up"—build a home, make improvements, and farm continuously for five years. By the 1870s, however, William Holman became concerned at how few farmers were benefitting from government land disposal. Instead, legislators found it too easy to give away land to large companies, such as railroads. Any individual transaction had an economic justification—for example, encouraging railroad-building exponentially increased the value of nearby homesteads—but taken together, the corporate giveaways encouraged monopolies. They detracted from the founding fathers' goal of a vast, relatively equal middle class. In pursuit of growth, legislators ended up encouraging concentrated land ownership, the very problem that American democracy had been designed to oppose.

In the Holman philosophy, an equitable homesteading policy would have been a particularly valuable form of social engineering in the late 1800s. It was needed to counter the income disparities created by the technological developments of the Industrial Revolution. Instead, Holman saw, monopolists tilted homesteading policies in their favor, worsening the divide. It happened not only with railroads and farms, but also forests; in one case, 100,000 acres of California coastal redwood trees went from the public domain directly to a single firm.[9] Although he was colorfully adamant about it, Holman was hardly alone in his dismay. Indeed, if you were an aspiring statesman seeking to improve broad societal issues—if you were, say, a young Theodore Roosevelt or an even younger Gifford Pinchot—then you would want to address how some people and companies were too big and powerful. They had too much money, they owned too much land, and they controlled too many economic and natural resources.

Pinchot's particular flavor of statesmanship—forestry and conservation—went beyond William Holman's concerns about inequality to another set of problems posed by the faulty federal land disposal model. America's land itself was running short.

In Jeffersonian terms, the supply of farmable homesteads ran out. After Midwestern states filled up, aspiring famers farther West struggled with poorer rainfall, climate, or soil quality. In response, Congress tried to extend homesteading laws: The Timber Culture Act of 1873 offered an additional 160 acres if homesteaders on the treeless high plains would plant 25 percent of their acreage in trees. The Desert Land Act of 1877—and subsequent revisions, plus broader acts in 1904, 1909, and 1916—increased grants to 320 or 640 acres for irrigated farming, dry-farming, or stock-raising in areas with insufficient rainfall. Furthermore, given that some

Western lands proved better suited to trees than crops, the Timber and Stone Act of 1878 sought to apply the homesteading model to forests, while the Free Timber Act of 1878 authorized anyone to take timber from public mineral lands for building, mining, or domestic purposes.

The result: a disaster. Even when successful, homesteading had generated a huge amount of fraud. These extensions accelerated the swindles to ridiculous proportions, to the level of legalized plunder. For example, the purpose of the 1878 acts was to provide woodlots for the personal use of nearby homesteading farmers, so that they could have a source of timber for cabins, fences, and fuel. That theory made little sense on real-life landscapes in a real-life economy that was transitioning from Jeffersonian farming to industry. The law ended up supervising the giveaway of millions of trees with no agriculture in sight. Instead this timber addressed industrial demand from mines, railroads, and faraway cities. Logging was a scale-based industry, in which trees were worth far more to a big company than they ever could be to a smallholder. Thus some aspiring monopolists encouraged people to file claims they otherwise wouldn't have bothered to; some bribed the land agent to make transfers directly, without the fiction of a middleman. Quickly, entire forests were transferred from the government to private monopolies for practically nothing.

Beyond the collapse of Jeffersonian ideals, conservationists were dismayed at the effects on the environment. Under traditional homesteading, once a tract of land became private property, it was planted with relatively sustainable crops; from an economic view, at least, it had been enhanced.[10] But when forests were homesteaded, the land was often too cold, steep, or thin-soiled to be farmed. Financial incentives demanded that all the trees be cut down immediately—and once that happened, there was no incentive to replant trees because the next harvest would be decades away. America's private lands thus seemed headed for mass deforestation and devastation. The land itself, once seen as free for many uses, became disposable, a waste product of the timber industry. And short of overthrowing entire economic systems, there didn't seem to be much anyone could do to save it.

Most anyone who believed in science saw a choice: America could either conserve forests or watch them turn into deserts. George Perkins Marsh, the prophet who first shared this view, was arguably the most important environmental thinker of the 1800s. As a diplomat in the Mediterranean, Marsh observed devastated, desertlike landscapes in places that had once cradled civilization. His 1864 book *Man and Nature* argued that this environmental catastrophe had resulted from historical failures to steward the forests. "Man is everywhere a disturbing agent. Wherever he plants his foot, the harmonies of nature are turned to discord," he wrote.[11] Marsh wasn't merely a scholar of ancient history: he'd seen the same patterns in his youth in Vermont, when many of his cash-strapped neighbors cut down their forests or abandoned the state for richer Midwestern farms.

Marsh saw such disturbances as immoral, a violation of the close-knit Puritan town ideal that had ruled New England for two centuries. Puritan theology—as later embodied in Gifford Pinchot—emphasized obligation to community over individualistic expression. If some Vermonters moved to Iowa homesteads, then what remained of the Vermont community might not be strong enough to enforce that obligation. And Vermont was a microcosm of America in general. Some force—perhaps the government—needed to establish limits on individual freedom in order to save the collective resources. As a good Puritan, Marsh embraced the passages of the Bible that said that human management could improve on nature—but successful human management would require some sort of authority figure to constrain human greed. The excesses of the robber barons proved a handy symbol of what needed to change.[12]

Gifford Pinchot received Marsh's *Man and Nature* as a twenty-first birthday present from his parents. The book showed Pinchot how to combine his father's outdoor interests with his mother's religious ones. However, Pinchot was late to arrive at these ideas: the book was older than he was. By the time Pinchot read it in 1886, Marsh had already influenced dozens of nature-lovers, from the Harvard horticulturalist Charles Sargent to the park designer Frederick Law Olmsted to the German-born forester Bernhard Fernow to the hunter-editor George Bird Grinnell to the California naturalist John Muir. Unfortunately for their cause, however, this influence came out piecemeal. Each of these individuals pursued their own passions and interpreted Marsh in their own ways. For example, Sargent liked Marsh's call for a moral authoritarianism but believed that only the military had the necessary distance from human weakness to save the forests. Olmsted applied Marsh's idea to work with nature to recondition land trashed by humans, but only in the context of urban parks. Fernow loved the science but was more oriented toward research than politics. Grinnell embraced the principles but tended to apply them only to hunting and fishing, as when he distilled *Man and Nature* into: "No water, no game; no woods, no water; and no water, no fish." Muir liked Marsh's science, but Muir's spiritual individualism never meshed with Marsh's view of an obligation-based society. Thus, as a whole, the pre-1890 conservation movement lacked a leader, someone who could tie together its multifaceted view of nature; tie forests to water, fish, game, and other resources; tie conservation to anti-monopolism. [13]

Lacking such a leader, the movement to redefine the nation's relationship to forests and nature careened from Congress to the executive branch, from park to public domain, from preservation to conservation, from poorly thought out laws to unexpected consequences. We can next follow it back to greater Yellowstone.

John Muir might have more enjoyed his 1885 visit to the Yellowstone National Park if he'd known about his counterpart, another brilliant geologist who loved wandering obscure corners beyond park boundaries. The two didn't meet that year because during Muir's visit, Arnold Hague was on a backcountry adventure in the Absaroka Mountains east of the national park. "Nowhere in the northern Rocky Mountains do I know grander and more rugged scenery than can be found in the Absarokas," Hague later wrote. [14]

The son of a Baptist clergyman and professor from an old New England family, Hague was what you might get if you crossed Muir with an establishment-friendly intellectual. Hague had a high forehead and prominent nose atop a bushy beard. His manner was reserved and gentle-manly. Born in Boston in 1840, he graduated from Yale, studied geology in Germany, and then began a long career with the U.S. Geological Survey (USGS). Hague examined volcanoes in the Pacific states and Guatemala, and in 1883 was appointed to head USGS efforts to study Yellowstone's geysers, especially their relation to ancient volcanoes. He spent seven straight summers in Yellowstone, with interests growing beyond geology. He loved Yellowstone's scenery: mountains, sunsets, "sequestered nooks, and enticing grassy parks." Having frequently followed elk trails in his travels, he believed that elk "have an appreciation of the picturesque and the grand."[15] Later in his career, USGS would publish his study covering more than 3,000 square miles as a book and atlas titled *Geology of the Yel-lowstone National Park,* which is still lauded today by geologists as one of the most in-depth Yellowstone studies ever performed.

Like Muir, Hague wasn't content to merely describe natural features—he wanted to make sure they weren't destroyed. He started working in Yel-lowstone in the same year that the railroad arrived, and the new acces-sibility promised the first big test for Yellowstone's sustainability. During Hague's tenure, whenever concessionaires, big-game hunters, or rail tycoons sought inappropriate uses—hotels too close to natural features, lax enforcement of poaching regulations, or a railroad through the park's Lamar Valley—Hague fought against them. He supported Yellowstone's transfer to army supervision, and worked well with his military counter-parts. During his winters in Washington, D.C., he developed networks of scientists, generals, and policymakers that could stop threats to the park's integrity.

Like Muir in Yosemite, Hague in Yellowstone quickly saw that natural wonders brimmed beyond the arbitrarily drawn park boundaries. When early explorer Ferdinand Hayden had sought to preserve the geysers and other thermal features—of which he knew he'd seen only a portion—he suggested that the park's eastern and southern boundaries be set ten miles beyond the edges of Yellowstone Lake. Now that Hague and others had more fully explored and mapped the territory, they found that, for example, the rugged Absarokas, the scenic Tetons, and the actual headwaters of the Yellowstone River all lay beyond those lines. Why not protect these marvels too? In exchange—to demonstrate the ignorance in which Hayden had proposed those first boundary lines—Hague even flirted with rationalizing the park's northern and western borders to match those of the Wyoming territory, rather than spilling into slivers of Montana and Idaho.[16]

The idea of expanding Yellowstone was not Hague's alone. In 1882, General Phillip Sheridan proposed stretching the park 40 miles east and 10 miles south. The hunter-activist George Bird Grinnell highlighted Sheridan's plan in Grinnell's *Forest and Stream* magazine. Early in 1883, a Senate bill proposed that extension. It failed to pass. But Hague's scientific credentials, on-site experience, and insider network could offer weight when advocates tried again.

Where Muir had a gift for talking about nature in spiritual terms, Hague's gift was to do so in scientific terms. As an intellectual, he rarely called on sentimental arguments. Instead, he used concerns about dwindling natural resources to argue for Yellowstone. For example, in an 1883 letter to the Yellowstone-friendly Senator George Vest, Hague noted the expense and complications of the state of New York's quest to provide uniform water flow in the Hudson River by buying or controlling Adirondack forests. To secure similar protections for the vital rivers arising in Yellowstone, Hague suggested, the time to act was now, before settlers arrived. As Hague summarized for *The Nation* magazine in 1888, "Remove the forests from the sources of the Yellowstone and Snake, and the region would become a barren waste. . . . If left alone, [forests surrounding the national park] will soon be invaded by the lumberman, charcoal-burner, and railway-tie cutter, the advance guard of a rapidly increasing population."[17]

Hague also endorsed Grinnell's efforts to preserve scarce game animals. Like trees and water, wildlife habitat was a dwindling resource that needed protection, especially in the era when bison, elk, and other charismatic, once-common animals were threatened with extinction. Although not a hunter himself, Hague was able to describe greater Yellowstone in terms of habitat. "In midsummer[, elk] cows and calves frequent the picturesque park-like country near the sources of the Snake River," he wrote in a piece commissioned by Grinnell. "In my opinion, the head waters of the Snake furnish one of the best breeding grounds for elk anywhere to be found . . . they exist in numbers sufficient to put to rest all fear of extermination if they shall only be protected and allowed to wander undisturbed."[18] For work in protecting elk in and around Yellowstone, Hague and his attorney colleague William Hallett Phillips became the only two non-hunters ever elected full members of Grinnell's Boone and Crockett Club.

Hague thus made multiple arguments in favor of expanding Yellowstone's boundaries: scenery, hydrology, timber, habitat, and a sense that these high-elevation lands, lacking minable metals, were worthless for any commercial purpose. Indeed, as a geologist for the mining-friendly USGS, Hague could speak with authority about the region's lack of mining opportunities. And he had political savvy: he shrank Sheridan's proposal to leave in the public domain Jackson Hole meadows that were desirable as private grazing lands.

Hague's combination of arguments could attract a diversity of advocates in the political sphere. The combination also demonstrated the very reason that conservation could only be addressed in the political sphere—it was a task so big and diverse that it was beyond the purview of any single private landowner. The scenery, habitat, and forests around Yellowstone were all so diverse and sprawling that they dwarfed even George Vanderbilt's Biltmore. A place like Yellowstone—and, similarly, the Sierra Nevada, Mount Rainier, the Grand Canyon, and other sweeping tracts of nature—needed coordinated management. These places served different goals than the farms, mines, and private forests that had previously covered the entire American landscape. These places protected rivers, habitat, scenery, recreation, and sustainability—goals that could be accomplished only by a landowner bigger than America had ever encountered. Just as monopolistic industrialists like the Carnegies and Rockefellers were discovering the value of scale, so too were the advocates of nature.

Hague failed to expand Yellowstone's boundaries in four consecutive congressional sessions through the 1880s. Each time, lobbying by railroads altered the proposed bill to allow construction of a rail line through Yellowstone's Lamar Valley. Railroads sought access to potentially lucrative mines at Cooke City, Montana, just outside the park's northeast corner. Hague and other Yellowstone defenders believed that such a railroad would defile the meaning of the national park, so they refused to support the bills as amended. They took a principled stand, which helped establish the integrity of the national park idea, even at the risk of failing the broader conservation goals that the expanded boundaries represented.

Hague and his allies believed that they simply needed to keep trying and hope that either luck or changing political dynamics would allow them to eventually expand Yellowstone. In the spring of 1891, Hague developed yet another boundary-expansion bill. It too died. Then the Great Objector, Congressman William Holman, unexpectedly stepped in.

During the 1880s, Holman had become especially infuriated at the way that railroads and big timber companies ended up acquiring so much of the public domain. One of the very few times Holman changed a bill to *increase* its appropriation was for a study of fraudulent entries on public land. Late in the decade, he proposed various tweaks to homesteading laws that could limit fraud. He didn't want to eliminate homesteading itself—it was the best method of disposing of public lands, which was essential to his small-government ideology. Instead, Holman's tweaks insisted that genuine homesteaders be the only beneficiaries of that disposal. For example, one proposed tweak would reserve a homestead's coal deposits: smallholders could use coal for their own purposes but not sell those rights to a big coal mining company. Another demanded that railroads forfeit land grants that they weren't using for construction. A third required that as the former Indian Territory in Oklahoma was opened to white settlement, no land be used for the benefit of any railroad. Few of Holman's proposals made it into law, but they did help establish the terms of the debate.

Meanwhile, other congressmen were carrying bills for activists concerned about forests. Given that wood was so essential for so many purposes, would massive immediate logging create a subsequent timber famine

ABOVE: John Muir was a mountain wanderer, glaciologist, defender of Yosemite National Park, and co-founder of the Sierra Club. *Helen Lukens Jones photograph, in Kings Canyon in 1902, courtesy of the Library of Congress LC-USZ62-52000.* BELOW: His hair and beard were untrimmed, but John Muir's personality showed in his lively, kindly-looking eyes. *Courtesy National Park Service, RL_01339.*

LEFT: Gifford Pinchot was a close advisor to President Theodore Roosevelt and founded the U.S. Forest Service to promote sustainable use of timber resources. *Circa 1910 photograph courtesy the Library of Congress LC-DIG-ggbain-18121.* BELOW: When he met Muir in his 20s, Pinchot was handsome, wealthy, intelligent, and dedicated. *Frances Benjamin Johnston photograph from the early 1890s courtesy the Library of Congress LC-DIG-ppmsca-19459.*

RIGHT: In 1893, Pinchot and Muir first met at the Pinchot family mansion at #2 Gramercy Park in New York City. *2018 photograph by the author.* BELOW: The night that Muir and Pinchot met, Muir told the story of exploring Alaska's Brady Glacier with the dog Stickeen. Although the glacier has likely retreated since then, this photo still portrays the immensity of the country. *Photo courtesy National Park Service.*

ABOVE: The youthful Muir was intense and outdoorsy, a spellbinding storyteller with a thick Scottish brogue. This picture was used in a magazine in 1883. *Courtesy John Muir National Historic Site, JOMU 3521.* BELOW: With his marriage to Louie Strentzel in 1880, John Muir moved onto this vineyard in the Alhambra Valley near Martinez, California. *George H. Knight photo, undated, courtesy Yosemite National Park, RL_01363.*

ABOVE: An editor at *Century* magazine, Robert Underwood Johnson was Muir's friend and lobbyist. *Albert Bigelow Paine photograph, from* The Critic *magazine, vol. 42 (1903), courtesy Wikimedia.* BELOW: In 1889 at Tuolumne Meadows, high above the Yosemite and Hetch Hetchy valleys, John Muir arranged Johnson's blankets as if tucking a child into bed. *Steve Dunleavy photo courtesy Wikimedia.*

ABOVE: John Muir, aged 57, near the Hetch Hetchy valley in 1895, photographed by conservationist Theodore Lukens. Lukens departed the Yosemite valley looking for Muir, and found this man, lacking food, pack animals, or companions—and perfectly content. *Courtesy Wikimedia.* BELOW: In 1885, this map identified routes to the remote Yosemite valley via rail and stagecoach. The map also shows Martinez, on the northeast edge of San Francisco Bay, the home of John Muir. *Doxey & Co. map courtesy Wikimedia.*

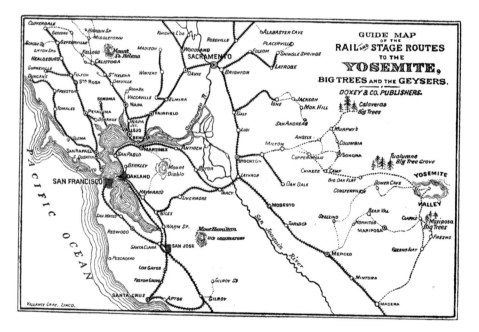

ABOVE: Muir was a captivating storyteller, especially in outdoor settings. Here he's instructing at front left, probably on the 1909 Sierra Club summer outing to Hetch Hetchy. *George R. King photo first published in the Sierra Club Bulletin, Vol. 10, No. 1 (Jan, 1916), 4; courtesy National Park Service, RL_01344.* BELOW: In a famous 1903 photograph, John Muir and President Theodore Roosevelt posed at Overhanging Rock in Yosemite National Park, with a view of Yosemite Falls behind them. *Courtesy Wikimedia.*

ABOVE: President Roosevelt (third from left), John Muir (next to Roosevelt), and others gathered at Yosemite in 1903. The man in back is sometimes mis-identified as Gifford Pinchot, but is in fact Dr. Presley Marion Rixey, Roosevelt's physician. *Joseph N. LeConte 1903 photograph courtesy National Archives 7002905. For full list of names see https://www.loa.org/news-and-views/1190-john-muir-save-the-redwoods, accessed Jan 25, 2018.* BELOW: To protect a grove of redwood trees north of San Francisco, William Kent donated them to the federal government in 1908, and insisted that they be named Muir Woods. *Eric Poelzl 2005 photograph courtesy Wikimedia.*

TOP LEFT: William Kent is shown here between Muir and J.H. Cutter of the Tamalpais Conservation Club at Muir Woods National Monument, circa 1912. *Courtesy Golden Gate National Recreation Area, GOGA 32470-0314.* CENTER LEFT: Although Muir, shown here at Muir Woods, loved nature as a holistic spiritual presence, gigantic redwood and sequoia trees were physical representations of nature's wonders. *Courtesy Golden Gate National Recreation Area Park Archives, GOGA 32470-0292.* BOTTOM: In this photo from the early 1900s, the Tuolumne River flows through the lower portion of a remote Yosemite valley called Hetch Hetchy. John Muir famously opposed building a dam in this valley. *Isaiah West Taber photo originally published in the Sierra Club Bulletin, Vol. VI. No. 4 (Jan, 1908), 211, courtesy Wikimedia.*

John Muir and President William Taft (in the center, with other unidentified men) pose at the Grizzly Giant in Yosemite in 1909. Muir showed Taft the Hetch Hetchy valley, persuading the President to personally oppose the dam, although he never quite killed it. *Courtesy National Park Service, C27AD878-155D-4519-3E4980889538DE19.*

Nature writer John Burroughs, at age 70, and John Muir, age 72, in Yosemite in May 1909. Frustrated by Muir's quixotic argumentativeness about Hetch Hetchy and the spirituality of nature, Burroughs said, "I love you, though at times I want to punch you or thrash the ground with you." *Fred Payne Clatworthy photograph courtesy Yale University Art Gallery 2011.164.4.*

RIGHT: At Yale, where he graduated in 1889, Gifford Pinchot was voted "Most Handsome." *Courtesy USDA Forest Service, Grey Towers NHS.* BOTTOM LEFT: Vermont's George Perkins Marsh wrote *Man and Nature*, a seminal book on conservation that Pinchot received for his 21st birthday. Marsh poses here in 1850 for a daguerreotype by Matthew Brady. *Courtesy Library of Congress, 2004664024.* BOTTOM RIGHT: The landscape architect Frederick Law Olmsted hired young Gifford Pinchot for his first real forestry job, at the Biltmore mansion in North Carolina. *Courtesy Wikimedia.*

ABOVE: In 1895, the Biltmore estate was in its infancy. The job of Frederick Law Olmsted and Gifford Pinchot was to turn the scraggly trees and exhausted soils of the surrounding area into a landscape that would match the opulence of George Vanderbilt's newly-built chateau atop the hill. *Harry Shartle photograph courtesy Library of Congress LC-USZ62-71822.* BELOW LEFT: German-born Bernhard Fernow, Pinchot's predecessor as chief U.S. government forester, was a knowledgeable scientist who struggled to implement forestry ideals in the political arena. *Courtesy Library of Congress, cph 3a49593.* BELOW RIGHT: In addition to founding the U.S. Forest Service, Gifford Pinchot spent the Roosevelt administration as the President's chief advisor on environmental issues. They're shown here on a riverboat in 1907. *Courtesy Library of Congress, ppmsca.36197.*

THE CONFUSION OF TONGUES.
SAD FINISH OF THE REPUBLICAN TOWER OF BABEL.

This cartoon from the humor magazine *Puck* compared 1912 Republican party infighting to the Tower of Babel. Theodore Roosevelt jumps hysterically atop a block labeled "Me-ism"; below him, a toga-clad President Taft gestures at Gifford Pinchot while standing atop a block labeled "Conservationism." In the aftermath of the Pinchot-Ballinger affair, everywhere people are arguing while the tools and blocks that would build their legacy sit idle. *L.M. Glackens in Puck Vol. 71, No. 1841 (Jun 12, 1912), courtesy Library of Congress, 2011649355.*

Gifford Pinchot, second from left, acts as an elder statesman observing his acolytes' implementation of forestry principles at a 1921 forestry convention. "Keep your hillsides wooded," says the sign, with the model on the left demonstrating how vegetation retains water and soil compared to the flood- and erosion-prone bare hillside on the right. *P.C. Crass 1921 photograph courtesy National Archives 7002905.*

ABOVE: Pinchot, shown here in the 1925 inaugural parade, had a rich post-forestry career including two terms as governor of Pennsylvania. *1925 photograph courtesy National Archives 7002540.* LEFT: Congressman William Holman of Indiana, "The Great Objector," inserted a forestry clause into an 1891 bill designed to prevent homesteading fraud. *Brady-Handy photograph collection, Library of Congress, Prints and Photographs Division, LC-DIG-cwpbh-03815.*

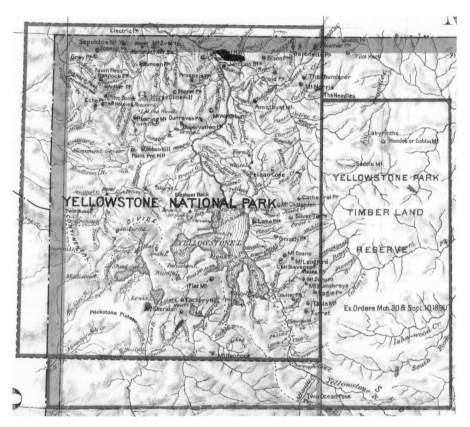

Yellowstone geologist Arnold Hague persuaded President Benjamin Harrison to use Holman's Forest Reserve Act to set aside the Yellowstone Timber Land Reserve, the world's first national forest, east and south of the park. *1892 General Land Office map courtesy WyoPlaces and WyoHistory.org.*

ABOVE: Hague wanted forest reserve status for the scenic, habitat-rich Absaroka mountains east of Yellowstone as a stepping-stone to add these lands to the national park. *2015 Sunlight Creek photograph by the author.* BELOW: On May 10, 1891, President Benjamin Harrison visited Glenwood Springs, Colorado. Five months later, he created the nearby White River Timber Land Reserve, with unclear purposes that split the town politically. *Courtesy Glenwood Springs Historical Society's Frontier Museum.*

ABOVE: Was the White River Timber Land Reserve set aside for sustainable logging and water supply, or was it intended to become a national park? *Carol M. Highsmith 2017 photograph courtesy Library of Congress, LC-DIG-highsm-48495.* BELOW: When the hunter, conservationist, and editor George Bird Grinnell helped the federal government purchase a portion of the Blackfeet Indian Reservation—for a forest reserve, which was later converted to a national park—he demonstrated the drawbacks of early public land models. *Photo from Popular Science magazine, 1893, courtesy Wikimedia.*

An aerial view of the Crown of the Continent, or Backbone of the World, in Glacier National Park. In 1891, George Bird Grinnell stayed at a cabin between the Upper and Lower St. Mary Lakes, at the right of the picture, and conceived a plan to take the land from the Blackfeet Indian reservation and convert it to a national park. *Joe Mabel photo-panorama courtesy Wikimedia.*

ABOVE: The horticulturalist Charles Sprague Sargent chaired the National Forest Commission of 1896 because he knew more than anyone in the country about plants. But his imperious personality made him a poor political influencer. *Thomas E. Mori photo (c. 1904) courtesy Library of Congress, 91784665.* BELOW: In their 1896 visit to what would eventually become Glacier National Park, Muir, Pinchot, Sargent, and other members of the National Forest Commission took the steamboat F.I. Whitney, shown here at a dock, nine miles up Lake McDonald to their hotel. *1896 photograph courtesy Glacier National Park Archives.*

ABOVE: From the steamboat, Muir, Pinchot, and company gazed into the heart of the wilderness now enshrined in Glacier National Park. Their shared love of natural landscapes enabled them to overcome their differences and work together for public lands. *2017 photograph by the author.* BELOW: At Lake McDonald, most of the National Forest Commission stayed here at the Snyder Hotel, site of the present Lake McDonald Lodge. Gifford Pinchot chose instead to camp nearby. John Muir joined him. *1896 photograph courtesy Glacier National Park Archives.*

LEFT: On their last day in office in 1897, President Grover Cleveland and his Interior Secretary, David Francis, faced a momentous decision about the future of public lands. Six years later, Cleveland (left) and Francis (right) posed with then-President Theodore Roosevelt. *Courtesy Library of Congress, LC-DIG-ppmsca-35675.*

RIGHT: This map of national parks and forest reserves as of 1901 was published in John Muir's book *Our National Parks.* At the time there were just five national parks (in black: Yellowstone, Yosemite, General Grant, Sequoia, and Mount Rainier). More than half of the forest reserves (shaded)—including what are now Glacier, Olympic, and Grand Teton National Parks—resulted from the work of the 1896–97 National Forest Commission. *Courtesy Sierra Club John Muir exhibit website, from* Our National Parks *by John Muir, 1901.*

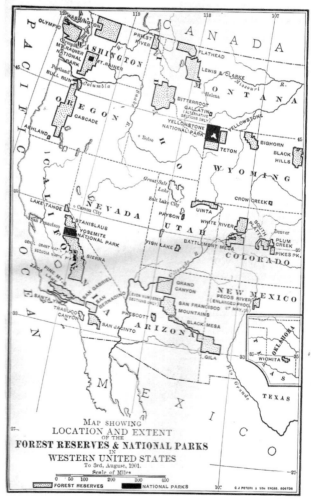

MAP SHOWING
LOCATION AND EXTENT
OF THE
FOREST RESERVES & NATIONAL PARKS
IN
WESTERN UNITED STATES
To 3rd, August, 1901.
Scale of Miles

that would cripple the economy? Were timber monopolies as dangerous as those in railroads or steel? How could the nation prevent forest fires from destroying valuable resources? Could forests enhance downstream irrigation and agriculture?[19] In 1888 alone, more than two dozen bills were proposed to *reserve* some of the forests still remaining on public-domain lands in the West. In the Senate, one of the most promising bills was authored by chief government forester Bernhard Fernow, the German-trained scientist who would later serve as both mentor and nemesis to Gifford Pinchot. But like the other forestry bills—like so many bills seen as unimportant—Fernow's was sent to a Senate committee and never made it back out.

On the House side, Holman saw that Fernow's ideas could support his own homesteading reform goals. He included them in an omnibus bill. To accomplish its varied goals, the bill classified the public domain into "agricultural, timber, mineral, desert, or reserved" lands and developed detailed policies for each category, thus meeting some portion of both the Holman and Fernow agendas.[20] The bill underwent lengthy debate and revision, with discussion centered on issues that demonstrated the promise of combining forestry and anti-monopolism: protecting watersheds, creating timber reserves, selling timber from government lands by sealed bid to the highest bidder, preventing the assembly of large landed estates from the public domain, and ensuring settlement by actual settlers rather than corporations. The bill eventually passed the House, but with the Senate version lost in committee, it died.

In the 1890–91 session Holman tried again, with an omnibus homestead reform "act to repeal timber-culture laws, and for other purposes."[21] It passed the House, was amended in the Senate, and got sent to a joint House-Senate conference committee—another common graveyard for unimportant bills. Even though Holman was part of that conference committee, the bill languished there for five months. When it came out, just three days before the end of the session, the committee had added a single extra sentence, Section 24. The way Congress was supposed to work, Section 24 should have been referred back to the originating committee and then assigned to formal printing and debate. The tedious procedures might have addressed flaws like an apparently missing noun that made Section 24 grammatically incoherent. In the end-of-session rush, however, these time-consuming actions would have killed a potentially useful bill. So the bill sailed through, with promises from its sponsors that all of its issues, including Section 24, had already been debated.[22] On March 3, President Benjamin Harrison signed it into law.

Section 24 allowed the president to reserve forested lands from homestead entry. It was a surprising concession of power from the legislative to the executive branch—especially surprising for a small-government Democrat like Holman to be granting such power to the Republican President Harrison. Given the surprise, and the confusing nature of how it became law, historians have debated: Who inserted Section 24, and why? Years later, South Dakota Senator Richard Pettigrew and Interior Secretary John Noble both tried to take credit. Other people were tempted to give credit to Bernhard Fernow, who once drafted the idea, but Fernow admitted that he was not at all involved in the 1891 law. One hundred years later, historian Ron Arnold showed that Section 24 was actually an awkwardly rewritten version of a clause from William Holman's 1888 bill; the House had indeed debated it during that previous session. The Great Objector presumably reinserted it here because of his concern for how fraud, monopoly, and speculation were ruining the homesteading principle. Homesteaders needed access to fencing and home-building timber, as the Timber and Stone Act of 1878 had tried to give them, and Section 24 seemed like a less corruptible approach. The desire to improve homesteaders' prospects outweighed even Holman's reluctance to give a president too much power or a federal government too much land. Holman must have expected presidents to act prudently, reserving small forests near homesteaded lands to keep them for neighbors' use rather than monopolists' profits.[23]

Holman never publicly took credit for Section 24. He was then sixty-nine years old. His wife's health was failing, his career was winding down. He lost an 1894 election amid the Populist revolt that decimated northern Democrats, and although re-elected in 1896, he died just a few weeks into the new term. He may not have appreciated the significance of Section 24;

more likely, he hadn't even intended for it to be significant. However, the implementation of what is now known as the Forest Reserve Act of 1891—Section 24 having proved by far the most significant clause in the law—would kick off the most important conservation story of the century.

Arnold Hague had not been involved with William Holman's bills, since they had nothing to do with Yellowstone. Indeed, Hague had previously clashed with Holman, who'd shown little interest in protecting or expanding Yellowstone. "Old Holman is a good deal of a fraud," Hague once wrote.[24] But several days after President Harrison signed Holman's bill, Hague discovered Section 24. He consulted William Hallett Phillips, his attorney colleague, to confirm that it gave legal authority to accomplish their aims. On March 16, 1891, Hague and Phillips took their idea to Interior Secretary John Noble. Noble concurred, asking them to draft a proclamation creating the nation's first Forest Reserve, the 1.2 million–acre Yellowstone Park Timber Land Reserve. In the proclamation, Hague used the exact same boundaries that he had previously proposed for the expansion of Yellowstone park. President Harrison signed that proclamation on March 30, 1891.[25]

As always, Hague spoke of actions in scientific, unsentimental terms. This reserve, he said, was unsurpassed "for its advantage as a natural reservoir for the storage of water."[26] But he very much envisioned the reserve as a temporary status for land that needed to be included in the national park. National park status would not only secure forests from being chopped down, it would also secure the other benefits, such as scenery and habitat. In short, Hague's idea of conservation was a preservationist one, tied to national parks. Hague's interpretation of Section 24 could thus appeal to John Muir and his editor-lobbyist Robert Underwood Johnson—Section 24 offered a potential new tool to use in protecting nature. But Hague's interpretation was not at all what the anti-monopolist William Holman had envisioned: it wasn't small or local; it didn't benefit nearby homesteaders; and it did nothing for the equitable, Jeffersonian distribution of land.

Which meant that it was doomed.

8

No Trespassing

O n May 9, 1891, President Benjamin Harrison arrived in Glenwood
Springs, Colorado. Short and stocky, with a reddish tinge to his full
gray beard, Harrison was not a particularly outgoing, man-of-the-
people type. He stopped in this growing city on Colorado's Western Slope
only because he was returning home from California by train and it was
Sunday so he needed to go to church. Glenwood Springs pulled out all
the stops. Preachers from Denver and Leadville volunteered to help lead
worship at First Presbyterian. A "Natatorium" at the hot springs gave free
lifetime passes to every member of Harrison's party, which included his
extended family plus political hangers-on. At a six-course dinner, gifts for
the president and his wife included elegant bathing suits for a post-dinner
swim. Alas, Harrison chose not to enter the pool—a decision that seemed
somehow tied to his insistence on keeping the Sabbath as a day of rest—but
he did consent to make brief public remarks, in which he commended
Glenwood Springs for "now launching into great prosperity."[1]

Established just eight years previously, Glenwood Springs served as a commercial center and rail hub for the silver-mining boomtowns of Aspen and Leadville. Miners came to Glenwood on regular Sunday "laundry trains" to bathe, wash clothes, and visit saloons and brothels.[2] Glenwood also boasted its own economy: dozens of coal mines in the low, dry hills around town evolved into neighborhoods that attracted immigrant miners, many of whom later homesteaded area farms and ranches. As Glenwood grew, its leading citizen, a Princeton-educated silver baron named Walter Devereux, developed sophisticated ambitions. A handsome thirty-eight-year-old with level eyes and a ginger beard, Devereux constructed the 600-by-150-foot Natatorium at the hot springs; inside its sandstone bathhouse he opened a casino where gentlemen were required to wear a white tie and tails. Adjacent to the pool, he would soon build a luxury hotel featuring Victorian gardens, a bird sanctuary, a Florentine fountain, and a private railroad spur. As part of his plan to make Glenwood a resort for the cream of society, Devereux even bought 10 acres south of town for a polo field.[3]

But the Devereux-Harrison vision of a booming, wealthy future competed with other visions. Tensions often centered on government land policy. And these tensions, like similar ones across the West, exemplified problems with the Forest Reserve Act of 1891—ways in which well-meaning interpretations of that law actually made the crisis worse.

Western Colorado gave President Harrison a warm reception because he was a silver guy. Unlike his rival Grover Cleveland, Harrison cautiously supported backing U.S. currency with silver as well as gold—a policy that would bring windfalls to the Aspen and Leadville silver mines. Silver was the only partisan issue most Coloradans cared about. But Harrison's visit may have had a hidden agenda: to support the research that his administration was already doing into another policy change, with arguably greater long-term impacts.[4]

The results became evident five months later, on the afternoon of October 8, 1891. A telegram arrived at the Glenwood registry of the General Land Office (GLO), where a clerk administered paperwork for prospective homesteaders all over northwest Colorado. In the telegram, the GLO commissioner instructed the clerk to withdraw from homesteading eligibility 1.2 million acres near the headwaters of the White River, north of the city. Most of this land was located on a heavily wooded, high elevation plateau with scenic lakes and good wildlife habitat, a "sportsman's paradise."[5] Ever since March, when a team of GLO agents spent a month allegedly investigating illegal timber cutting, rumors had suggested that the government might take some action on the White River Plateau. But the scope of these withdrawn lands, including many valleys on the edges of the plateau, far exceeded expectations. Eight days after the telegram, the purpose of the withdrawal was revealed: these tracts would become the White River Plateau Timber Land Reserve, second in the nation after Yellowstone.

The move was controversial because it might thwart area growth. If homesteaded, the lands would have been farmed, grazed, mined, or logged, and all of those activities would have boosted the Glenwood-area economy. Indeed, before the withdrawal was even announced, the nearby Leadville *Herald Democrat* published an article titled, "It May Cause Trouble." The article asked what would become of homesteaders on the reserved lands. If you were still enmeshed in the homesteading process, if you had not yet proven up on your land, the article said, your claim might be denied. Although Harrison's official proclamation clearly allowed such claims, you did need to have flawless paperwork, a potentially intimidating requirement. Could you be sure you'd complied—even if you were illiterate, or an immigrant? If your family had come to America because they felt their property rights had been abused in the Old Country, you were predisposed to the fear that "They're coming for our lands."[6]

The strongest opposition to the reserve arose in smaller towns outside of Glenwood, closer to the reserved lands and with less-diversified economic bases. For example, in Yampa, northeast of the White River Plateau, Routt County commissioners protested that the reserve's boundaries were too big, that all of the reserved Routt County lands were needed for agriculture. In Meeker, northwest of the plateau, the *Herald* called the reserve a "damnable outrage! Will you sit still and let that government outfit drive you from the homes that you have acquired by years of toil?" To accomplish conservation goals, the *Herald* said, rather than restricting settlers' rights, the government should be punishing campers who started wildfires and Native Americans who killed game.[7]

By contrast, within Glenwood itself, two of the town's three newspapers supported the reserve. Walter Devereux welcomed it "as a protection for the many against the few." Devereux had an economic interest: preserving scenic views in adjacent mountains might aid his goal of turning Glenwood into a world-class spa. Yet Devereux and his brothers also owned a large area ranch, so the dispute couldn't be pigeonholed as tourism versus agriculture. It was more city versus country, or upper-class versus working-class, cosmopolitan versus hermit. Devereux and those who shared his silver-and-tourism vision would thrive by connecting Glenwood to the world; Meeker- and Yampa-area smallholders would prefer the world to leave them alone.[8]

Devereux, like others of his class, used the accoutrements of outdoor recreation as status symbols. An outdoorsman, hunter, and photographer, Devereux belonged to national organizations, such as the Boone and Crockett Club and the American Forestry Association.[9] These groups called for protecting forests and recommended federal authority as a method of protection.

What shape would that authority take on this land? When asked about the White River Plateau Timber Land Reserve, Devereux endorsed President Harrison's action, saying, "I am in favor of that land being turned into a national park." Others also called the forest reserve a *national park*. For example, the *Pueblo Daily Chieftain* editorialized, "The few who are opposing the establishment of this great national park are simply doing so on political and personal grounds." The Glenwood *Avalanche-Echo* puzzled over the town of Meeker's opposition to "the national park scheme." One Aspen correspondent recommended that the plateau be "set aside as a national park under state control," thus mischaracterizing the very idea of a national park, which would necessarily put national interests ahead of local ones.[10]

Similar thoughts were expressed about the Yellowstone reserve—even by John Muir. As late as 1901, Muir was writing that Yellowstone National Park "was to all intents and purposes enlarged by the Yellowstone National Park Timber Reserve." Because of the reserve's elevation, dearth of minable minerals, and lack of nearby population, Muir said, "The withdrawal of this large tract from the public domain did no harm to any one." Meanwhile "its geographical position, reviving climate, and wonderful scenery combine to make it a grand health, pleasure, and study resort."[11] Just as the world's first national park had been reserved in 1872 with a negative vision—*we can't say quite what it should look like, but* not *Niagara Falls*—so nineteen years later were the world's first national forests reserved with little agreement on what they were. Muir thus could interpret the reserves as resort-like parks in the service of spiritual contemplation, while Glenwood-area smallholders could see them as government overreach in the service of class warfare.

For opponents stoking fears of federal authority, calling the White River reserve a national park could specifically associate it with the Kaweah socialist colony, which had recently been dispossessed at Sequoia, or with James Hutchings, who'd been ejected from his claim in the Yosemite Valley. Yet proponents also benefitted from calling White River a national park—they wanted the nationwide honor and tourism potential. Indeed, in creating the reserve, President Harrison was following the wishes of the Colorado legislature, which in 1889 had formally requested that the plateau be withdrawn from homesteading so that Congress could declare it a national park.[12]

At the moment, Congress wasn't interested in declaring new national parks, as Muir was learning in Kings Canyon. But the idea that a reserve could be an end in itself, something other than a park, was slow to take hold. In July 1892, Colorado state forest commissioner Edgar Ensign tried to explain to Coloradans that "forest reserves and national parks are two separate and distinct things." Ensign believed that no national park would ever be created in Colorado. On the other hand, Ensign said that a forest reserve was intended to be *used*, which meant that it would most benefit the very grazing and logging interests who seemed most upset by it. "Advocates of forest reform do not seek to hinder the rational and economical use of forest products," he wrote. Reformers wanted only to prevent waste and destruction. [13]

In other words, Ensign rejected Arnold Hague's interpretation of Section 24, in which forest reserves were stepping-stones to national park status. Yet Ensign also rejected William Holman's view of small forests being used by adjacent homesteaders. As an experienced forester who had helped Bernhard Fernow and the American Forestry Association lobby for national legislation, Ensign interpreted Section 24 as ushering in large-landscape forestry. With this legislation, he believed, intensive management by a cadre of professionals would avoid a future timber famine and make sure that benefits were evenly distributed across all sectors of society. Although Gifford Pinchot had not yet arrived on the national scene—in these years he was devoted to Biltmore and private forestry—Ensign expressed the philosophy that Pinchot would later come to champion. Indeed Pinchot would later assert that the Forest Reserve Act of 1891, "the most important legislation in the history of Forestry in America," was the crest of a forestry-and-conservation groundswell. [14] At the time, however, Ensign was a lonely voice among many other interpretations.

On October 1, 1891, the General Land Office in Washington, D.C., received a petition from California's Tulare County, home to the recently established Sequoia and General Grant National Parks. The petition noted that the San Joaquin Valley had been barren before irrigation began in the 1870s, and now was successfully shipping its wines and fruits worldwide. The valley's new prosperity was nurtured by the streams of the southern Sierra, and thus endangered by timber speculators and sheepherders. So the petition requested that the government protect 7,000 square miles, or 4.4 million acres, stretching from the southern edge of Yosemite to the southern tip of the mountain range.

The arrival of the petition was a puzzling development. It was a two-year-old document and the people of Tulare County thought that it had been lost. Fifteen months previously, Visalia *Delta* editor George Stewart had announced that by unwisely inviting neighboring counties to partici-pate, they had lost track of the papers, which had probably never reached Washington. Privately, Stewart had also concluded that the petition was too ambitious, and advocates should start by reserving smaller groves of sequoias. Now that Stewart and his allies had indeed succeeded in getting Sequoia and General Grant National Parks set aside—now that condi-tions were ripe for more ambitious reservations—the petition magically reappeared, forwarded to the GLO by chief government forester Bernhard Fernow. Nobody would ever learn what had happened to it. [15]

Acting on the petition, the GLO assigned special agent B. F. Allen to investigate. Allen quickly recommended that the 4.4 million acres be temporarily withdrawn from homesteading while he built the case for a reserve. His work gradually excluded several lower-elevation parcels, as well as those that in the intervening years had become national parks or private lands. Allen orchestrated support for the reserve from Visalia's Board of Trade, a former state forestry chairman, and a newly established Bay Area organization called the Sierra Club. When *Century* editor Robert Underwood Johnson wrote to the GLO proposing a similar reserve, "not . . . for Park purposes, of course, but to save water supply for irrigation below and to preserve timber," the GLO was able to assure him that Allen was already on top of it. The only real opposition came from sheepherders; Allen dismissed them as primarily immigrants who didn't speak English, didn't own property, and hardly paid any taxes. [16]

Although slowed by limited budgets, Allen's efforts were successful. In February 1893, President Harrison proclaimed a Sierra Forest Reserve totaling four million acres, the heart of the High Sierra. Activists such as Stewart and Muir got nearly everything they wanted. Yet at the same time it was nearly nothing.

A forest reserve was a paper designation, its rules meaningless without enforcement. For the next several years, an estimated half-million sheep continued to graze across the Sierra reserve. When the military superin-tendent of Sequoia National Park traveled north through the Sierra reserve in 1894, he found it so overgrazed by sheep that his pack animals couldn't even find enough grass for their daily feed. He posted a hundred notices to warn scofflaws off the land, but all the notices were quickly torn down.[17]

Yellowstone faced similar problems. In 1894 Yellowstone's superintendent complained that the adjacent reserves were too remote, too expansive, too rugged, and too frequented by hunting parties to be effectively policed with his limited manpower. A Yellowstone official report in 1897 noted that at least one hundred prospectors and twenty-five ranchers were spending the summer in the forest reserve, all of them illegally hunting, in areas too remote to patrol without increased budgets.[18] But at least the Yellowstone and the Sierra reserves had the opportunity to rely on military patrols from the nearby national parks.

As President Harrison and his successor Grover Cleveland created new forest reserves—the White River Plateau, the Cascade (in Oregon), the Pacific (at Washington's Mount Rainier), and a dozen more—the GLO asked the military to patrol these acreages as well.[19] But the War Department declined. It did not want troops serving as a domestic police force. The GLO would need to patrol the reserves itself. But in 1893, Congress cut its investigation budget by 10 percent, and in 1894 by another 50 percent.[20] The GLO faced increased responsibilities but declining budgets: even if in passing Section 24 Congress meant to say that it wanted forest reserves, its subsequent budget appropriations showed that it wasn't willing to pay anything for them.

In late 1893, memos started circulating around the GLO. Staffers were incredibly frustrated with the Forest Reserve Act. What was the point in setting aside forestlands without protection or management? The GLO joined the American Forestry Association in lobbying Congress to pass new legislation that would establish some clear policies. However, a dysfunctional Congress failed to act.

President Cleveland's interior secretary, Hoke Smith, eventually reached two conclusions. First, his department would not recommend the establishment of any new reserves until such designations became meaningful. President Cleveland agreed, and proclaimed his last reserve in September

1893. Second, Smith decided on a new interpretation of the Forest Reserve Act: "the object in creating [the] forest reserves [was] to preserve the lands and timber and undergrowth thereon in a state of nature, as near as possible." He talked about *preserving* the lands: if America was ever stymied by a preservation-versus-conservation divide, it was at this moment, on an issue that neither Muir or Pinchot was paying attention to. *Preserving:* the GLO decided that since Congress hadn't defined what a legal use of the forest was, it must have meant to ban all uses. *Preserving:* no trespassing would be allowed on any forest reserve; all of the lands' resources would be locked up.[21]

Legally, the GLO's interpretation was as valid as any of the others then floating around. Section 24 had given the president authority to *create* forest reserves—to withdraw the land from homesteading—but was silent on what to *do* with them. Previous acts reserving lands from homesteading had prescribed a *use*: most famously, the Yellowstone National Park was intended as "as a public park or pleasuring-ground for the benefit and enjoyment of the people."[22] But Section 24 didn't describe what the land was for. It didn't say what was permitted or prohibited.

On the other hand, philosophically, the GLO's interpretation was crazy. The whole point of American democracy had been for land to be used, ideally by common people in the private sector. Furthermore, in a democracy, the government was supposed to be simply an expression of the will of the people. So an ethos of "Government Land: Keep Out" shouldn't have even been possible. In America, it was the people's land. If it wasn't given to individual people for private enterprise, it should have been capable of use by the people collectively.

But "No Trespassing" was clearly what the GLO intended. One staff memo read, "trespassing on the public lands within these forest reserves will not be tolerated under any pretext."[23] Formal regulations confirmed the no-trespassing policy, which in the spring of 1894 was posted on reserve boundaries throughout the country. Public protests arose. The GLO responded that it would enforce these regulations because that's what Congress wanted.

The GLO's reinterpretation may have been power politics, an attempt to force Congress to do something. And Congress did try. A bill "To Protect Forest Reservations" was introduced in 1893 by Thomas McRae, Democrat of Arkansas, a member of the American Forestry Association and chair of the House Committee on Public Lands. Similar to Bernhard Fernow's previous, unsuccessful bills, the McRae bill sought efficient use of forests. It would allow logging, grazing, and other uses—but would regulate them. It had support from the Eastern establishment. In the West, however, where the reserves were located, both sides protested. Miners and stockgrowers wanted more-unfettered access to public lands, while downstream farmers and residents believed that any mountain logging would jeopardize their water supplies. Buffeted on all sides, McRae's bill died.[24]

That meant the GLO was stuck trying to enforce a No Trespassing policy that nobody wanted. William Holman had drafted Section 24 because he wanted natural resources to be used; he just wanted them to be used by homesteaders rather than big business. Edgar Ensign was telling Coloradans that the resources could be used, just not wasted. Arnold Hague had seized on Section 24 because he wanted greater Yellowstone's habitat and scenery to be protected; he believed they could be best protected while being used like a national park. And the rural people who wanted to use the land despaired at a faraway government getting between them and their homesteading, logging, mining, grazing, hunting, vacationing, or other uses.

Of course, Section 24 hadn't prescribed any penalties for violations, and the GLO had no budget for enforcement, so the No Trespassing policy was utterly toothless. People could do whatever they wanted on the reserves without punishment. Even if they were caught, an authority could only eject them from the reserve, not send them to jail. In effect, the forest reserves were no better protected than the un-reserved public domain. Or actually—given that the forest reserves had been withdrawn from the privatization process that might eventually provide such lands with some property rights—they were *worse* off than the rest of the public domain. So Section 24, under the variety of interpretations that sought to protect forests in crisis, had instead made forests more vulnerable than ever. The law was an utter failure.

Section 24 didn't fail merely because it was a last-minute rider that Congress hadn't debated or understood. It failed because neither Congress nor society at large knew how to resolve the underlying issue. The idea of public land went to the heart of inherent conflicts in American values—nature versus development, market versus government, rich versus poor, city versus country, farm versus ranch, efficiency versus fairness, logic versus sentiment, practicality versus spiritual fulfillment, and individualism versus community. What *was* the purpose of these lands?

Although the era is sometimes described as a crisis for *forestry*, it was really a crisis in *ownership*. The American public was thinking about retaining permanent ownership of many different tracts of land, to fulfill many different purposes. But it was trying to invent these ideas on the fly, without a model, an organizational template, or even a set of stories to articulate the vision.

On September 17, 1891, about six months after the passage of Section 24, George Bird Grinnell, the conservation-minded New York magazine editor, sat outside a log cabin in northern Montana, soaking in the stunning mountain vistas. The cabin sat between the Upper and Lower St. Mary Lakes, deep fjords on the western edge of the Blackfeet country, beneath bare mountain peaks that were known for abundant wildlife. Grinnell was an older version of Gifford Pinchot: fashionable mustache, wealthy Puritan background, Yale education, and outdoor enthusiasms. At age forty-one, Grinnell was not yet married, in part because he'd spent each of the last nineteen summers on expeditions in the West. He had a fascination with Plains Indian culture, and published several books about the Blackfeet and Cheyenne tribes. His greatest passion was wildlife. He organized the first Audubon Society, designed to protect birds and their habitat. Then he joined with his young friend Theodore Roosevelt to form the Boone and Crockett Club, designed to do the same for big game. Grinnell loved animals because he loved to kill them—he was a hunter. He sought to protect habitat so that it would conserve a sustainable annual harvest of game. He also loved grand scenery and sought to preserve it from development such as logging or mining. [25]

The previous day, Grinnell had returned from a lengthy trip into the mountains. The next day he would climb another mountain. On this day he let his companions go hunting while he stayed behind at the cabin to develop a map of this little-known mountain country.

While hand-drawing the map, Grinnell also jotted some notes in his journal. "How would it do to start a movement to buy the St. Mary's Country, say 30 x 30 miles from the Piegan [Blackfeet] Indians at a fair valuation and turn it into a National reservation or park." Grinnell was not the first to have this idea—Charles Sargent proposed reserving a similar area eight years previously—but Grinnell was in a unique position to bring it about. Like Robert Underwood Johnson, Grinnell's job as a magazine editor also involved plenty of congressional lobbying—in Grinnell's case, the magazine was *Forest and Stream*, and the wildlife-oriented lobbying helped save Yellowstone bison from extinction, among other accomplishments. Given these interests, it's not surprising that the next few sentences in Grinnell's journal pondered how various political actors would respond to this idea. "Certainly all the Indians would like it," he wrote. [26]

The phrase *National reservation or park* again reveals the uncertainty surrounding government land management designations. Did Grinnell want this area to become a national park? Yes: the following spring he wrote to Johnson's *Century* magazine suggesting an article on "The Crown of the Continent," which "some day I hope may be set aside as a National Park." (*Century* expressed interest, but waited nine years to publish the article.) Grinnell was a big supporter of national parks; earlier that year he and Johnson had corresponded about possibly creating an organization called the Yellowstone and Yosemite Defense Association. [27] So why didn't his journal entry just use the phrase *national park*?

Grinnell was particularly well-informed about politics, so he surely understood that a national park would require congressional approval, which could prove difficult. Conversely, a forest reserve could be accomplished by executive order. Indeed, at that moment, Bernhard Fernow and the American Forestry Association were preparing a petition that asked President Harrison to set aside 2.2 million acres of Montana forest as the "Flathead and Marias [River] reservation." This forest reserve, which was also endorsed by Sargent's *Garden and Forest* magazine, would extend from foothills south of Grinnell's current location more than 50 miles straight west to the Kootenai River. Because the region was poorly surveyed, the proposed reserve boundaries apparently included a lot of farmland. A GLO investigation later that fall showed it to be profoundly unpopular with the area's white settlers, and the petition went nowhere.[28]

Yet Grinnell's use of the word *reservation* is especially curious because he was at the time *already on a reservation*. The cabin was on Blackfeet land—the Blackfeet Indian Reservation. The only reason Grinnell could sit in a cabin here was that his host, Hank Norris, had married a Blackfeet woman and been adopted into the tribe.[29] Although Grinnell mused about purchasing the land from the Blackfeet, Fernow's petition simply reclassified these Blackfeet lands as part of a new forest reserve. As one of the protesting white settlers put it, "Timber Reservations may (by proper authority) be declared upon Public Lands, but I do not understand Indian Reservations to be 'Public Lands.'"[30] True enough: these lands had been reserved from homesteading for tribal use. Only through profound disrespect for this racial minority could someone imagine that the lands were available to be reserved again for forestry.

A further irony: the Blackfeet were actually taking a remarkably conservation-minded approach to managing this western strip of their reservation. After all, Blackfeet had been living here for centuries, and understood far better than whites the need to conserve natural resources for their grandchildren's use. Few tribal members lived fulltime on the mountainous western strip, but they did access it for hunting, fishing, and selective timber-cutting. They set controlled burns to improve habitat. They also attached deep spiritual significance to the peaks above Norris's cabin, which they called "The Backbone of the World." Yet when Grinnell saw the Blackfeet living out on the plains, he mistook their relatively judicious, conservation-minded use of this western strip for indifference. He assumed they would be happy to trade it.[31]

Grinnell failed to recognize indigenous conservation values; other whites actively worked against them. In a bizarre extension of the homesteading ideal, politicians nationwide were at that time demanding that Native Americans stake homesteads on their own reservations. Opposing the notion that a tribe could own land collectively, the 1887 Dawes Act called for *allotment*, in which each tribal member would select ("be allotted") a homestead. Then any leftover land within the reservation could be made available to other homesteaders, to meet the demand from whites for more homestead-able land. Proponents of the Dawes Act believed they were acting in the Native Americans' best interests, helping them assimilate into the dominant culture. Most tribes, however, hated allotment. It was yet another land grab, which used a lame justification relying on yet another paternalistic refusal to acknowledge either the tribes' unique cultures or their sovereign rights to practice those cultures on their own lands.

For the era, Grinnell had a remarkably enlightened attitude toward indigenous people. He advocated for the Blackfeet, including helping the tribe delay allotment. Grinnell also tried to improve the quality of the tribe's Indian agents, the typically incompetent or corrupt white men assigned to oversee tribal finances. Grinnell became concerned about rumors that the "St. Mary country," this western strip of the reservation, enjoyed a wealth of copper, gold, or other minable minerals. As places around the nation had proven, an inflow of prospectors would make it nearly impossible for indigenous people to hold on to their lands. In response to the rumors, in 1895, a federal commission was assigned to negotiate potential sale of the strip. At the request of the Blackfeet, Grinnell was named one of three commissioners.

Grinnell didn't want the job: it was a no-win situation. He reluctantly took it, and it indeed remains the most controversial aspect of his legacy. The Blackfeet entered negotiations with a price of $3 million for the strip. Grinnell told them that would never fly. They stood firm. He responded that agreement was not required, he wouldn't force anything on them, he could go home empty-handed. When they asked, he suggested a price of $1 million. The two sides finally settled on $1.5 million.

Thanks to Grinnell's involvement, the 1895 commission did provide the Blackfeet with more than they might have otherwise received. For example, allotment was permanently banned. Also, when the $1.5 million was converted to a ten-year extension on a previous treaty's annuity, the commission made sure the tribe received interest. Additionally, the Blackfeet gained employment preferences, a sort of government-job affirmative-action program that sadly was never enforced. Grinnell's work to protect wildlife habitat on the strip also protected water resources, thus aiding Blackfeet farmers and ranchers downstream. And given that miners never found anything close to $1.5 million in minerals, one could have argued at the time that the Blackfeet got a good price.[32]

But Grinnell also failed his Blackfeet friends. In the negotiations, the Blackfeet demanded that the treaty give them the inalienable right to hunt, fish, and cut timber on the strip—in effect they were wisely ceding its "ownership" without ceding their traditional conservation-oriented use. Then Grinnell apparently reworded the clause after they signed the agreement, to say that these rights would exist only on public land, subject to Montana state laws. Given that Montana law then prohibited all elk hunting, this was clearly not what the Blackfeet had in mind.

Furthermore, as soon as the Blackfeet agreement was finalized, Grinnell lobbied his longtime friend Arnold Hague, the Yellowstone geologist, to include the strip in a forest reserve. Doing so was clearly not in the Blackfeet's best interests, because at the time the reserves were governed by the No Trespassing policy. Grinnell and Hague apparently believed that Congress would soon resolve that ill-advised philosophy, and the Blackfeet would indeed be allowed onto their old lands. Nevertheless, Grinnell's lobbying indicates his loyalty to white notions of forestry on the ceded strip, a loyalty that caused him to downplay Blackfeet views of conservation and self-determination. The Blackfeet had to bend to the state laws and white legalities of ownership, rather than the laws bending to their traditions. Likewise, the Blackfeet had to become cattle ranchers, rather than becoming miners or tourism entrepreneurs. The Blackfeet had to live on the plains, because Grinnell's wilderness ideal could not accommodate collective tribal ownership of lightly used lands.

Grinnell had always thought that the rumors of mineral wealth were unfounded. He supported the land purchase in hopes that prospectors would come up empty. He sought forest reserve status because once the prospectors departed, the land would retain habitat and watershed protections. That was precisely what happened: In February 1897, the ceded strip became a forest reserve. In 1898, it was thrown open to miners. By 1901 it was abandoned. That was the year that *Century* magazine finally published Grinnell's Crown of the Continent article, kicking off a nine-year campaign to establish Glacier National Park, with the ceded strip as its eastern half.[33]

The worst repercussions for the Blackfeet came with the transition to national park status. The legislation establishing the park extinguished the tribe's right to hunt, fish, and cut timber on its former lands. When the Blackfeet protested, the government basically argued that a "national park" was not "public land." Specifically, it claimed that the 1895 treaty had given the Blackfeet rights on the *public domain*—the not-yet-given-away lands for which no purpose had yet been declared. Because Glacier National Park had a purpose, it was not public domain. Although upheld by subsequent rulings, such legal hair-splitting was not at all how the Blackfeet had interpreted the treaty. Grinnell, now acting as a national park advocate rather than a Blackfeet ally, said nothing. He now perceived the Crown of the Continent scenery as a spiritual haven for white people, which somehow left little room for the Blackfeet's Backbone of the World.[34]

To be fair, Grinnell *wanted* to support both the Blackfeet and park preservation; he probably never grasped how those two objectives conflicted. He was not a bad man, and for his time, he treated the Blackfeet with more respect than most of the white men in Washington. Nevertheless, he was caught in the middle of a fumbling societal move toward the notion of a government collectively owning land. Because the idea was still so poorly understood, his actions ended up opposing an indigenous government's collective ownership structure that should have been his very model.

On December 16, 1894, Gifford Pinchot entered the story. With his work at Biltmore largely complete, and the death of his fiancée now ten months in the past, Pinchot had hung out his shingle in the United Charities Building in New York City as a "consulting forester." But clients weren't materializing as fast as he wanted; he needed to do some marketing. He needed to convince people that forestry was worthwhile. To that end, on this day he agreed to attend a meeting at the Brevoort Mansion, a Greek Revival brownstone house at 24 Fifth Avenue in New York. The meeting had been organized by Charles Sargent, the patrician Harvard horticulturalist. Also present were William Stiles, editor of Sargent's *Garden and Forest* magazine, and Robert Underwood Johnson, editor and policy wonk at *Century* magazine.[35] Pinchot, who had already engaged with Sargent on several long talks, served as secretary, consolidating the group's discussion into a formal outline that he and Johnson could later present to groups like the New York Chamber of Commerce.

Since the early 1880s, Sargent had been calling for action to protect American forests. Philosophically, Sargent was a disciple of George Perkins Marsh's conservation ideas, but practically, he favored the draconian measures of the No Trespassing policy. From his ivory-tower perspective, he believed that forests should be locked up and the army deployed to protect them. Stiles, a Yale graduate who had come to prominence writing editorials for the *New York Tribune*, could temper Sargent's position with a bit more worldliness. A thin, timid-looking man, Stiles was a stylish writer with a keen eye for politics and a Frederick Law Olmsted–style appreciation for the value of parks.[36] The other editor in the room, Johnson, was likewise interested in practical applications of conservation ideals. For a forthcoming edition of *Century*, Johnson was asking Sargent to lay out his plan for the future of the forest reserves so that a variety of experts could comment on it.

In the Brevoort meeting, the attendees agreed that if Congress couldn't reach decisions about forestry policy, maybe a more dedicated deliberative body could. They proposed that the president appoint a commission of three men who could prepare a plan to manage public forests. In Pinchot's recollection, the idea was that all three would believe in "the principles of Forestry." In other words, Pinchot saw this as a step forward for the discipline he loved, rather than a narrow attempt to resolve a congressional stalemate or protect any one specific place. [37] But his was just one of many opinions. The following month, publication of Johnson's *Century* symposium "A Plan to Save the Forests" demonstrated the wide divergence of experts' differing opinions on forests.

Johnson began that article with an explanation of the specifics of Sargent's plan: The military academy at West Point should instruct cadets on forestry, complete with a nearby forest dedicated to experimentation. The best-educated officers would supervise forest reservations across the country, while enlisted men would serve as a "forest guard." Sargent's vision of a sort of Army Forestry Corps was not as improbable as it might seem today; the Army Signal Corps had recently been operating 4,000 miles of telegraph lines and a weather bureau, while the Army Corps of Engineers played a visible role in rivers, canals, roads, seawalls, and railroads. The federal government then did so little management that *any* management function was a good candidate for military administration. Although military leaders had expressed reluctance to take on these responsibilities, Sargent expected that they would embrace the new mission if Congress demanded it. [38]

Of the fourteen experts that Johnson asked to respond, all agreed with the need to manage forests. Even an Arizona lumberman believed that Sargent's plan would prevent "wanton destruction." However, Bernhard Fernow, the chief federal forester, thought the army was exactly the wrong body to perform such a civilian function. Pinchot likewise gave only lukewarm support to the army, expressing concern that a single seminar would be insufficient training and a dedicated "Forest Service" might be better. And others had diverse but penetrating questions: How would the chain of command work? Shouldn't forestry classes be a distinct school at West Point, or at least an optional postgraduate course of study? What about adding the National Guard? Given how much of the remaining forestlands were located in the arid West, was New York's Hudson River Valley really the best place for an experimental forest? In an accompanying editorial Johnson himself acknowledged many drawbacks, but argued that the Sargent plan would be a quick and inexpensive solution to an important problem.

The symposium exposed conflicts, but in such a situation, conflict could be useful. Addressing difficult questions would make the solution stronger, and a process that listened to differing factions would gain their buy-in. Even the fact that all these experts were talking to each other, instead of past each other in the press, was a constructive development. So was their recognition of young Pinchot's talent and passion, and their decision to bring him into the movement. A formal commission could continue such discussions.

On the other hand, Johnson's editorial suggests a note of exasperation at his experts' squabbling. Despite the importance of the forest issue, and the continued failure of Congress to act, many of his symposium contributors seemed more concerned with pontificating for their own egos than uniting behind a solution.

One contributor, however, gave selfless, unqualified support. He wrote that Sargent had proposed "a complete solution to all our forest troubles." Citing the War Department's success at managing Yosemite National Park, he called it "the most reliable, permanent, unpolitical, and effective department of our Government. . . . One soldier in the woods, armed with authority and a gun, would be more effective in forest preservation than millions of forbidding notices." Although that sentence used the word *preservation*, he made it clear that he was not a mere preservationist, that he saw various forest issues in a bigger picture. "It is impossible, in the nature of things, to stop at preservation. The forests must be, and will be, not only preserved, but used . . . the forests, like perennial fountains, may be made to yield a sure harvest of timber, while at the same time all their far-reaching beneficent uses may be maintained unimpaired."

That contributor's name was John Muir.

9

Lake McDonald's Delight

V isiting Holm Lea, the Brookline, Massachusetts, mansion of horticulturalist Charles Sargent, Gifford Pinchot was overwhelmed by the magnificence of the rhododendrons and azaleas. He arrived at 9:30 A.M. on June 5, 1895, to encounter Sargent's manor in full bloom. Sargent and his charming, kindhearted wife, Mary Ellen, had created an effortlessly pastoral landscape, with open pastures of grasses and wildflowers framed by groves of trees and the occasional grazing cow for scenic effect. John Muir, on his own visit two years previously, described it as "the finest mansion and grounds I ever saw. The house is about two hundred feet long with immense verandas trimmed with huge flowers and vines, standing in the midst of fifty acres of lawns, groves . . . acres of rhododendrons twelve feet high in full bloom, and a pond covered with lilies."[1]

The Holm Lea grounds were Sargent's creation, his magnum opus. In his twenties, before taking the job at the nearby Arnold Arboretum, he'd designed the plantings, built the pond, and laid out the finely manicured lawn. Like his friend and neighbor Frederick Law Olmsted, Sargent used plants to create art, to spur emotional reactions. Sargent designed Holm Lea for visual fulfillment, with long sweeping views focused on trees of profound color or bloom. He planted naturalistic flower borders, as if creating a huge patch of English countryside in a near suburb of Boston. Closer to the house, alongside the porch where he and Pinchot likely sat, bloomed azaleas, hydrangeas, and June-flowering clematis.[2]

The twenty-nine-year-old Pinchot, returning from a five-week trip to Europe with his mother, had put this meeting at the top of his agenda. This chapter shows how it brought the Dream Team together.

Pinchot saw Sargent as a mentor, and to that end had already contributed a dozen articles to Sargent's *Garden and Forest* magazine. He also saw Sargent's crusade for a rational forest policy as a career opportunity. When Pinchot's replacement Carl Schenck arrived at Biltmore, Pinchot was troubled by Schenck's Prussian arrogance toward the surrounding "peasants," and may have been reminded of his old missionary impulses. Like Congressman William Holman, he wanted the American system to benefit regular people.[3] Furthermore, as a consulting forester, Pinchot now needed clients, and the federal government would be a desirable customer, with deep pockets and the opportunity to make a difference. Meanwhile, Sargent admired the younger man's talent and saw him as a potential field assistant whose traveling research could improve botanical knowledge across the continent.

On this day, Sargent and Pinchot met with the *Garden and Forest* editor William Stiles and Professor O. Wolcott Gibbs, a retired Harvard chemist who served as president of the National Academy of Sciences. Gibbs was tall, erect, and dignified. Although shy, he was an avid gardener who must have been thrilled with the grounds of Holm Lea.[4] At first, Sargent likely recapitulated the story for Gibbs: The forests were in crisis and the politicians didn't know what to do. It was now four years since President Harrison had created the first forest reserves, and they still had no official charter or purpose. Because they were unmanaged and unprotected, no more were being created. Great swaths of forest still moldered away in the public domain, potential clear-cuts in need of some sort of resolution.

Having watched politics make a hash of his science in the Adirondacks (as discussed in Chapter 4), Sargent believed that only the army, isolated from political pressures, could succeed at defending forests. So he needed to somehow convince politicians to remove this issue from political influence. Pressure would have to come from both scientists and constituents. The issue should be put in front of the public continually, in the form of lectures, endorsements, and articles. Constant discussion, Sargent hoped, would lead to popular enlightenment.[5] To that end, he, Pinchot, and Robert Underwood Johnson had spent six months pushing the idea of a three-man commission to advise Congress on public timberlands. But they weren't gaining much traction.

Professor Gibbs responded with a suggestion. Instead of an independent commission, why not use the National Academy of Sciences? Congress had incorporated this institution precisely to report to the government on scientific subjects. A National Academy of Sciences Commission would by definition be made up of scientists, not politicians. It would be free of pressure from profiteers. It could evaluate the best path forward. Even if Congress didn't immediately act, the process could advance public understanding of the issues. Stiles endorsed the idea immediately, and by the end of the meeting Pinchot and Sargent climbed on board as well.

However, to do the study, the academy would require some government official to request it. Some politician had to care about the issue, without wanting to control the result. Gibbs endorsed a Sargent-Pinchot plan to keep up the public pressure, especially by seeking to influence commercial associations. They had already received endorsements from the New York Board of Trade and New York Chamber of Commerce; now they went to work on the American Forestry Association. There they encountered skepticism—chief government forester Bernhard Fernow didn't see the point of more study, when any scientist could see what the answer would be, and what was needed was action on legislation—but they eventually received an endorsement. The editor Johnson, facing the public in *The Century*, kept up a drumbeat of editorials that something ought to be done, although he kept specifics intentionally vague. As Pinchot said to his mentor Dietrich Brandis, "*What* ought to be done, and how, and who is to do it, are questions of another stripe," of less interest to the general public. Once the public endorsed the need for *something* to be done, the Academy Commission could debate specifics. [6]

In November 1895, Johnson wrote to Interior Secretary Hoke Smith to urge that he request Academy assistance before the next session of Congress. Enclosing a *Century* editorial, Johnson hinted, "I have reason to think that the President is very much interested in the general subject, and that any action you might take in the direction indicated would meet with his approval." Meanwhile, Pinchot composed a draft of the letter of request that Smith could send to Gibbs. [7]

Smith, Pinchot later wrote, was "a big, smooth-faced, powerful, confident man of real capacity." Smith was a Southerner, a Georgia newspaper publisher and personal-injury lawyer. Thus Johnson and Pinchot hoped that he would be immune to political pressures regarding Western forests. But the same forces that made Smith impartial also put the issue low on his list of priorities. It would be another three months before he got around to sending the letter.

The pinnacle of late-1800s Boston Brahmin intellectual society was the Saturday Club. Starting in 1855, Ralph Waldo Emerson gathered writers, scientists, philosophers, historians, and other notable thinkers at the Parker House Hotel on the last Saturday of every month for dinner and conversation. Early members included novelists Nathaniel Hawthorne and Henry James, Henry's philosopher brother William, biologist Louis Agassiz, poet Henry Wadsworth Longfellow, and *Atlantic Monthly* editors James Russell Lowell and William Dean Howells. Forty years later, the club had lost some of its luster, with most of its early members having passed away. Nevertheless, an invitation to address the club still marked a rite of welcome to a world where ideas mattered.

On November 30, 1895, Pinchot stood in front of the Saturday Club to lecture about forestry. Only nine of its thirty-six members were present.[8] But Pinchot, Johnson, and their coconspirators wanted to speak to every influential body they could, in an effort to gain endorsements for rational management of forest reserves. In this case, Pinchot was surely invited by Professor O. Wolcott Gibbs, the club member who also sponsored Sargent for membership the following year. Pinchot's speech to the Saturday Club is particularly interesting because where Johnson or Sargent would have been merely making a policy argument about the type of legislation that would lead to the best management of forest reserves, Pinchot had larger ambitions. He wanted the intellectuals to accept forestry as a profession.

These were the years of Social Darwinism, when every potential competition—even short-term rivalries among people in the workplace or trees in the forest—was seen through the lens of relentless evolution, of the triumph of desirable qualities. Thus Pinchot lauded forestry's removal of "undesirable kinds of trees, such as willows and poplars," because such human intervention was "encouraging the growth of better individuals." A better individual tree, like the better individuals of the Saturday Club, came from good stock. Pinchot's definition of desirability, it went without saying, was expressed in terms of human benefit, such as the strength or durability of lumber. It also went without saying that wise humans would put a thumb on the Darwinian scales, aiding the hemlocks, spruces, and maples in their competition.[9]

Especially in this distinguished crowd, Pinchot saw himself as a man of science. To the extent that forestry was known at the time, it was often seen as a sentimental movement to save trees. Inspired by George Perkins Marsh, "foresters" sought to cut fewer trees and plant more of them. Pinchot understood that crisis, and sympathized with the response, but believed that only dispassionate science could solve it. The *scientific* forestry he'd learned in Europe did involve cutting some trees, because it was driven by reason, not sentiment. To show that he was embracing science, Pinchot spoke of his disapproval of the interest in preserving trees. Scientific forestry aimed at utility, primarily timber production. Pinchot did not see any utility in preserving what would later be called "old growth" forests, ones that had never been logged. Although some people saw "a chance for preserving primeval forest for its aesthetic value," he said to the Saturday Club, he disagreed. "As a matter of fact, the quality is a totally different one. It must be taken for granted that in all the great forest regions of this country the timber will be utilized in spite of everything that may be done to prevent it. Nor do I see any reason it should not be so."[10]

Over the past century, some of Pinchot's critics have seen him as too idealistic, setting up a large Progressive bureaucracy that he believed could manage public lands better than any market or private party. Other critics have seen him as too political, too willing to accommodate public opinion rather than holding old-growth forests inviolate. The combination of criticisms is unusual—the notion of a craven idealist seems paradoxical. It arises partly from Pinchot's statesmanlike quest to find a middle ground where all parties compromised: *you have to accept use*, he told the preservationists, while telling the loggers, *you have to accept regulation*. Furthermore, this speech shows how those views fit together. Pessimistic about individual greed, Pinchot believed that people would always use all the timber they could. But optimistic about the mitigating value of systems, Pinchot believed that with education and regulation, a system of forestry institutions could redirect greed toward sustainability rather than self-destruction. His instincts resembled those of America's founders in the Constitution: rather than hoping that people could become more virtuous, he would design a system that accommodated the lack of virtue. When you look only at the resulting government institution—the Forest Service—Pinchot's system design appears to fall short of the founders' ideals because this executive agency doesn't have enough checks and balances, and thus fails to account for potential lack of virtue in foresters themselves. However, Pinchot saw the Forest Service as merely one institution in a system of professionalization. In his system, other institutions—universities, professional organizations such as the Society of American Foresters, and science in general—would provide forestry's checks. Compared to the lawlessness of the existing situation and Sargent's preferred solution of an unrestrainable military authority, it was a compromise both fair and full of potential.

This philosophy was the heart of Pinchot's rivalry with Muir. Muir the evangelist was optimistic about individuals. If he could get an individual out in nature—especially in Yosemite—he believed that person would become fulfilled, and thus act for the good of all. But he was skeptical that any institution or system could substitute for individual transformation in accomplishing meaningful goals. He often argued with his friend John Swett about the value of public schools, and with his in-laws and neighbors about the value of the farmers' institution known as the Grange.[11] To Muir, any such institution was a form of social conformity—and he was an individualist. To Muir, nature was the home of individualism, and thus had to be set aside from human society, including human-designed government institutions. Although Johnson had dragged him into politics, Muir had no interest in statesmanship, saw no point in designing virtuous systems. Individual salvation could offer so much more.

Of course, Muir was not at the Saturday Club meeting that evening. He preferred his discussions of weighty ideas to take place under the stars.

The National Academy of Sciences never worked quickly. Its previous project, to provide Congress with meaningful scientific definitions of new electrical terms like *ampere* and *volt*, had dragged on for months despite an utter lack of controversy. Hoke Smith's request for help on the forest reserves finally reached Professor Gibbs in February 1896, just a few weeks before the end of the congressional session. It took Gibbs those few weeks merely to come up with a roster and budget for the Committee on the Inauguration of a Rational Policy for the Forested Lands of the United States, commonly known as the National Forest Commission.

But the academy did know how to ask powerful questions. Smith had vaguely requested advice on "a policy of forest conservation" on the public domain. Apparently discarding a response that Pinchot had drafted for him, Gibbs rephrased the assignment. He noted that the first issue was to consider "the question of the ultimate ownership of the forests now belonging to the Government." Pinchot kept asking, "How are we going to *use* these lands?" but Gibbs realized that the first question was "How are we going to *own* these lands?" If Congress was going to decide how to administer forests, it first needed to decide to hold onto them. Since Yosemite in 1864, Congress had fallen into an almost accidental pattern of behavior. Now it needed to actively confirm that Americans wanted some lands to be collectively and forever owned by their democratic government. Pinchot and Sargent had wanted the commission to confirm a question of science, "Is conservation doable?"; Gibbs understood that the country also needed to address a question of political philosophy, "How can the *federal government* do conservation?" Sadly, however, Gibbs was only an ex officio member of the commission, and never followed up to make sure his question was fully answered.[12]

Gibbs named Sargent the commission's chair. Sargent was a scientist, he was removed from politics, he had developed the most comprehensive surveys of American forests, he knew more about trees than anybody in the country, and the whole notion of a *rational forest policy* was basically his idea. The other members spanned scientific disciplines: Geologist Arnold Hague knew Yellowstone, and had helped establish the first forest reserve adjacent to its borders. Botanist William Brewer had conducted the first-ever nationwide census of American forests in 1870, and given what many considered the first-ever American lectures on forestry—indeed he was the Yale professor who had most inspired Pinchot. Civil engineer Henry Abbot knew stream hydraulics, which were important to the forest-as-reservoir philosophy; as a general in the Army Corps of Engineers, he could also speak to military administration. Zoologist Alexander Agassiz, son of the famed biologist and geologist Louis Agassiz, might have contributed perspectives on wildlife habitat, but he ended up attending only one commission meeting.

They were all respected scientists, already elected to the academy for their professional achievements. Sargent also insisted that another man be added to the roster, even though he was far younger and not an academy member: Gifford Pinchot. Sargent wanted Pinchot to be the commission's secretary. Because such a position was typically reserved for an older, esteemed scientist, Sargent saw himself as doing Pinchot a huge favor, although the well-born Pinchot, used to such favors, didn't seem to notice. Pinchot was, however, plenty eager to help. Indeed he and Sargent had already started planning a trip that summer to the Rocky Mountains. Now they would have an official charter.

Sargent could have written the commission's report without leaving home—for that matter, so could Brewer or Pinchot. They'd seen Western forests in person, and they had plenty of Western correspondents willing to provide more evidence. For example, George Ahern, an army lieutenant with forestry training, wrote in 1894 that Montana's Blackfoot River Valley was littered with timber waste: "One firm alone cuts fully 50 million feet annually and about 30 million feet reach the mills on the lower river; the rest remains rotting where it fell." Anyone could have assembled observations like these from the front lines—indeed Hague and Pinchot compiled a preliminary report that spring. Then the commission's work could have involved deliberation about what these facts meant for science and policy. [13]

However, Hague, Brewer, and Abbot liked the romantic notion of joining Sargent and Pinchot on a four-month tour of the American West. They would see these forests in person, and have dialogues with the Westerners who used them. Such a trip could both publicize their cause and give it legitimacy in the eyes of locals who often complained about arbitrary, distant federal decisions. Although none of them mentioned it, they may have also hoped that the social dynamics of traveling together would make them better able to collaborate on reaching their final recommendations.

Sargent was surprised that the commission wanted to travel. When he and Robert Underwood Johnson negotiated with Congress for a $25,000 expense account ($750,000 in 2018 dollars), he'd expected only himself and Pinchot to visit the West. [14] But once the commission gained the potential to become a sort of rail-borne forest salon, Sargent committed to make the discussion as lively as possible. He decided to get John Muir to join them.

The Sargent-Pinchot relationship started deteriorating in that spring of 1896, even before the commission got on the road. Some of their troubles stemmed from differences in ambition and scheduling. The eager young Pinchot wanted to wrap up the commission's work—which he expected to change the world—by early autumn. That meant completing a lot of work ahead of time, and ideally traveling in spring rather than late summer. There was good reason to act quickly: Hoke Smith had expected a report within a matter of weeks. But after being appointed in March, the commission didn't even have its first meeting until six weeks later. There were bureaucratic delays, but Pinchot blamed Sargent.

Furthermore, Pinchot became increasingly alarmed that Sargent didn't want to do any "real forest work." To Pinchot, forestry was a site-specific discipline, requiring detailed surveys and valuation studies of any given acreage. He believed that Hoke Smith had asked the commission to do this work: collect detailed data in order to determine what to do with the forests. Sargent disagreed. He wanted to "go slow and feel our way, not to attempt too much and to take plenty of time." Sargent likely grasped that it would be impossible to crank out dozens of forest surveys in just a few months, using a collection of senior citizens not trained in forestry valuation techniques. However, that left Pinchot wondering what, then, was the purpose of the trip. If they were just going to look at the edges of forests from a nearby train station or luxury hotel, then they wouldn't really advance knowledge.[15]

Pinchot proposed that he would conduct a valuation survey himself. He would do it on the ceded strip recently taken from the Blackfeet reservation, east of what George Bird Grinnell called the Crown of the Continent. In proposing this survey, Pinchot may have been primarily motivated by his desire to go hunting and hiking there. He had already hired two of Grinnell's favorite guides, Billy Jackson and Jack Monroe.

Sargent disliked the idea. He doubted that detailed valuation surveys should be part of the commission's work, but if so, he wanted them done in Colorado. Sargent himself had already seen the Crown of the Continent, back in 1883. Furthermore, there just wasn't time: the commission couldn't leave on its Western excursion until its congressional appropriation became active on July 1. At that point, the commission would have to hurry to squeeze in South Dakota's Black Hills, Wyoming's Yellowstone, Montana's Bitterroot, the Washington and Oregon Cascades, and the California Sierra before autumn snows limited high-elevation travel. Finally, Pinchot told Sargent that he would make the Crown of the Continent trip on his own. He would leave a month early and pay for it himself.[16]

Beyond policy differences, the Pinchot-Sargent squabble also had an uncomfortable personal dimension. For the past few years, with his consulting practice failing to take off as he'd hoped, Pinchot had been writing a book called *The White Pine*. He and his assistant Henry Graves had taken measurements and performed calculations on the growth and yield of that species in central Pennsylvania. Despite the subtitle, *With Tables of Volume and Yield*, Pinchot seemed to believe that his book might be a new direction in the literature of natural history, might start him down a poetic path similar to John Muir's. That ambition was sheer fantasy; the book was at best a dully competent technical forestry primer. Even for such a limited purpose, Pinchot struggled to make this site-specific study relevant or interesting to foresters in other regions. Worst of all, when Sargent read the book—the Eastern white pine was his own favorite tree—he found an error. The white pine, Sargent said, did not grow with the red maple, as Pinchot asserted. That paragraph should be deleted.

Pinchot pushed back. He'd seen the two trees growing together.

Sargent responded, "It is always better to omit the statement of a fact than to state a doubtful one, and I do not see how you will improve your essay on the White Pine by saying what tree grows with it."[17]

Sargent was wrong. The two trees did grow together.[18] Worse, there was no arguing with him when he was sure he was right. Sargent's high-society background added to the emotional coldness; as biographer S. B. Sutton wrote, "Apologies were beneath his dignity."[19] Similar conflicts had engulfed Sargent and many of his previous underlings: he was stubborn, imperious, demanding—a bully.

Meanwhile Pinchot was unduly sensitive to criticisms of *The White Pine*. He was devastated when Bernhard Fernow published a review criticizing its methodology. Pinchot's correspondence with John Muir later that fall was dominated by Pinchot's dismay at Fernow's critique and his desire to strike back. Muir counseled him to forgive, move on, stop seeing the world through the lens of his ego and personal relationships. "Never mind Fernow," Muir wrote in October. "Go ahead with your own work and very soon he will become polite and good." And in December: "You do just right 'going ahead full steam' with other work instead of wrangling with Fernow or any other fellow."[20] Despite aspiring to work in politics, the young Pinchot was sensitive and egotistical, and capable of petty personal rivalries.

Pinchot's split with Sargent, however, also encompassed substantive issues that divided the commission as a whole. On one side were Sargent and Abbot; on the other, Pinchot, Hague, and Brewer. The division could be characterized in many different ways: Forest management by the military versus professional foresters. Relatively restricted use versus relatively open use. Harvard versus Yale.[21] Theory versus practice. As Pinchot wrote to his mentor Brandis, "Sargent seems to think we should devise the best possible solution without regard to whether it can be given effect or not through Congress. My own desire is very strongly in the other direction."[22] In a sense it all came down to leadership style: as Pinchot wrote to one of Brandis's disciples, "We are going into the summer's work with nothing but the most hap-hazard conception of what there is to do and how to do it."[23]

The commission's first huge failure was that Sargent didn't address this split. Indeed he showed little sign of even recognizing it. Given his privileged background and omnipotent position at the arboretum, was he incapable of recognizing or managing disagreements? Was he simply conflict-averse? Was the policy debate too big to be decided by any National Academy of Sciences Commission? Whatever the issue, before it even embarked on its research-gathering trip, the three-month-old commission was already a troubled body.

Back in January, while Hoke Smith was sitting on the request to the National Academy of Sciences, Robert Underwood Johnson had filled in John Muir on the potential commission as a "short cut" to meaningful forest policy. Although Johnson wasn't a scientist and thus couldn't be a member of the commission, he was lobbying intensely for it. At his urging, Muir and the Sierra Club did the same. After Smith finally made the formal request, Muir told Johnson, "The glorious news of the National Academy of Sciences Commission has kept me happy ever since I heard of it. This sure enough is a move direct towards permanent forest management and cannot fail."[24]

Soon Muir started gearing up for another cross-country trip. In Wisconsin, his mother was dying. And in Massachusetts, Harvard University wanted to give him an honorary degree. "Heavens, what an honor for a tramp & how it surprises & excites me," Muir wrote to Johnson. Muir didn't want such a formal honor for himself, but he understood that Johnson had engineered it as a way of increasing Muir's public influence. Muir had to accept.[25] Sargent was delighted that his friend would come East and receive this honor. Sargent also pointed out that since the Harvard ceremony was in late June, Muir could travel back West with the commission in early July.

Although the arrangements were tentative, events broke favorably for the commission. Muir saw his mother, told stories that made her laugh, and then while at Harvard received a telegram that she had died peacefully in her sleep. After the Harvard ceremony he raced back to Wisconsin for the funeral. The timing then worked out for him to meet the commission's train in Chicago, on July 3, 1896.

If Muir was spending the month out of his element, so was Pinchot. On June 7 his train arrived in Blackfoot, Montana, at 2:00 A.M. There waited the Blackfeet guide Billy Jackson, a tall, slender man with high cheekbones. Jackson had been a scout for Major Marcus Reno at Custer's Battle of the Little Bighorn in 1876, and over the last twenty years had become a widely acclaimed guide, scout, and packer. He brought horses to the train station for Pinchot and his assistant Henry Graves to ride before dawn to Jackson's ranch on Cut Bank Creek. From there it was only a few miles to the St. Mary country, Grinnell's old haunt, which was no longer Blackfeet territory but not yet a forest reserve. Joined by an aspiring forester with photography skills named Walter McClintock, they stalked a site that they'd baited with a dead horse, hoping to see a grizzly. "Very cold, and at times very exciting," Pinchot wrote in his diary. One day they heard the bear shuffling and scratching, and crawled forward with rifles ready. The sounds, they discovered, had been made by birds. [26]

After a few weeks of hunting, hiking, photographing, and surveying, they moved west of the Continental Divide, to the South Fork of the Flathead River and then to Swan Lake. Then Pinchot sent Graves back to Michigan, to work on a forestry plan there. Jackson returned to his ranch, inviting McClintock to accompany him. (The experience led McClintock to become fascinated with the Blackfeet; he would forsake forestry to become a noted anthropologist of Blackfeet culture.) Pinchot joined with guide Jack Monroe—a small man, about thirty years old, a former jockey who had come to northern Montana in search of gold and stayed after marrying a Blackfeet woman—to set out southward through the Swan Valley on foot.

"To me it was a fairy land," Pinchot later wrote. Overwhelmed by mosquitoes, "The only chance we had to sleep was when the cold of the short July nights moderated their [the mosquitos'] zeal. But the country more than made up for everything . . . There is a freedom in the pathless woods, if you are there on your own feet and on your own resources. It was a gorgeous trip—the best I ever made on foot." [27]

Pinchot was finally achieving the sort of carefree wandering that Muir kept suggesting for him. While hunting deer and bear, while marveling at the thick western larch, western yellow pine, and Douglas fir, while admiring the nearby streams and high peaks, Pinchot felt his responsibilities utterly fall away. Because Pinchot lacked Muir's gift for language and storytelling, we can see only scraps of what this trip meant to him. For example, although he talked about mosquitos, and fording huge rivers, he never told the story of how he and Monroe almost ran out of food. Monroe finally shot a young colt for its meat. Pinchot ate the steak and admitted to enjoying its taste. Monroe later implied that Pinchot was marvelously torn: morally queasy about eating horseflesh, but caught up in the magic of living by their wits in the wilderness. [28]

Indeed, Pinchot apparently lost track of what day it was. One evening he realized that there was no way to make it to the train station in Belton, Montana, by the time that he had arranged to meet Sargent and the commission there. Worse, the last person they'd seen had told them that they were crazy to try this trip, that they would drown trying to cross the Swan River. When they made that crossing, Monroe's dogs had instead turned around and likely returned to that ranch. When the rancher next visited the regional center of Kalispell—which he expected to do at about the same time that Pinchot and Monroe were scheduled to arrive—he would report them likely dead. Upon that realization, Pinchot and Monroe hiked 52 miles in twenty-six hours, mostly without a trail, to try to get back to civilization ahead of reports of their demise.

At Belton, Montana, just 20 miles below the Continental Divide, the Great Northern railroad snaked through thick pine forest, alongside the Middle Fork of the Flathead River. The seventh U.S. transcontinental route to be built, the Great Northern was the northernmost, traversing rugged country with long winters. It was slow to attract settlement: Belton itself consisted of three houses marooned in the vast, nearly uninhabited forest. Its "station" was an abandoned boxcar. When dawn reached this village on July 16, 1896, surprises awaited for nearly everyone.

At 5:35 A.M., a train chugged down from Marias Pass, carrying members of the National Forest Commission. After a midnight transfer in Shelby, John Muir had not gotten to bed until 1:00 A.M., and he was up again at 4:00 A.M. to marvel at the spruce, pine, and larch blanketing the pass. At Belton, Muir, Sargent, Hague, Brewer, and Abbot got off the train—and were surprised to see Gifford Pinchot waiting to meet them. Sargent had notified Pinchot of their itinerary in a telegram he sent to Kalispell, but Pinchot hadn't responded. Indeed Sargent had sent a week's worth of telegrams to Kalispell about the commission's continually delayed arrival at Belton, and Pinchot hadn't responded to any of them. Pinchot had been off in the Swan Valley, battling mosquitos. Given the limits of frontier communication, Sargent wasn't yet worried for Pinchot's safety but did expect that they would miss each other here. In fact, Pinchot had arrived in Kalispell in time to receive, if not respond to, the final telegram. So he was able to meet the train. Pinchot and Jack Monroe invited everyone down to their camp by the river for coffee.[29]

Muir expressed particular approval. "Meet Pinchot with delight," he recorded, present-tense, in his journal.[30] This was only his second in-person encounter with Pinchot, three years after the Gramercy Park dinner. They'd become regular pen pals, full of encouraging warmth. Muir liked Pinchot's mind, and also his appreciation for adventure. At age fifty-eight, Muir was younger than anyone on the commission, and the thirty-year-old Pinchot promised outdoorsy companionship. It was probably obvious even in the way Pinchot now carried himself: This was a man who'd spent the last five weeks in rugged northwest Montana, the last two weeks on that epic trip through the Swan. This was a man closer to Muir's wild sensibilities than anyone he'd seen in months. Muir's trip East had brought him into the company of relatives, academics, scientists, and editors; although he loved them all, what he treasured most was unfettered exploration of the natural world—and here was Pinchot embodying that.

Pinchot was equally astonished. He was pleased to have made it back to Kalispell in time to receive the telegrams, to realize that he would not be late, to meet up with these learned men and embrace the work of the summer. Most significantly, as he wrote in his autobiography, "To my great delight, John Muir was with them." John Muir! Muir's presence was a complete surprise. Muir had not decided to join the commission until mid-June, long after Pinchot had left for the West.[31]

John Muir! Pinchot was equally thrilled to find someone young and outdoorsy among the elderly scientists. Muir—not an academy member, lacking in earned degrees or the desire to acquire them, more interested in people and storytelling than dry scholarship—promised to be an ally of Pinchot's against stuffiness. John Muir! Muir was a hero to Pinchot. Pinchot understood that Muir had qualities that he himself lacked: eloquence, keen observation, deep feeling, the courage to embrace freedom. Pinchot had always molded himself through intimacy with older men he admired—Forstmeister Meister, Dietrich Brandis, and until recently Charles Sargent. Muir was the obvious next great mentor. And now here he was in the flesh, totally unexpected.

In Pinchot's autobiography, he wrote that "I took to him [Muir] at once." In an early draft, that sentence was preceded by, "It was the first time I had met him."[32] Obviously, Pinchot soon remembered that they had met three years previously at Gramercy Park—but that dinner had been dominated by his parents. Pinchot had been such a quiet listener that Muir thought he was merely a student. Now, here he was: self-confident and independent, located in Muir's home turf of the West, having just completed a Muirish ramble through pathless territory. It was the first time Pinchot had met Muir as himself rather than his father's son, as an outdoorsman rather than a socialite, as an individual rather than an acolyte.

Their shared delight did not imply that they were carbon copies of each other. They still had all of their differences in appearance, class, and religion; their differing relationships to people, power, politics, and society. But these differences could attract rather than repel.

After coffee, they rode from Belton—which is now known as West Glacier—on a scant, swampy trail through dark, dense cedars three miles to the village of Apgar. As he always did, Muir noted in his journals the trees, which also included western white pine, larch, Engelmann spruce, and white poplar. He noted almost a dozen species of shrubs and wildflowers, including "glorious beds of *Linnaea*, best ever saw." Without mentioning the huts at Apgar, or the forty-foot steamboat *F. I. Whitney* that they boarded there, Muir did record his impression of the 10-mile lake that steamboat traversed: Lake McDonald was "one of finest ever saw." Summarizing in a letter to his wife several days later, he repeated, "This is one of the most beautiful of all the glacier mountain lakes I have yet seen, more beautiful [in] some ways even than Tahoe."[33]

Lake McDonald fills a deep glacial valley, and thus has no islands or sandbars, few shallows or reed-beds. Unbroken forests approach its shores, end with a strip of gravel, and then begin again as mirrored reflections. If you look straight down, the water is deathlessly clear, the lakebed pebbles crisp and sharp. If you look across, the water turns blue, a vibrant shade competing with the evergreens and mountain snowfields to make the endless sky seem pale. Today, the lake is a centerpiece of Glacier National Park. But during the commission's visit, it was just another stretch of the public domain. The rocky ground and long winters made for poor farming, no prospectors had found any minerals on this western side of the Continental Divide, and the timber was as yet too far from mills to bring much profit. The tall, thick forest provided little nourishment to hunters' favorite game, making this area less attractive than the eastern, Blackfeet side of the divide.

A few Montanans clustered around Apgar to trap, hunt, fish, and cater to tourists. As the *F. I. Whitney* pulled out into the middle of the lake, it quickly left them behind, entering a simple majesty of mountains. This was a classic U-shaped glacial valley, so fresh and pristine that you could almost picture the "Back in Five Minutes" sign that the glacier would have tacked up in its retreat. Muir had complained that Helena, Montana, was "set nestlike amid high bare hot hills" and the rolling plains between there and Shelby were a "dull treeless bunchgrass region." Here, he was delighted by the wet forested glacial valley, thrilled to "be with the blessed mosquitoes & pines." [34]

Muir's great loves were glaciers and trees—and here the forests matched the wonder of the glacially carved terrain. With the divide squeezing moisture out of eastward-moving rainclouds, the Lake McDonald region supported pockets of western red cedar and western hemlock, a rare inland rainforest. Taller and deeper than anything the commission had yet encountered, the trees felt like they could go on forever. And, as the commission's mapping showed, ridgeline after ridgeline to the west did unfurl in nearly unbroken forest. None of the mountain ranges to the west were as epic and craggy as the ones to the north and east—the Crown of the Continent—but they represented precisely what the commission had come to study: a seemingly inexhaustible supply of trees that, recent history suggested, might soon become exhausted.

Close to the far end of the lake, at the site of today's Lake McDonald Lodge, the *F.I. Whitney* docked. A recently built two-story log structure offered bunk beds and meals. This would be the commission's home for the next few days.[35] Nearby, Pinchot and Jack Monroe set up camp. Although Monroe was the commission's official guide through this country, a guide always stayed in camp, not a hotel. Fresh off their Swan Lake trip, Monroe and Pinchot—also accompanied by Henry H. Garr, a fishing-obsessed justice of the peace from nearby Columbia Falls—may have actually preferred sleeping outdoors. What was the point of a bunk bed in a stuffy building when you had come all this way for the glorious natural aesthetics?

Muir had the same mindset. His journal for July 16 recorded "fishing trout," which was not a common pastime for him, likely an excuse to be out on the lake with the brilliant fly-fisherman Pinchot. He stayed to watch the sun set behind the ridge across the lake: The cool arrived suddenly, on a vanishing breeze. Distant birds sailed single-file along the lakeside shadow-line. Above, the sun still bathed the upper peaks in light. Muir compared the color of the sunset reflections in the still lake to *nemophila*, the wildflower known as "baby blue eyes."[36]

The next day Muir headed upstream, past the head of Lake McDonald, alongside a creek strewn with enormous deadfall and round boulders. The waters bounced noisily in the cool morning, here white with cascades and there funneling down a moss-encrusted gorge. After about 6 miles, his trail turned right, through a huge grove of thousand-year-old red cedars. For the next 2 miles it climbed steeply, following the playful, bounding Avalanche Creek. Then, rather suddenly, the trail emerged at what Muir called a "grand amphitheatre." At the far side, multiple waterfalls leaped, danced, and plunged down cliffs more than three thousand feet high. Directly in front of him, lakewater was "milky from small [glacier] not in sight."[37]

Just two years previously, in 1894, Dr. Lyman Sperry had been one of the first white men to see the lake. "It constantly reminds one of the Yosemite;

and yet it is as unlike that famous valley as a bewitching waltz is unlike an inspiring march," Sperry wrote. One of Sperry's first thoughts was to file a homestead claim. Instead, he later arranged for the Great Northern railroad to sponsor additional explorations, and came to advocate for a national park. Today the lake attracts an overwhelming stream of tourists, but for Sperry, as for Muir, "It [was] an ideal spot for one who wishes to withdraw from the haunts of men."[38] Much satisfied with Avalanche Lake, Muir's only regret was that the epic cliffs made it impossible for him to explore the glaciers themselves.

In the essay Muir later wrote about Avalanche and McDonald Lakes, he advised, "Wander here a whole summer, if you can . . . [in] the best care-killing scenery on the continent—beautiful lakes derived straight from glaciers, lofty mountains steeped in lovely *nemophila*-blue skies and clad with forests and glaciers, mossy ferny waterfalls in their hollows, nameless and numberless, and meadowy gardens abounding in the best of everything. . . . Give a month at least to this precious reserve. The time will not be taken from the sum of your life. Instead of shortening it, it will indefinitely lengthen it and make you truly immortal."[39] But he himself was on a far tighter and more social schedule. He was up to Avalanche Lake and back to Lake McDonald in a single day.

The next morning the commission took the steamboat back down Lake McDonald to Apgar, although Muir chose, instead, to walk along the shore. Then they all headed 20 miles down the Middle Fork of the Flathead to Columbia Falls. The guide Monroe and the fisherman Garr took Pinchot by boat; Muir would have joined them too, except that Sargent insisted he accompany the adults on the train.[40]

But those two magical evenings on Lake McDonald! Returning from Avalanche, Muir's July 17 diary records that he spent the evening "with Pinchot on lake, lovely, ethereal." As Pinchot wrote, "The scenery was grand, gloomy, and peculiar, and in one way nearly as fine as the Yosemite"; he and Muir "saw two wonderful evenings on the water." The campers served Muir freshly caught trout, while the old fogies on the commission "had them fried to a crisp at the hotel."[41]

Muir and Pinchot were out in nature together, communing with some of the most glorious scenery in the nation. They bonded. They became part of a team. Muir told his stories, and Pinchot listened ("a most fascinating talker," Pinchot called him). Pinchot told his own stories (the two were "talking vigorously a good deal of the time," Pinchot wrote). Pinchot fly-fished the productive waters of Lake McDonald, and Muir tried it too, to be social. ("It amazed me to learn that he never carried even a fishhook with him on his solitary explorations. He said fishing wasted too much time," Pinchot wrote.) As on Muir's later Sierra Club outings, the grand natural setting inspired not solitary contemplation but camaraderie and community. There's no record of what exactly they talked about, but we can imagine weighty ideas emerging under the stars. [42]

Time together in the outdoors did not eliminate their rivalry. It did not make them think alike. Maybe it caused them to avoid potentially controversial topics: maybe Pinchot didn't talk about selective logging or how to harness these lands for production, while Muir didn't complain about development or greed that ruined opportunities for spiritual growth. But more likely, they did discuss these topics—after all, both men enjoyed expressing opinions—and the setting helped make those talks constructive. They could agree that they shared a greater priority. This land must be handled rationally and fairly. Politics-as-usual wasn't working. A new system was needed, one with enough foresight to preserve the scenery of Lake McDonald while also allowing for growth and development. Within this new system, their goals might still conflict. But in the ethereal sunset, under the *nemophila* sky, the two men could find mutual respect. Each could understand and appreciate the other as an individual with great intellect and integrity. Each could see that the rival perspective was valid, was equally deserving of triumph.

10

The Public Good Forever

🌰

On July 21, 1896, Gifford Pinchot awoke in the Spokane Hotel, a charming five-story Arts and Crafts–style building anchoring the downtown of that booming timber city in eastern Washington. After Lake McDonald, the commission had endured three long days of grueling travel, but today they had the morning free. "A beautiful happy day," Pinchot wrote in his diary. "I dreamed of my Dearest last night . . . I am very thankful."[1]

The dutiful Pinchot had spent some time the previous evening writing home: "Dear Mother and Father, In my last letter I forgot to thank you for the last deposit of $500, and to refer to a lot of other things . . ." By contrast, John Muir arrived in Spokane "weary and feverish," and went to bed early. He spent his morning writing a detailed letter that updated Louie on all that had happened since he'd left Helena a week previously. He also decided to leave the National Forest Commission.[2]

Muir had long been planning a summer trip to Alaska. He was glad to have crossed the country with the commission, and to have experienced Lake McDonald. He still intended to show the commissioners around California in September. But at this point, as the commission turned back east for study of Montana's Bitterroot Mountains, neither Sargent nor Pinchot was going to convince him to skip Alaska. Muir decided to depart for home, see his family, and get ready for the trip north.

Before leaving, he raised a possibility with his young friend. Would Pinchot like to join him in Alaska?

Pinchot was thrilled. As with his experiences with Dietrich Brandis, the opportunity for long, intense interactions with an accomplished older man could make for great personal and professional development. In his diary for this beautiful happy day, Pinchot wrote, "plan was suggested by him [Muir], and approved by Sargent." In a letter Muir sent Pinchot upon returning home, he suggested some logistics and urged, "Let nothing on earth hinder you in this icy Alaska business."[3]

However, Arnold Hague objected to the plan. Pinchot's diary doesn't say why, but Hague likely didn't want his ally Pinchot to be absent from so much of the commission's trip, given how its members remained so split. Sargent and Abbot weren't wavering from their belief in military control, while Hague and Pinchot insisted on professional forestry. Brewer could end up a swing vote. Remove Pinchot for several weeks, and Hague alone might lose the argument.

If the Muir-Pinchot interactions at Lake McDonald demonstrated the potential of collaboration among commissioners, these dynamics show the forces working against that potential. The scientists rarely put themselves into situations of genuine team-building. Although the trip allowed them to see many beautiful forests, and perhaps compare notes on botany or geology, they spent too little time immersed in nature. Critics accused them of rarely leaving the comfort of railcars, steamboats, and downtown hotels; although that was an exaggeration, their hardships generally consisted of arduous stagecoach rides or crude country lodgings. They didn't all fish together on Lake McDonald, or hike together to Avalanche Lake, or float together on the Middle Fork of the Flathead, or philosophize together around a campfire. They weren't jointly engaging in the mind-body stimulation of outdoor life. If the commission's trip wasn't going to be about building those kinds of relationships in order to find creative solutions, what good could it accomplish?

Muir and Pinchot were part of the problem. Muir was a marvelous storyteller and engaging companion, but because he wasn't a member of the commission, his presence detracted from their group bonding. It accentuated the idea that the trip was just an excuse to see some pretty places, rather than a working retreat. Meanwhile, Pinchot spent his first six weeks in the West basically on vacation, hunting and hiking in northwest Montana. Now after three weeks of work he wanted another vacation, to Alaska. Bernhard Fernow had opposed the entire endeavor, saying the trip would be a boondoggle, and now Muir and Pinchot seemed intent on proving him correct.

To Pinchot's credit, he was conflicted. Although he wanted to visit Alaska with Muir, he also wanted to work on forest surveys. Hague and Sargent suggested a survey in the Bitterroot. So Pinchot wrote his regrets to Muir and summoned his assistant Henry Graves from Michigan. With three other men, they explored the "wonderfully rough country" on the Montana-Idaho border, which, Pinchot later claimed, "in consequence soon became the Bitterroot Forest Reserve." He may be right to take credit, since he certainly knew more about those mountains than the rest of the commission, which saw them only from the valley-bottom Missoula-to-Hamilton train. However, plenty of other reserves would be created with less personal knowledge; indeed Pinchot's Bitterroot trip caused him to miss the commission's entire Washington State itinerary, which resulted in creation of the Washington and Olympic Forest Reserves. [4]

So it continued all summer: the commission viewed forests, mostly from trains and stagecoaches, and never quite succeeded at engaging with each other's perspectives. Pinchot (from the Bitterroot) and then Muir (from Alaska) rejoined the crew in Oregon, in time to jointly experience the wondrous Crater Lake. Nobody complained about the company; for example,

Pinchot wrote that on the way to Crater Lake, "John Muir and Professor Brewer made the journey short with talk that was worth crossing the continent to hear." But nobody made any progress toward achieving a unified vision of forest policy. Pinchot was still frustrated that Sargent didn't fish or hunt or otherwise *use* mountains, and thus didn't *know* them the way Pinchot did. In his autobiography's description of the Oregon/California portion of the trip, Pinchot highlighted how he deplored the wasteful logging of giant sequoias, and how he sent Graves to study the effects of sheep grazing in the Cascades. In other words, he was showing how his work incorporated the perspectives that he learned from Muir—dynamics that were sorely missing from interactions among the rest of the commissioners. Indeed after Crater Lake, their ambitious agenda required them to split up: Hague and Brewer to see Mount Shasta; Sargent, Abbot, and Muir to see the coastal redwoods; and Pinchot to take a solitary ramble through the central Sierra. How would they ever find common ground?[5]

The commission continued south through California, then turned east to the Grand Canyon, and finished its tour at Colorado's Pikes Peak in early October. Covering so much country gave members some confidence that they knew the West well enough to offer advice about forest policy. But among the great road trips of American history—from Lewis and Clark to Alexis de Tocqueville to Jack Kerouac—it hardly rates a mention. The commissioners didn't learn much that wasn't already known, and certainly didn't feel transformed by their experiences. Only a few incidents shine like flecks of gold in the dross, all related to the curious interactions of Muir and Pinchot. For example, there was a moment at Crater Lake when Muir, enduring a heavy overnight rainstorm in his tent, realized that Pinchot was still sleeping outside in the downpour. It was a remarkable man, Muir's notation implied, who would so eagerly withstand outdoor rigors that daunted Muir himself.[6]

Then, at the south rim of the Grand Canyon, while the others drove to a designated scenic point, Muir and Pinchot hiked along the canyon's rim to appreciate the endlessly changing views. They came across a tarantula, and when Pinchot went to squash it, Muir told him not to. "He said it had as much right there as we did," Pinchot wrote, still fascinated decades later by that unusual perspective. They had packed a lunch, and by dinnertime, each still had a small sandwich and a hard-boiled egg. Rather than go back to the hotel, they found a campsite out of the wind. They collected cedar boughs to sleep on. The temperature dropped near to freezing, but the campfire kept them warm. Muir "talked until midnight," Pinchot wrote. "It was such an evening as I have never had before or since."[7]

They dozed until about 4:30 A.M. Then they returned to the hotel for breakfast, and to allay the others' concerns that they might have fallen into the chasm. Pinchot remembered feeling like "guilty schoolboys," as if Muir was the rascal who tempted him away from obligation into his true self.[8]

The trip was just research; the real work of the commission would be writing a scientific report. Upon their return, they were slow to take up that work. First the commissioners had to readjust to home life after almost four months away. Then Sargent sprained his ankle. Their sponsor Hoke Smith left the Department of Interior, although his replacement, David Francis, did pledge support. William McKinley won the presidential election, which meant that come March, the administration would shift from Democratic to Republican. Then a wing of Sargent's mansion burned down.

When the commission members finally got together in January, they could see two purposes for their report: First, identify forests that should be reserved, based on their travels and other research. Second, recommend a management plan for those and the previously established forest reserves—a set of policies that would describe how forests could be used and how those rules would be enforced. For the first purpose, they had unanimous agreement, recommending thirteen new reserves that totaled 21 million acres. That would more than double the acreage of forest reserves, adding territory from the Black Hills of South Dakota to the Olympics in Washington, and from the Flathead around Lake McDonald to the San Jacinto in Southern California. For the second purpose, they remained divided. On some issues they inched toward agreement: public access (trespassing) should be allowed, timber should be sold, and grazing should be regulated.

Although Sargent may have privately wanted to keep everyone off all 21 million acres, he seemed capable of compromise.[9] But he did hold his ground on the issue of how to kick off this new era of government land management. How do you gain authority? To Sargent, the only answer was to replace the patronage-riddled GLO with the efficient, incorruptible military.

But Hague and Pinchot were concerned about deploying the army across large swaths of the West. It would look like a military occupation of the countryside, Hague said. Instead, they put their faith in this new trend of professionalization. A forestry bureau could pay employees well enough to inspire both expertise and incorruptibility. An organization of foresters could adopt military-style structures and philosophies—as Pinchot had seen in Europe—but not have to use actual soldiers. Soldiers were for fighting wars, Hague and Pinchot said; forest overseers should be engineer-managers with an ethical code all their own.[10]

As they debated, the commission faced a potential deadline: Could they finish the work while Grover Cleveland was still in office? Eager Pinchot especially wanted to. Muir expressed a similar sentiment in letters to both Pinchot and Sargent.[11] The argument for acting quickly was that Cleveland was a clear fan of forest reserves. The blunt, quick-tempered president, so hefty that he'd once been nicknamed "Uncle Jumbo," was nearing the end of the second of his two nonconsecutive terms. He'd established two reserves in Oregon before realizing that such actions were pointless without a policy to administer the reserves. Why not give this hunter and fisherman the chance to protect more land? Furthermore, Sargent started realizing that the longer forests lay unreserved, the more people would use them—in other words, the longer the commission waited, the more opposition it would face.[12]

The argument against acting quickly was that Cleveland wasn't the only decider. The commission needed to work with Congress. Because Congress was the body that set policies for government-owned land, Congress needed to be included in the political processes of compromise. Managing a scientific commission's relations with Congress was a unique art, and Pinchot, the inexperienced statesman, hadn't yet found the right approach. Indeed, at one point Pinchot suggested to Hague that they simply ask someone in Congress what forestry policy would be likely to pass and recommend that. Hague gently scolded Pinchot for such a terrible idea. First, he said, the commission had to write its report based on science. Then the politics would come in. Eventually, Hague believed, the greater knowledge provided by science would enable Congress to endorse a forestry policy it couldn't yet even conceive of.[13]

Of course this strategy would work only if Congress listened. The cynical Sargent found that prospect unlikely, and thus took the opposite extreme.[14] He refused to engage with politicians or the public at all. His scientific judgment would be pure. He kept the commission meetings private, he held no public hearings, he barely spoke to the press. He thus laid no groundwork for public or congressional understanding of what the commission might suggest.

In late January, the commissioners decided to meet the Cleveland deadline. Because Sargent kept meetings confidential, it isn't quite clear why they chose this path, although impatience seems likely to have played a role. The commission had consensus on one of its two purposes, so it could mark the first half of its assignment as complete. Pinchot drew up formal boundaries for the new reserves, and following a unanimous commission vote, Sargent included descriptions of the thirteen proposed reserves in a letter to Interior Secretary David Francis. A brash, plainspoken former Missouri governor with a noble, prominent nose, Francis eagerly endorsed the commission's plan and suggested to President Cleveland that proclamations creating the reserves would be a great way to commemorate George Washington's 165th birthday.

Creating the "Washington's Birthday Reserves" was a grand statement—and in retrospect, stupendously ill-advised. Earlier, Cleveland had told the commission, "Let the plan be one that looks small . . . let it avoid points liable to attack." And, he added, "The bills necessary to carry out the plan should be prepared in consultation with someone thoroughly familiar with the temper of Congress."[15] Instead, the executive branch carried out a large-looking plan prepared without any congressional consultation. Worse, it had a point liable to gigantic attack: Without the second half of the commission's work, without its judgment on how to administer forests, the old policies would remain. No trespassing would be allowed on the Washington's Birthday Reserves. All the set-asides that Cleveland had refused to make piecemeal for the last three years, he made on February 22, 1897. It was perceived as an arrogant farewell gesture, a thumb in the eye of the West.

In response, a political storm engulfed the Cleveland administration, Congress, and the issue of forest reserves. The commission and its allies were blindsided.

At 2:15 P.M. on Monday, March 1—seven days after Cleveland's proclamation—Gifford Pinchot received a telegram in New York. Interior Secretary Francis was summoning him to Washington, along with Sargent, Abbot, and Brewer. (Hague already lived there.) Congress was on the attack, and the administration needed all the defense it could get.[16]

The Senate had even met on Sunday, almost scandalous in an era when most of the country enforced the Sabbath as a day of rest. "Ye Gods! What's to be done with the crazy Senate?" John Muir wrote when he heard the news. "Voting all on the holy Sabbath day for old-fashioned diabolical destruction of forests." Senators imagined conspiracies in which the commission was a tool of Wall Street, or an attempt to prevent the production of silver. By one account, Senators even discussed impeaching Cleveland—which seems unlikely, given that he was already set to leave office that Thursday morning.[17]

Legislators were angry because their constituents were angry. Letters, editorials, and condemnations from state legislatures were pouring in. After all, Cleveland hadn't warned any Western politicians about this major policy change. Congress had gotten no say in these dramatic proclamations. The very idea of a highfalutin commission passing judgment on land policy smacked of imperialism rather than democracy. While Western congressmen were outraged, Eastern ones saw little benefit in defending a lame-duck president four days before he left office forever. One scholar described "vituperative denunciation of the President in both houses of Congress that has rarely been equaled."[18]

Pinchot boarded a train within an hour of receiving the telegram. Although he intended to stay with the Hagues, he went straight to the Interior Department upon arrival, at about 8:00 P.M. There, Secretary Francis briefed him on the pressure Francis was getting to rescind the Washington's Birthday Reserves. Meanwhile, at the Capitol, Congress was meeting day and night to pass appropriations bills and finish other business before its term ended and the newly elected Congress was seated on Thursday.

Opponents of the new forest reserves decided to make their statement using the Civil Sundry Appropriations Bill, which funded civil works projects, such as river and harbor improvements. Civil Sundry was a major part of the federal budget; failure to pass it would be grave. The bill addressed a fiscal year beginning on July 1, and if in the next four months the new Congress still couldn't pass it, a government shutdown would ensue—although in the 1890s such a prospect was unthinkable. Nevertheless, the path to compromise was far from clear, because this Civil Sundry bill already featured some of the most extravagant spending to that date in history. Cleveland's Democrats were then the party of small government, and threatened a presidential veto of pork-laden appropriations. In response, congressmen continually discussed the provisions of Civil Sundry with Cleveland and his cabinet, trying to get as close as possible to a veto without actually causing one. The president would never identify the tipping point, although he did insist that he would need time to study whatever bill they presented.[19]

Late Sunday, senators attached a draft rider to Civil Sundry that would restore to the public domain "all the lands in the states of Wyoming, Utah, Colorado, Montana, Washington, Idaho, and South Dakota set apart and reserved by Executive orders and proclamations of February 22." It was a draft, likely to be modified, still open to debate. Some Western congressmen were so disgusted with forest reserves that they wanted to eliminate *all* reserves—even the ones like Yellowstone and White River that had been appointed by the Republican Harrison six years previously. On the other hand, California's congressmen *liked* the reserves, which were popular with their constituents. That's why California was excluded from the draft rider—unless it had been excluded in error. Colorado was included, even though the Washington's Birthday Reserves included no Colorado lands. And the draft referred to "21 million acres," although excluding the California reserves would bring it closer to 19 million. The draft needed rewriting—and Secretary Francis saw opportunities.[20]

One possibility would be for Cleveland to agree to alter the Washington's Birthday proclamation, rather than see it completely rescinded. Members of both houses, from both parties, urged Francis to get the president to somehow reduce the scope of the proclamations, to pacify Congress and eliminate its desire for a rider. However, the independent-minded Cleveland had long fought for presidential autonomy. He'd already issued a record-breaking number of vetoes and dispatched troops without congressional approval. He didn't like backing down to Congress. When Francis approached him with the idea of alterations, Cleveland glared at him and asked, "You have not changed your mind on the subject, have you?"[21]

Absolutely not, Francis replied. He believed in the Washington's Birthday Reserves.

Cleveland said he did too. He would not alter the proclamation. Francis relayed this message to allies in the Senate. He signaled that if the Civil Sundry bill tried to force Cleveland into backing down from the reserves, that would lead to a veto. Then Congress would have to start over, perhaps even in a special session, with only itself to blame.

Meanwhile, however, Francis and his allies tried to soften the rider. They feared that if the rider passed and Cleveland vetoed it, Congress might override the veto. Francis wanted the commission in town to participate in these negotiations, so that he and the debating congressmen could consult with experts. Another expert also happened to arrive in town: the editor Robert Underwood Johnson came to Washington for Inauguration Week, aiming "to give Mrs. Johnson and myself a rest." As an experienced park and forest lobbyist, he got pulled into the fight. Francis, Johnson, and Iowa Congressman John Lacey led a substitute rider—known as the Lacey Amendment—first through the House and then through the Senate. The Lacey Amendment "was not so bad," Johnson told Muir, "although we should have preferred not to make" its concessions in timber-cutting and mining. [22]

With his tireless work ethic and ambitions for statesmanship, Gifford Pinchot was essential to these efforts. On Monday, the day he arrived, he hobnobbed at the Capitol until midnight. On Tuesday, he shuttled among the Capitol, Interior Department, and Hague's office, developing an official commission statement endorsing the Lacey Amendment. By Tuesday afternoon he got the statement approved by Hague, Brewer, and Abbot—although Sargent felt that its concessions to development on *all* reserves, not just the new ones, made it worse than the prospect of annulling the new ones. On Wednesday night, Pinchot stayed up until almost 3:00 A.M., monitoring the Capitol discussion well past the hour when Sargent and Brewer needed sleep. [23]

By now it was early Thursday morning, just hours before inauguration, and still the Civil Sundry bill wasn't ready. Cleveland put his cabinet on alert: They would meet at the White House as soon as the bill arrived. Because there would be no time to read the bill as he had demanded, they would need to come to the meeting with knowledge of what it said. This was one of Pinchot's essential functions: keeping Francis up to date.

Thursday at 9:30 A.M., the cabinet assembled, standing in Cleveland's office. A few minutes later, the congressionally approved Civil Sundry bill finally arrived. It was fifty pages long, handwritten—there hadn't been time to type it. Cleveland was incredulous: How could he be expected to act intelligently on this bill? Nevertheless, he went around the room, asking each cabinet secretary two questions: Do you know the contents of the bill that affect your department? And is it satisfactory? [24]

The secretary of state responded affirmatively to both questions. So did treasury. Attorney general. War. Postmaster general. Navy. Then came interior.

Francis explained that the bill contained a rider withholding appropriations for guards of the public domain until the president revoked or altered the Washington's Birthday proclamation.

Then came a knock on the door. A messenger announced that President-elect McKinley had arrived at the White House. Tradition demanded that McKinley, Cleveland, and the outgoing cabinet ride together in carriages to the Capitol for the inauguration ceremony. Cleveland told the messenger to show McKinley to the Blue Room to wait. Then he asked Francis to explain the rider again.

The rider was indeed the Lacey Amendment. It would allow Cleveland or his successor to alter, rather than completely revoke, the Washington's Birthday proclamation. This was the compromise that Francis, Johnson, and the commission had been working toward: the required alterations weren't specified, but presumably could include a loosening of the no-trespassing regulations and/or a changing of the boundaries to allow more mining and logging. Still, Cleveland didn't like to be pushed around. And by now it was awfully late. The president-elect was waiting.

Cleveland frowned. He paused. Then he hurled the bill to the floor. Loose pages flew everywhere. He stood up and announced that it was time to leave for the Capitol.

In legal terms, the action is called a *pocket veto*. Cleveland didn't officially veto the bill, but since he didn't sign it, it didn't become law. Congress had no opportunity to override his decision, because the inauguration ceremony marked the end of its term, as well as Cleveland's. A new Congress would have to start from scratch. The nation was lacking a key component of its budget, but for now the reserves would remain as Cleveland had declared them.

In one view, Cleveland made a heroic gesture, taking a principled stand to save the forest reserves. In another view, he made a cowardly punt. Now McKinley and a new Congress would face the same issues on a new Civil Sundry bill. Congress was still furious about the Washington's Birthday Reserves, and would be even angrier about the pocket veto. Meanwhile, there was no reason to suspect that McKinley, a business-friendly Ohioan, had any affection whatsoever for forests.

In the optimistic view, maybe the hefty Grover Cleveland, in his moment of frowning contemplation, saw that the issue was bigger than he was. It was bigger than his disputes with Congress over appropriations, bigger than congressional fears of executive-branch overreach, bigger than a scientific commission that somehow got tied to petty politics. It was bigger, even, than forestry policy. The commission was really exploring a change in the relationship between the country and its land. Maybe Cleveland understood that a last-minute signature on an obscure appropriations bill wasn't the right way to settle such an issue.

In other words, Cleveland may have grasped that the commission's failure was even bigger than putting at risk the entire forest reserve system that it had been founded to bolster. Although the commission failed largely because it couldn't agree on military versus professional management, looming behind that dispute was the unsettled nature of its very scope. Hoke Smith had asked for "a policy of forest conservation." A typical National Academy of Sciences Commission might have responded by summarizing the best science with which individuals, such as George Vanderbilt, could manage private forests, such as Biltmore. Instead, Pinchot and Sargent were using the commission for an issue of far bigger scope: to solve the puzzle of forestry and management that had become a particular crisis on the forest reserves. Then Professor Gibbs both limited and expanded that scope by asking "the question of the ultimate ownership of the forests now belonging to the Government."

If it was about ownership, it wasn't just about trees, as Sargent had wanted. It wasn't just about forestry, as Pinchot had wanted. It wasn't even just about the forest reserves, as Hague and Johnson had wanted. Gibbs' question created an opportunity for the commission to redefine *public land*. The phrase hadn't meant much for America's first 120 years, when most public land was public only because it wasn't yet private. To truly solve the 1890s forest crisis, the commission had to get Congress to assert that land owned by the government deserved management and property rights. That assertion would be the first step in figuring out processes to manage land for multiple objectives, with democratic input and operative authority.

If such a solution was achievable, it could go far beyond forests. For example, overgrazing was then decimating public-domain grasslands in much the same way that overlogging was decimating forests. Grasslands, too, could benefit if the government decided that it would own this land forever and thus would require users to treat the land sustainably. Wildlife, rivers, marine fisheries, and other environmental resources were suffering from the same types of problems—what economists call *market failures*—that could be addressed if only the government would fully assert its ownership rights. The similarity of these environmental market failures was the eventual insight that drove Pinchot's definition of *conservation*, under which the government needed a comprehensive strategy to conserve many, varied natural resources. However, before it could implement such a strategy, the government, acting for the citizenry as a whole, needed to start by asserting the prerogatives of long-term land ownership.

In 1897, Pinchot hadn't yet arrived at that insight. Rather, he was attracted to conservation because he wanted to articulate a relationship between society and nature. He focused first on forestry because trees were his own story, from his wonderfully free rambles in wooded country to his grandfather's troubling legacy of riches through clear-cutting. Like William Holman, who sought to express statesmanship through his family homesteading experience, Pinchot sought to promote the welfare of all classes of society through forestry. Pinchot wanted society's relationship with nature to reflect a common good—and this redefinition of public land could accomplish that goal as well.

Muir was likewise driven by a desired societal relationship with nature—but he viewed the relationship as spiritual. Most of the forests and mountains that Muir most loved had not yet moved into private ownership, and he wanted their possibility of redemption available to all. This redefinition of public land could accomplish that goal as well.

Thus the needs and interests of the commission's two non-academy associates helped push it beyond science toward this expanded scope of *ownership.* Thanks to Pinchot and Muir, the commission was poised to endorse a new ideal, a democratically owned set of public lands to be used for diverse purposes, to express diverse views of society's relationship with nature. Here was the original link between *nature* and *public land.*

A Grover Cleveland aficionado might argue that, at least subconsciously, Cleveland recognized all this.[25] He recognized that the commission had sidled up to some magnificently ambitious ideas, but hadn't quite fully endorsed them. If he did reach that understanding, then in his frowning moment, Cleveland may have been asking himself how he should best counteract the commission's failure—how he could embrace as his legacy the potential of these ambitious ideas. Should he accept the late-night compromise with its uncertain effects, opening the door to forces that could undo the forest reserves that he took pride in? Or should he insist that the country bring this dialogue out into the open, and make a conscious choice for public land? If tossing the messy Civil Sundry bill on the floor was his answer to that question, it was an act not of petulance but faith: American democracy was big enough to figure this issue out.

Cleveland's pocket veto only increased pressure on the commission. As a new president and new Congress started their terms, commissioners knew that lobbying against the forest reserves would intensify. "A great onslaught will be made upon McKinley at once," Johnson predicted. Given the lobbying capabilities of anti-reserve miners and loggers, and given how few members of the public understood what the commission was trying to do, its work was in serious danger.[26]

So its members turned, unanimously, to John Muir.

On the day of McKinley's inauguration, Commission Chair Charles Sargent approached Walter Page, editor of the *Atlantic Monthly*, to suggest that Muir write a series of articles about "parks and reservations in the West." Here would be a direct result of the commission's trip: Muir's essays could ground their proposals in evocative depictions of the extraordinary places they had visited. Page loved the idea. In a letter to Muir, Page noted "the too general ignorance in the Eastern States of the beauty as well as of the practical value of these forest-reservations." Page wanted to take an editorial stance against congressional efforts "to annul Mr. Cleveland's action." He told Muir that his magazine was obliged to do "all that it can to build up an appreciative public sentiment—a duty that is made the more pleasant because the subject lends itself so happily to literary treatment in your hands." Muir had frequently written in support of the forest reserves for one of the *Atlantic*'s chief competitors, Johnson's *Century* magazine. Now those two rivals would unite behind the cause. Page was willing to let Muir decide exactly what to write, how and when to write it, and (within some limits) how much to be paid. With such an offer, Sargent told him, "you cannot very well get out of the job."[27]

A few days later, the commission's Arnold Hague similarly approached the editor of *Harper's Weekly*. Summarizing his angle for Muir, Hague wrote, "The fight will be renewed as soon as Congress meets or the new administration gets to work. In the name of the poor settlers much pressure will be brought to bear to throw these forests open to the great syndicates." To win that fight, Hague told Muir, "It is very necessary that the people be educated in this matter as to the importance of forest reservations."[28]

The editor and commission-advocate Johnson also beseeched Muir. "First of all we must have Western support," he wrote. The congressional battle was being depicted as East versus West, the reserves being foisted upon a region that didn't want them. Members of the commission believed otherwise—in touring the West, they'd heard from reserve supporters including water-users, recreationists, and those concerned about forest fires. So far, Congress was instead hearing primarily from corporate voices, especially mining syndicates. Johnson urged Muir to get the Sierra Club to assert "that the State of California is overwhelmingly in favor of the reservation system." California's senators had demanded that California get to keep its Washington's Birthday Reserves; now Johnson suggested a letter-writing campaign asking those senators to also save reserves in other states.[29]

Even Sargent, despite his distaste for politics, told Muir to generate regional publicity so that "we can get articles in California papers reprinted in the east." Like today's re-tweets, article reprints represented not only an opportunity for wider persuasion but also a metric for public sentiment. A few days later, Sargent wrote Muir with some added advice from editor William Stiles, his chief political adviser. "You want to make a public opinion as fast as possible," Stiles said. Muir should generate articles in the California papers describing the purposes of the reserves, "showing that they are not revolutionary and not hostile to the interests of the western people." Sargent gloomily concluded, "It is pretty evident to me that we are going to lose the outcome of all our work and that the reservations are going to be thrown open unless a back fire can be set in the west to check the universal condemnation which our action seems to have called for."[30]

Muir did as he was told. When he responded to the *Atlantic*'s Walter Page in late March, he explained his two-week delay by saying that "I am very busy at present writing for the reserves in the [San Francisco] newspapers. . . . Beds of lies are growing up thicker & taller than the redwood forests, & cutting them down seems an endless task."[31] Although Sargent had originally asked Muir to join the commission because he made a great traveling companion, in the crisis his writing talents turned out to be just what the commission needed.

In addition to a change in public sentiment, the commission desperately needed a published final report. The commissioners struggled to finish writing the report because they were still divided on what to say. Pinchot and Hague threatened to make a minority report unless they got significant concessions from Sargent about military versus professional management. "Hague, I fancy, has been working against us more or less from the start," Sargent complained to Muir. "He generally carries Pinchot with him." Later, Sargent would tell Muir that "I have no respect or esteem for either Hague or Pinchot and I am delighted that my official connection with them has come to an end. They have given me a good deal of anxiety and have done much harm in letting out the impression that the Commission was divided in its opinions."[32]

The feeling was mutual: Pinchot had only contempt for Sargent. Decades later, he wrote that Sargent's "greatest and most vital contribution to the forest movement in America came through his inexcusable mishandling of the National Forest Commission." Certainly Sargent's imperious manner made him poor at facilitating compromise or forging an innovative joint vision. However, Pinchot's critique centered on the strategy of recommending the Washington's Birthday Reserves before developing a plan to manage them. With this strategy, Pinchot charged, Sargent alone was responsible for the political crisis. [33]

Pinchot's retrospective attempts to pin everything on Sargent—"The whole forest movement paid dearly for Sargent's contrariness"—imply that Pinchot himself had objected to the Washington's Birthday strategy at the time. In fact, however, he'd endorsed it along with the rest of the commission. Indeed, a week after Cleveland's proclamation, Pinchot wrote British forester William Schlick, "I hope that our success in getting the reservation will react to our advantage when we come to ask for legislation." Pinchot's experience on the commission *taught* him about the dangers of the approach the commission jointly undertook. Pinchot was not born the legislative-relations genius he would be at the Forest Service—he became one thanks to participating in mistakes like this. [34]

Nevertheless, Pinchot's critique did contain a great insight: the commission's failure became its greatest contribution. With the Washington's Birthday furor, the long-simmering forest reserve issue came to a public boil. Which was a good thing: "For the first time in American history," Pinchot wrote, "the Reserves were widely, simultaneously, and here and there intelligently discussed by the press and the people of the country." [35]

For a decade or two, the need for a new national attitude toward nature had lurked in the intellectual shadows of the national consciousness. Only certain elites—the types who attended forestry conferences or read books by George Perkins Marsh—were truly invested. To change the culture, regular people and elites needed to better understand each others' concerns. They all needed to see rival interpretations of the future. The public needed conflict and controversy: Congress scandalously meeting on the Sabbath, the president throwing a bill onto the floor, rumors of divisions within a scientific panel devoted to finding the problem's one single answer.

Publicity surrounding these events could get people to think and talk about forestry and land policy. Out of that talk would emerge unity. Such an uproar might result in difficult times for the commission, but when is it ever easy to bring about lasting change?

Muir's essays from 1897 sound as if they have an unstated dual byline: Muir's rhetorical gifts are applied to Pinchot's ideas. For example, in *Mining and Scientific Press*, a San Francisco weekly on mining and industry topics, Muir argued for "a new departure in the Government's management of its forest property." Specifically, "Uncle Sam is trying to have his forests—what is left of them—at the same time trying to find out how best they can be put to use forever for the benefit of miners, farmers, lumbermen, and people in general."[36]

These were not new or insincere themes for Muir: even in his very first letter to Pinchot in September 1893, Muir discussed his plans to visit Washington, D.C., to "say a good word for the forests to [Interior Secretary] Hoke Smith and the President"—using the word *forests* rather than *nature* or *parks* or *wilderness*.[37] But after his summer listening to Pinchot talk about forestry, Muir was like the Dream Team's Larry Bird learning new tricks from Magic Johnson. He now trumpeted the non-spiritual uses of forests. Indeed, the diversity of forest use seemed to fascinate Muir; he harped on it constantly, like a dog playing with a new toy. For example, in July 1896, on his way to Alaska after camping with Pinchot at Lake McDonald, he gave an interview to the *Portland Oregonian*. He sang the praises of the commission, the scientific reasons for its appointment, the wisdom of its members, and its expected influence in Congress. He established the problem: "The destruction of the forests by the sheepmen and lumbermen would be an inexpressible calamity, as these forests protect the source of rivers. Every sawmill is a center of destruction, owing to the wasteful methods of lumbering practiced, by which the old trees and the saplings alike are destroyed. No civilized government under the sun leaves its forests to be destroyed without care, except the United States government." He warded off critics: "It will be no use for lumbermen or sheepmen to speak of the [commission] members as cranks who want to reserve all the forest lands on earth. They have the interest of the country at heart." And through all of it he sounded a great deal like what we think of today as a conservationist rather than a preservationist. He skipped the sermon on spiritual renewal. Instead, it was Muir, rather than Pinchot, who told the *Oregonian*, "The forests must be made to yield a perennial supply of timber, without being destroyed or injuriously affecting the rainfall, thus securing all the benefits of a forest, and at the same time a good supply of timber."[38]

Those themes continued in his California work in March 1897. Forests are the "fountains of our great rivers," he told the *Mining and Scientific Press*. Some kind of protective measures were needed to prevent forest fires. "The reform required is now being earnestly and thoroughly studied" by the commission.[39]

Like Walter Page, Muir also linked the forest reserves with the national parks. "No doubt you have noticed the savage attack made in the last Congress on our parks & forest reserves," began Muir's letter to a friend, urging political activism.[40] In policy terms, this characterization may not have been fair: the congressional rebellion hadn't said anything about Yellowstone, Yosemite, Sequoia, or General Grant (the only national parks then in existence). But when the commission asked Muir to speak up on their behalf, he spoke up on behalf of what he loved, parks and reserves—in other words, what we today think of as public land.

In early April, McKinley's new interior secretary Cornelius Bliss wired to summon all the commissioners to a meeting in his Washington office. The meeting's main purpose may well have been for Bliss to grandstand for the media: he told the *New York Times*, "The Commission will be asked to explain their reasons for setting apart such a large domain."[41] In fact the commission also secured a relatively friendly meeting with the president, who made a proposition: some of the reserves would be suspended for several months; meanwhile, a general forestry bill would give the Interior Department authority to manage the reserves for various purposes.

Sargent was appalled. The bill would "open reservations for all sorts of purposes but [provide] no machinery . . . to protect them." Westerners would get everything they wanted, he feared, and thus would never consent to any regulations. Pinchot, Hague, and Brewer saw it differently: the delayed implementation was regrettable, but the general forestry bill was the congressional authorization of forestry and land policy that forest-lovers had been working toward for decades. Indeed it closely resembled the McRae bill, including text from forestry bills that Bernhard Fernow had been fruitlessly sending to Congress for nearly ten years. The resurrection of these principles here suggests the influence of Hague. He rarely took credit for this sort of work, but this bill was arranged by Hague's supervisor, U.S. Geological Survey (USGS) Director Charles Walcott. Unlike Sargent, Walcott was a good candidate to negotiate with both sides. His agency was friendly to the mining industry, but he himself was trained as a paleontologist rather than an economic geologist; indeed, he was a member of the National Academy of Sciences. [42]

To shepherd the bill through Congress, Walcott recruited South Dakota Senator Richard Pettigrew, a Republican who had been one of the forest reserves' strongest critics. Pettigrew lined up Western senators behind the bill. They had three great reasons to vote for it. First, a nine-month delay in implementing Cleveland's non-California reserves would allow large corporations to cut as much timber and arrange for as many homestead claims as they could. Second, the well-regarded USGS, rather than the General Land Office, would undertake a detailed survey of the reserves, to make sure that they didn't include mining or agricultural properties. Finally, the bill firmly established the idea that the reserves were intended for *use*, rather than being "locked up." This had been the intent of Pinchot, Hague, and Johnson all along; Sargent's vehement objection to it, at this point, is hard to understand. Either Sargent had not been listening to his coconspirators, or he couldn't abide hearing their positions echoed by Western politicians.

For consistency, Pettigrew attached the forestry bill as a rider to the new Civil Sundry Appropriations Bill, replacing the one that Cleveland had pocket vetoed. The Pettigrew Amendment was so detailed that it no longer should have qualified as a rider to Civil Sundry appropriations, but nobody complained. Instead, debate on the rider offered senators the chance to spout plenty of anti-Cleveland invective. The Washington's Birthday Reserves were a "dastardly blunder," one said; Pettigrew himself thundered that Cleveland was "a disgrace to civilization and a disgrace to the Republic."[43] Such rhetoric against a now-vanished opponent gave Western senators cover to embrace forestry ideals in the bill itself.

Meanwhile, Sargent submitted the commission's formal report to the academy on May 1, 1897. In Sargent's recollection, he and Abbot wrote the whole thing, just before Abbot left the country for his new role as an expert on the proposed Panama Canal. However, the report's review of other countries' forestry practices, and its insistence that forestry could be profitable, sound a lot like Pinchot; its use of the phrase "hoofed locusts" clearly originated with Muir. The report did find a vague compromise on the Commission's core debate: it called for military administration of the reserves that would eventually—no timetable was offered—be replaced by a "permanent forest organization" organized as Pinchot had advocated. The report also included a lengthy section on "the unreserved forest lands of the public domain," which made clear its underlying principle to assert full property rights across all government lands, not only those in the existing reserves. Indeed, when the report urged that Mount Rainier and the Grand Canyon become national parks, it reflected a longtime belief of Muir and Sargent—but was clearly straying from the forestry principles that it had been chartered to examine. It was contributing to a larger theory of public lands.[44]

The report was "brilliant," in the retrospective judgment of a preeminent scholar of public land law, "a blueprint for the development of the forest policy for the next quarter-century." By contrast, a northwestern scholar called it "dogmatic, opinionated, undiplomatic, and pretentious."[45] Either way, the report didn't have much effect. A few Northwest editorialists got to complain about its elitism; most of the public ignored it. It was irrelevant. It didn't shape legislative debate, because the Pettigrew Amendment had already been hammered out. Pettigrew had introduced the amendment—which ignored the military option—in early April. Civil Sundry didn't pass the Senate until later in May, and McKinley didn't sign it until June 4. But during the time in between, Congress's debate on the amendment, and modifications to it, mostly reflected special interests trying to slip in favorable clauses, rather than serious reconsiderations of its principles informed by a scientific report. [46]

The report may have ended up being an anticlimax, but a document that could excite the public would be one designed especially for public consumption—a John Muir essay. Muir completed his *Harper's Weekly* piece, "The National Parks and Forest Reservations," in mid-April, although it wasn't published until June. Muir began the essay with a vivid scene of a horse "snorting, groaning, springing up on his hind legs and beating the air . . . plunging back and forth in a blind fury . . . his eyes staring wildly while he steamed and quivered and threw off splashes of froth from his widely distended nostrils." The horse's frightening behavior was explained only when a yellowjacket was found in his ear. The Washington's Birthday protestors were like that horse, Muir said, and their yellowjackets were greed for gold. In contrast to their loud complaints, he argued, 90 percent of Westerners favored some form of government protection for forestlands. In his memory, the commission on its tour had not met a single dissenter. [47]

In the *Harper's* article—along with the two he soon wrote for the *Atlantic*, "The American Forests," which was published in August 1897, and "The Wild Parks and Forest Reservations of the West," in January 1898—Muir was at the peak of his powers. He mixed travel narrative, scenic description, science, and humor in a way that encouraged people to think differently about nature without feeling like they were getting too radical. He excoriated industrial practices, spreading stories about how large corporations had abused homesteading laws. But he accepted the legitimacy of capitalism, writing, "Let right, commendable industry be fostered." He used religious imagery: "God began the reservation system in Eden, and this first reserve included only one tree. Yet even so moderate a reserve as this was attacked." But the *reserve* Muir wanted was a forest to be used for multiple purposes. He described the forest-thinning techniques that

Pinchot was so excited about, and repeated his comment to the *Oregonian*: "The forests must be made to yield a perennial supply of timber for every use." He painted the issue in black and white: "This forest battle is part and parcel of the eternal conflict between right and wrong." But the *battle* he spoke of was not for locking up wilderness—merely for "common-sense management."[48]

The key, Muir argued, was a change in policies toward "all that is left of the forest-bearing lands still in possession of the government." He wrote, "These lands now belong to all the people of the East and West alike, and in thus reserving them they are not taken out of the public domain, but kept in it for the benefit and advantage of everybody." In addition to the spiritual wonder that forests provided him, they could serve as a source of sustainable timber and riverflow. Thus, his essay concluded, "Every remaining acre of unentered forest-bearing land in all the country, not more valuable for agriculture than for tree-growing, should be reserved, protected, and administered by the Federal Government for the public good forever."[49]

For decades, the significance of Muir's 1897–98 articles has been hidden by what seemed, incorrectly, to be more important events that happened at the same time. At the Rainier Grand Hotel in September 1897, Pinchot allegedly betrayed Muir, sparking a feud that kicked off the preservation-versus-conservation divide. But as we have seen, Muir felt no such betrayal, and the Muir-Pinchot relationship experienced no such split. Yet because a preservation-versus-conservation divide requires Muir and Pinchot to be implacable enemies, some people have claimed that Muir's 1897–98 essays weren't representative of his overall views, or that he soon discovered the incompatibility of forestry and wilderness. For example, the eminent environmental scholar Roderick Nash argued that Muir's second *Atlantic* piece, in January 1898, "made no mention of forestry and wise use." Nash wrote that "in sharp contrast" to the August article, Muir was "withdrawing all support from the Pinchot school."[50]

However, Muir's *Atlantic* article itself presents much evidence pointing the other direction. When Muir discusses the most common tree in most Rocky Mountain forest reserves, the *pinus contorta* (lodgepole pine), he writes that it "is of incalculable importance to the farmer and miner; supplying fencing, mine timbers, and firewood." Similarly, the Douglas fir is "admirably suited for ship-building, piles, and heavy timbers in general." When Muir argues that the wilderness is less dangerous than a city home "with all the modern improvements," he notes that rather than Indians or bears you will meet loggers, "brown weather-tanned men with faces furrowed like bark, tired-looking, moving slowly, swaying like the trees they chop."[51] His arguments that Mount Rainier and the Grand Canyon should be made national parks echo the commission's final report. And Muir's opening declaration of his wilderness theme is that "mountain parks and reservations are useful *not only* as fountains of timber and irrigating rivers, but as fountains of life." In the article, Muir is indeed returning to an old theme of his, that vast spiritual wonders can accrue to humans from visiting forests. The dog has rediscovered his old favorite toy, and now plays with it and the new one together. The article shows Muir's belief that spiritual uses can coexist with other uses—which is the very essence of the Pinchot school. Muir's faith in that coexistence would later be tested at Hetch Hetchy—but Hetch Hetchy was the climax of a different story, which need not overwhelm this one.[52]

This story, the story of public lands, climaxed for Muir with these articles. Muir merged Pinchot's perspective, the commission's experiences, and his own rhetorical gifts into works of art that swayed public opinion. Finally, people came to understand the commission's intent, and the compromises that went into its proposals. People could see forest reserves as a newly empowered version of the old, meaningless phrase "public lands." Public Lands 2.0 was a product linked to national parks such as Yosemite, yet also capable of fulfilling the nation's continuing economic needs. Muir's moral voice, the voice of the aspiring prophet—as opposed to the legislative voice that Fernow, Sargent, Johnson, and others had been using to draft forestry proposals for years—made it clear that society had to act. Muir inspired people across the nation to support the Pettigrew Amendment and the gradual move to build diverse public lands in its image.

Muir himself didn't appreciate the climax because he was afraid his work would have little effect. Mystified by the seven-week delay at *Harper's Weekly*, he told Johnson that his article was "too late to do any good I fear." He may have been influenced by Sargent, who stepped permanently away from politics with his embittered prediction that none of the commission's land or policy recommendations would have any effect. Muir told Johnson that he too had little faith in politics, because "those Western Corporations with their shady millions seem invincible in the Senate." But Muir was wrong: In 1898, as the delay in implementation of the Washington's Birthday Reserves expired, corporate interests made another attempt to abolish the reserves. Supporters in Congress easily swatted it away. Public opinion, especially in the East, now firmly lay in favor of the commission's objectives. [53]

To Muir, the Pettigrew Amendment felt temporary and inadequate, like sandbags against a coming flood of greed and political power. But it held, thanks in part to his own buttressing work. Indeed, today legal scholars see this law as the story's legislative climax. By specifying purposes and granting authority, the Pettigrew Amendment gave the government the means to protect, manage, and regulate publicly owned forestlands. Because Pettigrew and its other supporters were Westerners, the reserves gained local legitimacy. Yet the Pettigrew Amendment proclaimed that the forests were "for the use and necessities of citizens of the United States"—a clause, absent from previous forestry bills, that identified the lands as belonging to a nationwide public, rather than local interests. More than Section 24 of the 1891 Forest Reserve Law, and more than the 1905 law that created the U.S. Forest Service, the Pettigrew Amendment provided foundational guidance to public land managers about their purpose and role. It has thus become known as the 1897 Forest Management Act, or the Organic Act. [54]

And yet any law is only as good as its implementation. Thus a rivaling version of the climax of this story would focus on a different set of actions from June 4, 1897, the day that President McKinley signed that act.

Because one selling point of Pettigrew's text was that it favored the USGS over other, less popular agencies—because, indeed, the bill had been authored by USGS director Charles Walcott—the USGS would implement it. The bill included no budget for the General Land Office or Fernow's forestry advisory service. Instead, funds were earmarked for USGS to conduct surveys on the temporarily suspended reserves to make sure they didn't include too much farmland.

The task was essential to the Pettigrew Amendment's success. For the six years that forest reserves had existed, the chief complaint about them was always that they were "hastily and improvidently drawn, including not only numerous towns, cities, and important developments, but millions of acres of land suitable for agriculture."[55] Fixing these errors had been one of Pinchot's goals for the commission, one that proved far beyond its scope. Now, USGS could try to survey the reserves correctly—and the future of public lands would rest on that effort.

Could a federal agency truly manage land? The first step in any management action is to define and measure the resource being managed. Thus, the first person USGS hired for this surveying task would arguably be the first-ever person with responsibility to implement this new vision of public land. It had to be someone with an immense and diverse skill set, with unbounded passion, with a grasp of both the discipline of forestry and the complexities of public policy. It had to be someone willing to selflessly commit to public service, someone who could make a real contribution to statesmanship.

Director Walcott and his employee Arnold Hague both had the same idea. On June 4, they each wrote to Gifford Pinchot in New York. They asked him to come to Washington immediately.[56]

EPILOGUE

❧

I n July 2018, I returned to Lake McDonald. Although I feared that Glacier's peak-season crowds would spoil my idyllic memories from the previous spring, I needed to experience this place again. On my previous visit, Lake McDonald served as the seed for my suspicion that the rivalry between John Muir and Gifford Pinchot was more complex and rewarding than most people thought. That seed sprouted and flowered through my time immersed in their lives. Now that I knew about the birth of America's public land ideals, the lake could serve as a shrine to their roles in that story.

Here Muir and Pinchot first sat around a campfire together. Here Muir's stories of woodsy adventures inspired Pinchot; here Pinchot's explanations of the practical applications of scientific forestry informed Muir. Here their rival backgrounds, rival philosophies, and rival views of the role of nature in society first fully engaged with each other. Here they articulated a shared belief that an American landscape could be productively managed, through democratic processes, for the benefit of all. Here the rivals' encounter offered hope.

Granted, the views of Muir and Pinchot would repeatedly converge and diverge until ultimately their friendship was drowned under a reservoir. That's the essence of great rivalries, and great partnerships. Granted also, as they met here, America already had several scraps of public land not destined for giveaway, such as Yellowstone and Yosemite. But at that moment, amid ineffectual management, political unrest, a wave of species going extinct, a depletion of resources, an explosion of income inequality, and a spiritual malaise, America needed a new way to think about nature. It needed to expand its commitment to protect many types of landscapes—not only unique landforms such as Yosemite but also the commonplace forests, watersheds, and prairies that were equally important in forging the nation's economy and character.

In retrospect, *public land* was an obvious choice to overcome these crises. Indeed, public land solutions were arising in settings as different as New York City's Central Park, the upstate Adirondacks, and the Canadian Rockies. Nevertheless, to simultaneously enshrine public land in both federal governance and the popular imagination was a feat staggering in its radical vision. So staggering, indeed, that Pinchot and Muir themselves may not have appreciated it at the time. They were caught up in their own quests for professional forestry and spiritual renewal. Yet it was the very intertwining of these quests that accomplished the goal.

The significance of Lake McDonald relies on the happy way that later events played out. One year after being appointed to the USGS surveying job, Pinchot succeeded Bernhard Fernow as the government's chief forester. Three years after that, Pinchot's friend Theodore Roosevelt ascended to the presidency to champion their shared philosophy. Roosevelt also promoted Muir's views on the spirituality of nature—for all of his much-discussed characteristics, one of Roosevelt's most underrated skills was uniting rivals.

Muir's moral authority and Pinchot's tactical genius made for an exceptional combination. As Muir continued to stoke the public's affection for forests and other natural places, Pinchot efficiently managed many such places, halting abuses. Muir wrote captivating books; Pinchot compelled loggers to use sustainable practices. Muir won hearts; Pinchot built trust. Furthermore, they were both able to shed the shackles that limited the commission's discussion to forest reserves—they expanded *public lands* to include more than forests. With Pinchot's encouragement, Roosevelt not only expanded national parks but also consecrated public lands in new formats, such as wildlife refuges and national monuments.[1] When the National Park Service was established in 1916, it rightfully credited the philosophical legacy of John Muir, but it also benefited from a legacy of federal managerial authority combined with public-relations genius—the legacy of Gifford Pinchot. The Park Service's relationship with the Forest Service subsequently developed as a sibling rivalry, in which the passion of their arguments sometimes obscured their shared genetic makeup. But the family also expanded to include the General Land Office, which slowly transformed its mission from land disposal to land custody, until in 1946 it was reorganized as the Bureau of Land Management.[2]

As governance evolved, so did ecological ideas. Aldo Leopold's innovative arguments made the question of how to balance uses on public land more complicated: it wasn't just about sustainable logging and water supplies, but also about humans' moral responsibility toward wildlife, ecosystems, and the land. Leopold's *land ethic*—an expansion of Muir's philosophy that Leopold began developing under Pinchot's influence as an early Forest Service employee—cemented the connection between public lands and nature.

Such evolutions couldn't solve some inherent problems with public lands. For example, Pinchot's oft-quoted dictum "the greatest good for the greatest number in the long run," doesn't say who gets to define the *greatest good*. Its faith in a single, pure, impartial solution creates a sort of romance of the bureaucrat, what historian Patricia Nelson Limerick in 1992 detailed as "the romance of the Executive Branch, the romance of rationality; the romance of expertise; the romance of reforestation and sustained yield."[3] While advocates of federal land transfer are good at highlighting such drawbacks, they struggle to show how a nation with reduced public lands would address deforestation, water quality, wildlife habitat, and other market failures, not to mention recreational and spiritual opportunities for people of all classes. [4]

Another problem emerged with increasing demands to use public lands. With more options for outdoor recreation, more free time, and a greater understanding of ecological needs, public lands today are far more complicated than they were for Muir and Pinchot. Incessant conflict among uses makes the situation messy, byzantine, and infuriating. The system to balance various interests never works perfectly. Each interest believes that someone else deserves less clout. For the past twenty years, in order to manage conflict and help various advocates find consensus, the Forest Service has embraced formal collaborative partnerships. Although admirably Pinchot-like in their process focus, these efforts are hardly a cure-all. [5] Indeed, it's tempting to dismiss them as dull and pointless, to instead self-righteously believe that all these underlying conflicts are a drawback of public land. Yet these struggles are not a bug in the public lands system, but a feature.

In Washington, D.C., on a frigid Friday morning in January 2018, I toured the U.S. Capitol. An enthusiastic intern led about two dozen of us on the standard circuit through that magnificent building's most renowned public spaces. I wasn't expecting much from the tour. I was spending a week at the Library of Congress, in Gifford Pinchot's archives, and decided to pop across the street for a quick break. But that break gave me a surprising insight.

On the tour, I was impressed at how hard Americans have worked, since the country's inception, to express cultural ideals with physical representations. For example, the Capitol's neoclassical architecture calls to Greek democracy. The "corn columns" so beloved by Thomas Jefferson—in which the Corinthian leaves of the capital part to show kernels of corn—announce that the Greeks' democratic foundations here have a uniquely American twist. Likewise, the capitol dome's interior is painted in the style of the Italian Renaissance, but with uniquely American historic scenes. The national statuary hall features nationwide heroes plus one from each of the fifty states. Outside the building, an 1873 landscape plan from Frederick Law Olmsted dignifies political processes, correcting an early optical illusion that the entire seat of government was about to slide off its hill into a swamp. Nearby, the Washington and Jefferson Monuments, the Smithsonian buildings, and the grand mall all likewise capture the nation's values using sculpture, architecture, and landscape design. The American idea was never simply theory. It has been constantly expressed in physical form, in hopes that such expressions will help future generations fully understand and reinforce it.

Muir and Pinchot, I realized, were part of a great innovation in the late 1800s to expand this movement to unmanicured terrain. With the 1872 declaration that Yellowstone was not merely a special place but a *national park*, America articulated and enriched its central theme: America is democracy, liberty, and natural wonder; America is a philosophy, a people, and a set of landscapes. Yellowstone's landscape-as-monument embodies the nation's values. But America is also commerce and recreation, water and wildlife, the pursuit of happiness and religious freedom. To express America's values on the land—in order to hand those values down to future generations—America needed to expand public lands beyond monumental preserves. In an expansion resembling that of the Smithsonian—which started as a museum for the hard sciences and later grew to include other forms of knowledge and art—land-based representations of America started in extraordinary icons and then expanded to forests, seashores, lakeshores, battlefields, wilderness areas, rangelands, and deserts.

Watching tourists bustle around Washington's iconic destinations helped me see public lands as a resource with symbolic value similar to that of the Capitol. We need public lands, despite their inefficiency, in the same the way that we need the Capitol, despite the fact that old buildings are always expensive to maintain. We shouldn't decrease the scope of public lands because they might have other uses, any more than we should start selling off buildings at the Smithsonian because the exhibits can be made available online. In an era when so many people feel so disconnected, we shouldn't give up public lands that serve as a springboard to a spiritual connection to nature. And we shouldn't reject the messy approach of democratic management of public lands—because that approach itself is one of the values we are using these lands to express. Public lands represent our appreciation of the equality, freedom, and responsibility inherent in the democratic process, plus our understanding of the role of nature in our collective lives. Democracy's lands, nature's lands: rival values, merging on America's landscape.

A century-plus of public lands history shows profound change: in landscape conditions, in philosophies used to manage the lands, and in how people perceive the lands' very purpose. Amid this change, I understand the desire to provide continuity by highlighting an alleged continuing preservation-versus-conservation divide. A Muir-versus-Pinchot dichotomy becomes a useful hook on which to hang debates. It has great explanatory power—but its continuity is an illusion. Just as Muir and Pinchot sometimes expressed that divide and sometimes didn't, so too did all the other characters in this story: Charles Sargent was Pinchot's mentor and then his enemy; Arnold Hague was Yellowstone's version of a free-wandering Muir who became Pinchot's biggest commission ally; Theodore Roosevelt was Pinchot's close friend who's best known for his Yosemite camping trip with Muir; and William Kent worked with Pinchot to donate Muir Woods but then opposed Muir at Hetch Hetchy. Preservation and conservation sometimes complemented each other and sometimes didn't—indeed, preservation and conservation sometimes appeared to be distinct concepts and sometimes meaningless lines drawn arbitrarily in the woods. If we could free public lands from the illusion of a preservation-versus-conservation dichotomy, we could free administrators to see public lands as a canvas for variable and changing visions of nature.[6] Sure, we would still argue about those visions. Sure, it would still be frustrating. But when the American idea works, rival perspectives reach an evolving set of specific compromises that add up to more than the sum of their parts.

That sum was the magic of the Muir and Pinchot story. These rivals rose above opposition to learn to briefly trust each other. One big lesson I take from the story is that it happened in a specific setting. Lake McDonald, their common ground, is the kind of glorious place where almost anyone could get along, as differences fade next to the wonders of nature. The rivals' interactions at Lake McDonald began a cascade of trust and transformation that helped the nation overcome its biggest problems: its rival needs for sustainable resources, special places, fairness, and opportunity. The vision of forests as timber rivaled the visions of forests as settings for water conservation, anti-monopolism, scientific advance, or spiritual renewal. In the birth of public lands, everyone gained from merging the visions. The apparent natural rivals were revealed as complementary and interdependent.

At Lake McDonald, I stake out a picnic site with the fresh clean smell of a sunny lakeshore. At midmorning, I'm alone with the birdsong and muted rush of a distant creek. Tall evergreens behind me cast a shadow onto the shoreline. Beneath the lake's clear waters, pebbles burst out in yellows, purples, and reds, as if the lakebed is lined with colored marbles. On the far shore, a hillside forest that burned a decade ago feels muted as the sun rises higher in the sky. Nearby, a pair of Harley Davidsons rumble along the road. I arrange myself with a view up-valley, toward the high peaks, breathtaking and impenetrable—but surprisingly light in snow cover.

Today's society faces its own environmental crisis: climate change. Scientists and intellectuals are concerned. They are calling to redefine our societal relationship to nature. Would such a redefinition ruin capitalism or the American spirit? Meanwhile, shouldn't society first address issues such as income disparity and corporate political influence? Amid such big questions, a dithering Congress and a tempestuous president won't take action. Blue-ribbon environmental commissions are ignored, sometimes because critics stoke rumors of dissension in their ranks.

What do we need to solve the climate crisis? It's easy to say we need more people like John Muir and Gifford Pinchot . . . and Theodore Roosevelt, Arnold Hague, and Frederick Law Olmsted . . . and even Charles Sargent, William Holman, and George Bird Grinnell. But we do have people like that today: brilliant, principled, creative, compassionate, eloquent, charismatic, and wise. Of course we do. As I gaze at the mirrorlike waters of Lake McDonald, I realize what this story is telling me: the existence of such people is not enough. How do we get them all pulling together?

I lose myself in a temporary fantasy of a modern Dream Team collaboration. What if today's counterparts of Muir and Pinchot were right now meeting at Lake McDonald? Maybe I'll see them in the campsite next to mine, or sitting on the veranda of the Lake McDonald Lodge, or telling stories as the *nemophila* twilight lingers. The specifics will vary: it might not be an immigrant who teams with a blueblood, a poet with a forester, an evangelist with a rookie, a straight white Protestant male with another one. Muir's individualism, mysticism, and promise of salvation could be expressed through many types of human forms, as could Pinchot's fairness, sustainability, and promise of community.

With this fantasy, I realize, I am imposing on this landscape my own ideas of the meaning of nature to our culture. I want to believe that people of intelligence and good will can solve the most difficult problems, that their power arises from their ability to collaborate, and that the richest collaborations take advantage of special natural settings. I want to see the legacy of the Muir-Pinchot collaboration expressed in physical representations, captured in the environment. Lake McDonald is just water and rock and trees and sky. The notion that it's a symbol of such harmony and political idealism is merely my interpretation.

But should I stop thinking this way? After all, this is the same type of exercise that Muir and Pinchot helped America perform as a nation: using landscapes to stand for values. I believe these exercises are useful. What does nature mean to you? Where do you look for meaning? As individuals, we all have our own ways of answering those questions. As a nationwide community we must find ways to share them with each other in order to build something greater than their sum.

My 2018 Glacier visit turns out to be just as memorable as the previous year. I hike at dinner- and breakfast-time, when the trails are less crowded. I nap at midday, when the campground is quiet. And I linger on the lakeshore long into the evening, which is as lovely and ethereal as Muir promised.

Even after the sun sets, its reflections shimmer on the not-quite-still waters. Bats emerge to dance and duel in the air above me. My eyes are drawn to the source of the waters, where alpenglow bathes the Crown of the Continent, the Backbone of the World. Darkness ascends the hillsides until just a single peak remains illuminated, glowing like a beacon.

In that beacon I see the other major lesson of Muir and Pinchot: to solve today's challenges, we need a marriage of morality and capability. We need a fresh, accessible story showing why we must take action combined with a powerful, visionary management framework that will go beyond culture wars to lead to better outcomes on the ground. We need a prophet collaborating with a statesman. Natural rivals, coming together to be revealed as complementary and interdependent.

ACKNOWLEDGMENTS

O nly after becoming immersed in this topic did I realize how well-suited it was for me. I grew up a preacher's kid and then moved to the mountains, so I identify with John Muir's perspectives on religion and nature. My family was Congregational, and then I majored in economics, so I also identify with Gifford Pinchot's perspectives on society. From childhood camping trips on a variety of public lands to twenty-nine years living fulltime in Montana, I've long experienced how these philosophies get expressed on the land. I've spent almost as much time in Glacier as in Yellowstone, often sharing the experience with friends and loved ones. So my deepest acknowledgments are to all who raised me and taught me and learned or traveled with me and brought me to this position.

This book is a work of nonfiction. All of its characters are real; nothing has been altered or embellished. The scholarship on both Muir and Pinchot is considerable and worthy; I am standing on the shoulders of giants. In particular, I started with, and often returned to, Char Miller's *Gifford Pinchot and the Making of Modern Environmentalism*, Donald Worster's *John Muir: A Passion for Nature*, Harold Steen's compilation of *The Conservation*

Diaries of Gifford Pinchot, and Stephen Fox's *John Muir and His Legacy: The American Conservation Movement*. But the breadth of my debt is indicated by the length of the Notes and Bibliography.

I first started expressing the ideas in this book through a series of articles for *The Montana Quarterly* and WyoHistory.org. My thanks to two great editors, Scott McMillion and Tom Rea, who prodded me on storylines and relevance. Thanks also to experts I interviewed for those articles—Amy Robinson, Terry Anderson, Dennis Glick, Mary Mitsos, Mike Clark, and Gloria Flora—who helped me develop ideas. Portions of Chapters 6 and 7 were previously published, in very different form, at WyoHistory.org as "John Muir in Yellowstone" and "Yellowstone Park, Arnold Hague and the Birth of National Forests," respectively.

I was gratified to be chosen as a scholar in residence at Grey Towers, the Pinchot mansion in Milford, Pennsylvania, which is now run by the U.S. Forest Service. For my time in Milford and at Pinchot's archives in the Library of Congress, thanks to Lori McKean, Bill Dauer, Melody Remillard, and the rest of the Grey Towers community. I gained great writing time from an artist-in-residence fellowship at the Absaroka-Beartooth Wilderness Foundation—props to David Kallenbach—and my research benefitted tremendously from a writer-in-residence gig at Montana State University–Billings—thanks to David Craig for the extension.

Amazingly, John Muir's letters and journals are available online. For making them available, thanks to Mike Wurtz and the staff of the Holt-Atherton Special Collections–Digital Archives Collections at the University of the Pacific at Stockton, California, a place I have visited virtually on an almost daily basis. Thanks also to volunteer webmaster Harold Wood, who maintains additional online archives of Muir books, essays, and scholarship at www.sierraclub.org.

For helping me pursue many other sources, thanks to librarian Anya Helsel and museum curator Deirdre Shaw at Glacier National Park, plus staff at the libraries and archives at the Library of Congress, Montana State University–Billings, the University of Wyoming, the East Tennessee Historical Society and Museum, the Obed Wild & Scenic River Visitor Center, the Montana Historical Society, the University of Hawaii–Manoa, Utah State University, Williams College, Montana State University–Bozeman, the University of Montana–Missoula, Rocky Mountain College, and at the cities of Denver and Fort Collins, Colorado; Cody, Wyoming; and Billings and Red Lodge, Montana. Several correspondents gave helpful information, including Bill Kight, Lou Salas Sian, Brooke Neely, Patty Limerick, John Auwaerter, Bill Swagerty, Mike Wurtz, Nicole Grady, Harold Wood, Edgar Brannon, Brittany Kropf, Jane Waldmann, Karen Nicholson, Ivy Gocker, June Can, Brendan Ross, Sara Azam, and Anne Marie Menta.

Chasmo Mitchell, Jeff DiBenedetto, Laura Nelson, Jackie Clayton, Lee Nellis, Mary Mitsos, Ken Coffin, Terry Jones, and Jeremy Tomkiewicz read the entire manuscript. Cathy Clayton, Paul Clayton, Bill Dauer, Edgar Brannon, Gloria Flora, Amy Robinson, Stephen Wilcox, the Rock Creek Writers, and Harold Wood read portions. They all saved me from misstatements, helped me organize storylines, and identified weaknesses. Of course, all errors that remain are my own responsibility.

This project builds on my previous book *Wonderlandscape: Yellowstone National Park and the Evolution of an American Cultural Icon* in both theme and team. Back again are agent Laura Wood, extraordinary editor Jessica Case, and Jessica's wonderful crew at Pegasus Books, including cover designer Charles Brock (formerly with FaceOut Studios), interior designer Maria Fernandez, copyeditor Mary O'Mara, proofreader Meredith Clark, and indexer Julie Grady. They make beautiful books, and were a delight to collaborate with.

I feel incredibly blessed to live in a wonderful place, surrounded by friends, doing work that I love. Words of acknowledgment feel insufficient to express my gratitude toward all in that world.

NOTES

Abbreviations used in the notes:

DPL = Denver Public Library.

GPP = Gifford Pinchot Papers, MSS36277, Manuscript Division, Library of Congress, Washington, D.C.

Grey Towers = Grey Towers National Historic Site library, Milford, Pennsylvania.

JMP = John Muir Papers, Holt-Atherton Special Collections, University of the Pacific, Stockton, California, https://scholarlycommons.pacific.edu/muir/, © 1984 Muir-Hanna Trust, used by permission.

USDA = U.S. Department of Agriculture.

If a citation lacks a page number, I used an online, unpaginated version of the source.

Prologue

1   A note on terminology: Experts have traditionally used the term *public lands* to refer only to Bureau of Land Management (BLM) lands; they call other federal-level public lands *federal lands*. (See Congressional Research Service

(CRS), "Federal Land Ownership: Overview and Data," March 3, 2017, accessed at https://fas.org/sgp/crs/misc/R42346.pdf on November 20, 2017, p. 1.) The distinction arose because the BLM mostly administers remnants of the *public domain*—a term generally used to refer to lands intended for homesteading but not yet claimed—where other agencies manage lands that at some point were reserved from homesteading and formally dedicated for parks, forestry, or other purposes. However, I find the public-versus-federal distinction counterintuitive and counterproductive. Avoiding the term *federal lands,* this book uses *public lands* the way most people understand it: all lands that are owned collectively by the American public and managed through any agency of our democratically elected government.

2   Most "public" lands on Indian reservations are known as "tribal lands," because they're not open to the general public, and/or as "trust lands," because the federal Bureau of Indian Affairs holds them in trust for tribes and their members. Given the many conflicts inherent in those relationships, plus the history of reversals in federal policy toward Native Americans and the fact that indigenous people also want a voice on public lands beyond reservation boundaries (as at Bears' Ears National Monument in Utah), the intersection of public land and tribal land is a complicated place. (See, for example, Rebecca Tsosie, "The Conflict between the 'Public Trust' and the 'Indian Trust' Doctrines: Federal Public Land Policy And Native Nations," *Tulsa Law Review* 39 (2003): 271–311.)

3   CRS, "Federal Land Ownership," 10. Montana's multiple-use lands receive about as much visitation as its national park lands. (USFS National Visitor Use Monitoring Program, https://apps.fs.usda.gov/nvum/results/A01002-A01003-A01008-A01010-A01011-A01012-A01014-A01015-A01016.aspx /FY2016, accessed September 5, 2018, and NPS Visitor Use Statistics, https://irma .nps.gov/Stats/SSRSReports/Park%20Specific%20Reports/Annual% 20Park%20Recreation%20Visitation%20(1904%20-%20Last%20 Calendar%20Year), accessed September 5, 2018).

4   Of course, a split between work and play oversimplifies. Is a hunter playing, or working the land to feed her family? Is a wilderness explorer playing, or pursuing a nature-based religion?

5   "Republican Platform: America's Natural Resources: Agriculture, Energy, and the Environment," at https://gop.com/platform/americas-natural-resources/, accessed November 20, 2017. Juliet Eilperin, "House GOP rules change will make it easier to sell off federal land," *Washington Post*, January 3, 2017. Juliet

Eilperin, "Trump orders review of national monuments," *Washington Post*, April 26, 2017. Hal Herring, "Can we make sense of the Malheur mess?" *High Country News*, February 12, 2016. https://twitter.com/search?l=&q=resist%20 %22public%20land%22%20since%3A2017-01-01%20until%3A2017-12 -31&src=typd, accessed September 5, 2018.

6 On jobs nostalgia, see Hal Herring, "The Changing Politics of Woods Work," *High Country News*, October 30, 2017. On litigation, note that some libertarians are so frustrated with wide-ranging litigation that their primary call is for new anti-lawsuit measures that "return land management to *federal and* state professionals." (Terry Anderson, "Land Of Many Uses Or No Uses?" Forbes.com, September 11, 2017, emphasis added.) For the exaggerations of opponents of federal land transfer, see Lena Felton, "Is America's 'Best Idea' at Stake?", *Atlantic Monthly*, November 24, 2017. I myself experienced the overstatement when I wrote an article about the history of national park campground concessionaires, and *Newsweek* (October 18, 2017) titled it, "Is Trump about to Sell Off our National Parks?"

Overstatements also clouded the question of control by state governments. Proponents of federal land transfer argued, reasonably, that state land management agencies are generally less bureaucratic than federal ones. Rather than counter with practicalities (e.g., how would a state pay for an increased management burden?), opponents acted as if state control would be equivalent to private ownership. The concern wasn't unreasonable, but it was an unproven exaggeration. Like people on all sides of many arguments today, defenders of public lands sought to win by highlighting the motives of the most extremist components of their opposition.

7 CRS says that Department of Defense lands comprise almost 2 percent of public lands. But discussions of public lands rarely include the Department of Defense lands—or, for that matter, lands administered by the U.S. Postal Service, tiny acreage-wise but in economically valuable locations. Why don't we hear more complaints that public ownership of these lands inhibits private economic development? Because people prefer to use the phrase *public lands* to mean *nature's lands*.

8 Each *individual*'s relationship with nature is unique, just as each marriage is unique. But in the same way that Americans fought over the definition of *marriage* in the context of same-sex relationships, we fight over a society-wide definition of *public lands* that can encompass different types of relationships to nature.

9   Compare the 2017 rhetoric about public *lands* with the 1980s debate about how the public-land actions of James Cason, appointed by Zinke as a chief Interior Department deputy, betrayed the public *trust*, in Adam Federman, "The Plot to Loot America's Wilderness," *The Nation*, November 16, 2017. For information on Ted Turner, see, generally, Todd Wilkinson, *Last Stand: Ted Turner's Quest To Save a Troubled Planet* (Lanham, MD: Lyons Press, 2013). For the Nature Conservancy, see www.nature.org, accessed November 20, 2017. For Bloomberg, see, generally, Michael Bloomberg and Carl Pope, *Climate of Hope: How Cities, Businesses, and Citizens Can Save the Planet* (New York: St. Martin's Press, 2017).

10 Granted, when public lands are used for a museum of natural history, they have some effect on people's relationships to nature. Indeed, to the extent that we want to integrate nature fully into society, any use of any land is about nature. However, these effects differ in scope and type from those associated with land management agencies.

11 "Greatest good": Pinchot quoted in Char Miller, *Gifford Pinchot and the Making of Modern Environmentalism* (Washington, D.C.: Island Press, 2001), 155.

12 The classic text for this tradition is Roderick Nash, *Wilderness and the American Mind* (New Haven, CT: Yale University Press, 2001) (reprint), chaps. 8 and 10. That book describes the Muir-Pinchot conflict with a fair amount of depth and nuance; subsequent interpretations, less so.

13 In its duality, the phrase "nature and society both" implies a divide. The question is how to get from our present state, where most people see nature and society in terms of a compare-and-contrast essay, to a state where we might see a nature-society unity. As noted below, I'm choosing a path that turns *enemies* into rivals, and a *divide* into multiple paths up a mountain.

14 http://www.pbs.org/nationalparks/history/ep2/2/, accessed November 18, 2018.

15 John Muir journal for July 16, 1896, JMP. Gifford Pinchot, *Breaking New Ground* (Washington, D.C.: Island Press, 1988) (reprint), 100.

16 The National Basketball Association sources its international popularity in the Dream Team at http://www.nba.com/history/dreamT_moments.html, accessed November 22, 2017.

17 Because the meaning of *wilderness* has evolved, it's actually quite tricky to apply to Muir and Pinchot. Pinchot rarely talked about wilderness. For example, the word *wilderness* appears only five times in his five-hundred-page autobiography: once metaphorically and four times referring to remote

or undeveloped country, with little of the ecological, political, or spiritual significance we attach to the word today. (Pinchot, *Breaking*, 23, 114, 125, 188, and 289.) Likewise, although Muir often used the word *wild* to mean the wonderful opposite of *civilized*, he rarely spoke of *wilderness* in the legalistic sense it has taken on since the 1964 Wilderness Act. Indeed, defenders of the Hetch Hetchy Valley never used the word *wilderness* in their arguments, as further discussed in Chapter 3.

18 Too often, Muir's and Pinchot's stories get told in organizational silos. For example, Samuel P. Hays's *Conservation and the Gospel of Efficiency* (New York: Harvard University Press, 1959) warps environmental history by focusing only on Pinchot, reducing Muir to a walk-on part, as Stephen Fox argues in *The American Conservation Movement: John Muir and His Legacy* (Madison, WI: University of Wisconsin Press, 1981), 289. Meanwhile, Lena Felton's *Atlantic* article "Is America's 'Best Idea' at Stake?" tries to summarize public-land history by focusing only on Muir, never mentioning Pinchot—and ends up warping Muir to fill the Pinchot role.

Part I: Natural Prophet, Natural Statesman
1: Gramercy Park

1 Robert Underwood Johnson (to K. Johnson, May 27, 1889), quoted in Fox, *The American Conservation Movement*, 87. Johnson, *Remembered Yesterdays*, 279.

Miller (*Gifford Pinchot*, 125) asserts that Muir and Pinchot previously spent a week hiking together in the Adirondacks in October 1892. Miller's source is a letter from Pinchot to Fritz-Greene Halleck that encloses a hunting knife for "John Muir" in appreciation of their time together (October 26, 1892, box 961, GPP). However, neither Pinchot nor Muir mention the encounter in their diaries, memoirs, or other letters. Muir's records show no evidence of a trip east that fall. And what would Muir—with his famously small appetite and large regard for wildlife—want with a hunting knife? Meanwhile, the estate where Pinchot stayed, Ne-ha-sa-ne, employed a caretaker-guide named George Muir. (See Gladys Montgomery, *An Elegant Wilderness: Great Camps and Grand Lodges of the Adirondacks, 1855-1935* (New York: Acanthus Press, 2011), 118.) Surely in the letter either Pinchot or his secretary misremembered George's name.

2 Gifford Pinchot and Harold K. Steen, *The Conservation Diaries of Gifford Pinchot* (Durham, NC: Forest History Society, 2001), 10.

3   Mark Stoll, "God and John Muir: A Psychological Interpretation of John Muir's Life and Religion," https://vault.sierraclub.org/john_muir_exhibit/life/god_john_muir_mark_stoll.aspx, accessed September 10, 2018. Mark Stoll, "'Sagacious' Bernard Palissy: Pinchot, Marsh, and the Connecticut Origins of American Conservation," *Environmental History* 16, no. 1 (January 2011): 4–37.

4   Mark Stoll, *Protestantism, Capitalism, and Nature in America* (Alburquerque, NM: University of New Mexico Press, 1997), 152.

5   For Muir's gait, see Fox, *The American Conservation Movement*, 11.

6   Tom Miller, "The James Pinchot House—No. 2 Gramercy Park," http://daytoninmanhattan.blogspot.com/2014/08/the-james-pinchot-house-no-2-gramercy.html, accessed September 8, 2018. Thomas Pike quoted in Robin Finn, "That's Some Key," *New York Times*, September 30, 2012.

7   John Muir to Louie [Strentzel Muir], June 13, 1893, in William Frederic Badè, *The Life and Letters of John Muir* (Boston and New York: Houghton Mifflin, 1924), chap. XVI.

8   Nancy P. Pittman, "James Wallace Pinchot (1831-1908)," *Yale FE&S Centennial News*, Fall 1999, 4–7.

9   Fox, *The American Conservation Movement*, 77–79.

10   Muir to Louie, June 13, 1893.

11   All Stickeen quotes from John Muir, *Stickeen: The Story of a Dog* (Boston and New York: Houghton Mifflin, 1909). See also S. Hall Young, *Alaska Days with John Muir* (Grand Rapids, MI: Fleming H. Revell, 1915), 131, 173–189. Obviously we can't be sure which details of the story Muir included in his rendition at the Pinchot home; over the years the story evolved from narrative to allegory. See Ronald H. Limbaugh, "Stickeen and the Moral Education of John Muir," *Environmental History Review* 15, no. 1 (Spring 1991): 25–45.

12   John Burroughs and Clifton Johnson, *John Burroughs Talks: His Reminiscences and Comments* (Boston and New York: Houghton Mifflin, 1922), 211.

13   Young, *Alaska Days*, 185.

14   Muir to Louie, June 13, 1893.

15   A few months later, in a letter to his mother about Laura Houghteling, Gifford wrote, "As Father said, all our interests are identical, and here especially." To my ear, that's a troubling description of family dynamics. Gifford Pinchot to Mamee [Mary Pinchot], October 20, 1893, box 961, GPP.

16 Pinchot quoted in James G. Bradley, "The Mystery of Gifford Pinchot and Laura Houghteling," *Pennsylvania History: A Journal of Mid-Atlantic Studies* 66, no. 2 (Spring 1999): 202.

17 Bradley, "Laura Houghteling," 200. Given the comprehensiveness of Pinchot's papers, the missing 1893 diaries and letters are mysterious. I heard speculation that the elderly Pinchot, his widow Cornelia, or another legacy-burnisher destroyed them to hide any scandal associated with the Houghteling romance, but was never able to confirm anything.

18 Gifford Pinchot to John Muir, June 19, 1893, and September 13, 1893, JMP.

19 Gifford Pinchot, *The Training of a Forester*, 1914, 66. Pinchot to Muir, September 13, 1893.

20 Muir to Pinchot, September 25, 1893, and June 16, 1894, box 961, GPP.

2: "Radiate Radiate Radiate"

1 Muir to Daniel H. Muir, November 19, 1866 (actually 1860), JMP. See also Muir to Sarah Muir Galloway, circa December 1–21, 1860, JMP.

2 Mrs. D. H. Johnson, "Interesting reminiscences of a celebrated naturalist." *Milwaukee Evening Wisconsin*, February 18, 1915, at http://www.wisconsin history.org/turningpoints/search.asp?id=1234, accessed October 27, 2017. Muir to Sarah Muir Galloway, October 1860, JMP. Linnie Marsh Wolfe, *Son of the Wilderness: The Life of John Muir* (New York: Alfred A. Knopf, 1947), 61–63.

3 Muir to Sarah Muir Galloway, circa December 1–21, 1860, JMP.

4 Muir to Emily [O. Pelton], January 29, 1870, JMP.

5 David Galloway to John Muir, December 21, 1860, JMP.

6 Fox, *The American Conservation Movement*, 54, 27–28.

7 John Muir, *A Thousand-Mile Walk to the Gulf* (Boston and New York: Houghton Mifflin, 1916), chap. 2. See also Donald Worster, *A Passion for Nature: The Life of John Muir* (New York: Oxford University Press, 2008), 35–37.

8 Muir, *Thousand-Mile Walk*, chap. 2. We have only Muir's side of this story.

9 Ibid.

10 Ibid.

11 Perry Miller, *Errand into the Wilderness* (Cambridge, MA:: Harvard University Press, 1984) (reprint), 208. See also 209–210.

12 Except as noted, all Emerson quotes from James Bradley Thayer, *A Western Journey with Mr. Emerson* (Boston: Little, Brown, 1884), 67–78. Emerson's

aphasia: Robert D. Richardson Jr., *Emerson: The Mind on Fire* (Oakland, CA: University of California Press, 2015) (reprint), 569.

13 Mark Stoll, "Milton in Yosemite: *Paradise Lost* and the National Parks Idea," *Environmental History* 13 (April 2008), 237–74. "Lofty images" quoted from Ralph Waldo Emerson, *Journals of Ralph Waldo Emerson* (Boston and New York: Houghton Mifflin, 1909), 44.

14 As discussed in Chapters 3 and 6, Olmsted had visited Yosemite before designing the Emerald Necklace.

15 Muir to Emerson, May 8, 1871, JMP. See also Wolfe, *Son of the Wilderness*, 145.

16 John Muir, *My First Summer in the Sierra* (Boston and New York: Houghton Mifflin, 1911), chap. 5.

17 Muir to Emerson, May 8, 1871.

18 Wolfe, *Son of the Wilderness*, 147.

19 John Muir, "The Forests of the Yosemite Park," *Atlantic Monthly* 85, no. 510 (April 1900): 493–507. Thayer, *With Mr. Emerson*, 108.

20 Muir's annotations of Emerson quoted in Fox, *American Conservation Movement*, 6, and Michael Cohen, *The Pathless Way: John Muir and American Wilderness* (Madison, WI: University of Wisconsin Press, 1984), 51.

21 The story in this section is drawn primarily from Wolfe, *Son of the Wilderness*, 194–97, and Worster, *A Passion for Nature*, 241–43 and 278–79.

22 Muir to Jeanne Carr, October 7, 1874, quoted in Badè, *Life and Letters*, chap. XI.

23 John Muir, "The Wild Parks and Forest Reservations of the West," *Atlantic Monthly* 81 (January 1898).

24 Mary Swett quoted in Wolfe, *Son of the Wilderness*, 196.

25 Muir to Asa Gray, June 19, 1880, JMP.

26 Although memoirs such as *My First Summer in the Sierra* were based on diary entries of a young John Muir, they were carefully crafted by an older, arguably radicalized John Muir. See Melanie L. Simo, *Forest and Garden* (Charlottesville, VA: University of Virginia Press, 2003), 66–69.

27 Muir to Louie, August 16, 1888, JMP.

28 John Muir, "Notes of a Naturalist," *San Francisco Daily Evening Bulletin*, August 29, 1879. Muir penned these words when he first saw Rainier from Puget Sound nine years before the summit climb.

29 Muir quoted in "Traveling Companions," *San Francisco Call* 82, no. 13 (June 13, 1897): 19. See also Aubrey L. Haines, *Mountain Fever: Historic Conquests of Rainier* (Seattle, WA: University of Washington Press, 2012) (reprint), 84–96.

30 "A Mountain Meadow," *Garden and Forest: A Journal of Horticulture, Landscape Art and Forestry* 2 (July 3, 1889): 314.

31 Sargent quoted in S. B. Sutton, *Charles Sprague Sargent and the Arnold Arboretum* (Cambridge, MA: Harvard University Press, 1970), 91. See also Shen Hou, *The City Natural: Garden and Forest Magazine and the Rise of American Environmentalism* (Pittsburgh, PA: University of Pittsburgh Press, 2013), 37–40.

32 Muir to Pinchot, June 16, 1894, box 961, GPP.

33 Muir to Pinchot, April 16, 1894, box 961, GPP. See also Pinchot to Muir, September 13, 1893.

34 The Sierra Club lists sixteen books authored by Muir, but that includes collections of letters and other posthumously assembled material. https://vault.sierraclub.org/john_muir_exhibit/writings/books.aspx, accessed September 16, 2018.

3: The Tragedy of John Muir

1 John Muir, *The Yosemite* (New York: The Century Company, 1912), chap. 12.

2 Robert Underwood Johnson, *Remembered Yesterdays* (Boston: Little, Brown, 1923), 279.

3 Johnson, *Remembered Yesterdays*, 280. Robert Underwood Johnson, "Destructive Tendencies in the Yosemite Valley," *The Century Magazine* 39 (January 1890): 478. In other words, Muir convinced Johnson of the value of protecting the valley in a parklike rather than "wilderness" state.

4 Johnson, *Remembered Yesterdays*, 281, 283. Muir describes their Yosemite trip in John Muir, "The Treasures of the Yosemite," *The Century Magazine* 40, no. 4 (August 1890), and John Muir, "Features of the Proposed Yosemite National Park," *The Century Magazine* 40, no. 5 (September 1890).

5 Muir, *The Yosemite*, chap. 16.

6 The conversation is recounted in Johnson, *Remembered Yesterdays*, 288. Johnson was recalling it more than thirty years later, and his text contains some factual errors, so some skepticism may be warranted.

7 John Muir, "The Mountain Lakes of California," *The Century Magazine* 17, no. 3 (January 1879): 416.

8 Johnson, *Remembered Yesterdays*, 288. For details on previous failures, see David Beasley, *Crow's Range: An Environmental History of the Sierra Nevada* (Reno, NV: University of Nevada Press, 2007), 112.

9   Johnson and Muir envisioned a large role for Olmsted, but Olmsted declined due to the press of other work. Then, when the governor of California defended the state's management by falsely claiming that Johnson was Olmsted's nephew ginning up work for his uncle, Olmsted responded in March 1890 by publishing *Governmental Preservation of Natural Scenery*, which generally contributed to Johnson's cause. See Frederick Law Olmsted and Charles E. Beveridge, *The Papers of Frederick Law Olmsted: The Early Boston Years, 1882–1890* (Baltimore, MD: Johns Hopkins University Press, 2013), 31–33, 778–82.

10   "Soda Springs cabin National Park Service," National Register of Historic Places nomination form, 1979, https://www.nps.gov/yose/learn/historyculture /upload/Soda-Springs-Cabin-lo-res.pdf, accessed December 5, 2017. See also William E. Colby, "Jean (John) Baptiste Lembert—Personal Memories," *Yosemite Nature Notes* 28, no. 9 (September 1949): 112–17. The inholding was purchased by the Sierra Club before 1914, and used for its (presumably preservationist) purposes until being donated to the national park in 1973.

11   Muir to Johnson, January 13, 1890, JMP.

12   Johnson to Muir, November 21, 1889, and February 20, 1890, JMP.

13   Muir to Johnson, December 6, 1889, JMP.

14   Muir, "The National Parks and Forest Reservations," Saturday, November 23, 1895, reprinted in *Sierra Club Bulletin* 1, no. 7 (1896): 271–84. Note that Muir uses the Pinchotian word *forest*, not *parks* or *wilderness*. See also Robert W. Righter, *The Battle over Hetch Hetchy: America's Most Controversial Dam and the Birth of Modern Environmentalism* (New York: Oxford University Press, 2005), 24–26.

15   Dennis C. Williams, *God's Wilds: John Muir's Vision of Nature* (College Station, TX: Texas A&M University Press, 2002), 46.

16   Johnson to Muir, May 4, 1896, JMP.

17   Muir to Louie, with original spelling, July 20 1901, JMP.

18   John Burroughs wrote about nature as a detached observer of tiny details in a Godless world—a style Roosevelt slightly preferred to Muir's more personal, spiritual flights. See Fox, *American Conservation Movement*, 119, and Worster, *Passion for Nature*, 368.

19   Muir to Johnson, September 21, 1902, JMP.

20   Muir to Johnson, April 11, 1895, JMP. In calling for Olmsted-style landscaping, Muir wasn't a single-minded advocate of *preservation* or *wilderness* in national parks.

21 *San Francisco Examiner* (headline, December 17, 1904) quoted in Jones, *Sierra Club*, 66.

22 He also called Muir a "pseudo naturalist who used to work in a saw mill," called Sierra Club member Charles D. Robinson a man "whose lack of the sense of harmony and color had incapacitated him as a house painter, and who therefore set up as landscape artist and painted pictures of the Yosemite which found no buyers," and accused Gifford Pinchot of colluding with Johnson on behalf of the national park. John P. Irish (January 9, 1893), quoted in the *Iowa Journal Of History And Politics*, July 1933, 435–38.

23 Jones, *Sierra Club*, 60.

24 Muir and Roosevelt quoted in Badè, *Life and Letters*, chap. XVIII. See also Wolfe, *Son of the Wilderness*, 289–94, and Douglas Brinkley, *The Wilderness Warrior: Theodore Roosevelt and the Crusade for America* (New York: Harper Collins, 2009), 536–48.

25 Muir to Johnson, July 16, 1906, JMP. See also William Colby to John Muir, March 5, 1906, JMP.

26 See letterhead in, for example, Muir [et al.] to James Garfield September 20, 1907, JMP.

27 "Sierra Club Board of Directors Meeting Minutes," August 30, 1907, http://www.oac.cdlib.org/ark:/28722/bk000775x57/?order=124&brand=o ac4 accessed December 10, 2017. See also reports in the previous pages in that collection, and Jones, *Sierra Club*, 94–96. Note that the board's activities had little to do with "wilderness." Frederick E. "Fritz" Olmsted was a cousin of Frederick Law Olmsted.

28 Pinchot wrote, "I had supposed from an item in the paper that the city had definitely given up the Lake Eleanor plan and had purchased one of the other water systems. If the possibility of a supply from the Sierras is still open, you should, I think, by all means go ahead with the idea of getting it." In other words, he was endorsing the Lake Eleanor compromise, as discussed below, not (yet) the damming of Hetch Hetchy. Gifford Pinchot to Marsden Manson, November 15, 1906, JMP.

29 Michael L. Smith, *Pacific Visions: California Scientists and the Environment, 1850-1915* (New Haven, CT: Yale University Press, 1987), 175–77.

30 Muir et al. quoted in *Sierra Club Bulletin* 6 (1907): 265.

31 Pinchot (to Colby, February 17, 1905) quoted in Jones, *Sierra Club*, 92–93. Henry Gannett to James Garfield, December 14, 1907, JMP. Muir to Johnson, March 23, 1905, JMP.

32 At the time of the meeting, even city engineer Marsden Manson had publicly suggested that Lake Eleanor might serve the city's needs for many years and Hetch Hetchy would not be needed. But after the meeting, Muir wrote President Roosevelt in opposition to damming Hetch Hetchy *or* Lake Eleanor. (Muir to Theodore Roosevelt, September 9, 1907, JMP.) See Righter, *Hetch Hetchy*, 69, 253.

33 Muir to James Garfield, September 6, 1907, JMP. Emphasis added.

34 Pinchot to Muir, September 6, 1907, JMP. (The telegram was dated the 5th but received the 6th.)

35 The story in this section is from Hal Rothman, *Preserving Different Pasts: The American National Monuments* (Champaign, IL: University of Illinois Press, 1989), 59–65. See also Lary M. Dilsaver, "Preservation Choices at Muir Woods," *Geographical Review* 84, no. 3 (July 1994): 290–305.

36 Kent to Pinchot (December 3, 1907) quoted in John Auwaerter and John F. Sears, *Historic Resource Study for Muir Woods National Monument* (Washington, D.C.: Olmsted Center for Landscape Preservation, National Park Service, 2006), 70.

37 An Act for the Preservation of American Antiquities, 16 U.S.C. § 431–33, 34 Stat. 225 (1906). Auwaerter and Sears, "Muir Woods," 296.

38 Kent's election resulted largely from the "altruism" of his gift (though his railroad and hotel investments benefitted from Muir Woods' tourism) and an ugly anti-immigrant plank. He was no saint, just a flawed man who made one magnificent gesture.

39 Roosevelt to Muir, September 16, 1907, JMP.

40 Worster, *A Passion for Nature*, 432.

41 The mountaineer and future Sierra Club president Francis Farquhar said that although he sided with Muir about Hetch Hetchy, "the idea that it was a second Yosemite, I did not quite agree with. It was nearly 1,000 feet lower than Yosemite and not as beautiful with its waterfalls." Francis Farquhar, "Mountains to Climb," Sierra Club Oral History Project, 1974, 15, http://digital assets.lib.berkeley.edu/roho/ucb/text/sc_reminiscences1.pdf, accessed September 26, 2018.

42 John Muir, "The Hetch Hetchy Valley," *Sierra Club Bulletin* VI, no. 4 (January 1908); Muir, *The Yosemite*, chap. 16.

43 Righter, *Hetch Hetchy*, 5–6, 107, 192, 206–11.

44 "The preservationist is not an elitist who wants to exclude others . . . he is a moralist who wants to convert them," wrote Joseph L. Sax in

Mountains Without Handrails, Reflections on the National Parks (Ann Arbor, MI: University of Michigan Press, 1980), 14.

45   William Kent quoted in Fox, *American Conservation Movement*, 144. John Burroughs quoted in Worster, *A Passion for Nature*, 432.

   Note that Gifford Pinchot never attacked Muir personally. Some sources suggest that Pinchot called Muir's views "sentimental nonsense" (e.g., Donato Bergandi, Patrick Blandin, "De la protection de la nature au développement durable: Genèse d'un oxymore éthique et politique," *Revue d'histoire des sciences* 65, no. 1 (2012): 103–42). But in fact those words belonged to Pinchot's more radical brother Amos, and were directed generally at the save-the-Hetch Hetchy cause, rather than at Muir personally. See Donald C. Swain, "The Passage of the National Park Service Act of 1916," *The Wisconsin Magazine of History* 50, no. 1 (Autumn 1966): 5.

46   These books—these memories—are thus the product of an aged writer at the height of his rhetorical powers, reinterpreting the events of his younger years through his radicalization over Hetch Hetchy.

47   Worster, *A Passion for Nature*, 457. Righter, *Hetch Hetchy*, 91–92.

48   Muir to Helen [Muir Funk], December 13, 1913, JMP. Muir (to "a friend") quoted in Johnson, *Remembered Yesterdays*, 313.

49   "A California Thoreau. A Chat With John Muir. The Hermit of the Glaciers," *San Francisco Call* 81, no. 118 (March 28, 1897): 17.

50   Muir left no evidence that he himself blamed Pinchot for Hetch Hetchy. The blame comes from others, such as Horace McFarland (to William Colby, December 18, 1913, quoted in Jones, *Sierra Club*, 167), Harold Bradley (to Norman Hapgood, December 7, 1913, quoted in Jones, *Sierra Club*, 168), and Robert Underwood Johnson (e.g., in *Remembered Yesterdays*, 307–10). Of course these people could have been reflecting sentiments that Muir privately conveyed to them. But McFarland and Johnson were upset at Pinchot for other reasons, which could have made them eager to pin the valley's loss on him.

4: "Sufficient Confidence in His Own Wisdom"

1   Robert H. Wiebe, *The Search for Order, 1877-1920* (New York: Macmillan, 1967), 28–32.

2   Although given the label by others, Pinchot never quite claimed to be "America's first forester," only that "Thanks to my Father's suggestion, I was

the first American to make Forestry his profession" and "The systematic study of American trees, by foresters for foresters, first started in 1896 with . . . [my book] *The White Pine.*" Pinchot, *Breaking,* 30, 306.

3   Gifford Pinchot, *Fishing Talk* (Mechanicsburg, PA: Stackpole Books, 1993), 74–75. See also Pinchot, *Breaking,* 2–3, and Miller, *Gifford Pinchot,* 18–20.

4   Mary Pinchot (to Gifford, 1880) quoted in Miller, *Gifford Pinchot,* 60. See also Stoll, "'Sagacious' Bernard Palissy," 4–37.

5   James Pinchot (to Gifford, 1880 and 1882), quoted in Miller, *Gifford Pinchot,* 59 and 63.

6   Stoll, "'Sagacious' Bernard Palissy," 23, 27.

7   Wiebe, *Search for Order,* 123–26.

8   Pinchot (to James Pinchot, February 9, 1890) quoted in M. Nelson McGeary, *Gifford Pinchot: Forester, Politician* (Princeton, NJ: Princeton University Press, 1960), 22. See also Pinchot, *Breaking,* 7–22.

9   Pinchot, *Conservation Diaries,* 36. Pinchot, *Breaking,* 15.

10 Pinchot's maternal grandfather Amos Eno was willing to give Gifford money—but only to go into business. Eno didn't believe in forestry. The Pinchot side of the family, the forest-loving side, was rich but not Eno-level rich. Their woodlands around the Grey Towers mansion weren't extensive enough for the scale of forestry that Brandis envisioned.

11 Pinchot, *Conservation Diaries,* 36.

12 Ibid., 36–39.

13 Eric Rutkow, *American Canopy: Trees, Forests, and the Making of a Nation* (New York: Scribner, 2012), 124–28.

14 Daniel Yergin, *The Prize: The Epic Quest for Oil, Money & Power* (New York: Simon and Schuster, 2011), 26.

15 Sargent quoted in Sutton, *Charles Sprague Sargent,* 96. The widely held belief that forests served as instruments to store water—their shade holding reservoirs of snow the way dams held reservoirs of water—was central to nineteenth-century notions of forestry-as-conservation. It explains conservationists' support for a dam at Hetch Hetchy. But when John Minto, spokesperson for Northwestern woolgrowers, challenged the connection between canopy and snowpack, Pinchot, to his credit, commissioned a scientific investigation that weakened the case for canopy. See Lawrence Rakestraw, "Sheep Grazing in the Cascade Range: John Minto vs. John Muir," *Pacific Historical Review* 27, no. 4 (November 1958): 376.

16 Pinchot, *Conservation Diaries,* 64.

17 Biltmore Village National Register of Historic Places nomination form, at http://www.hpo.ncdcr.gov/nr/BN0156.pdf, accessed January 12, 2018.

18 Bill Alexander, *Images of America: Around Biltmore Village* (Mount Pleasant, SC: Arcadia, 2008), 7, 21, 26. A great overview of Biltmore is in Denise Kiernan, *The Last Castle: The Epic Story of Love, Loss, and American Royalty in the Nation's Largest Home* (New York: Touchstone, 2017), 7–35.

19 For Catherine Hunt: USDA Forest Service, "Historic Structure Report: Grey Towers," FS-327, 1979, 10. For Natalie Dresser Brown, sister of Edith Dresser Vanderbilt: Pinchot to Pats of D'87 (a Yale club), February 23, 1893, box 3175, GPP. For Trix Farrand, niece of Edith Wharton: Bibi Gaston, "Apollo and Shooting Star: The Youthful Correspondence of Beatrix Jones Farrand and Gifford Pinchot," *Forest History Today,* Spring/Fall 2015, 14–20.

20 The Phelps Dodge assignment wasn't as attractive as it sounds. Pinchot received no salary, only expenses, and those perhaps only because his cousins sat on the company's board. Miller, *Gifford Pinchot*, 100.

21 Sargent quoted in Mark Antony De Wolfe Howe, *Later Years of the Saturday Club, 1870-1920* (Freeport, NY: Books for Libraries Press, 1968) (reprint), 187. See also Marc Landy, "Frederick Law Olmsted, Civic Environmentalist," in *Conservation Reconsidered: Nature, Virtue, and American Liberal Democracy,* edited by Charles T. Rubin (Lanham, MD: Rowman & Littlefield, 2000), 208–20. Note that Olmsted was not necessarily America's first landscape architect (Andrew Jackson Downing can better make that claim), but Olmsted's establishment of the discipline's first fulltime landscape architecture firm helped to *professionalize* it—much as Pinchot later professionalized American forestry. Additionally, Olmsted's parks weren't necessarily *governed* democratically: they were professionally designed and managed, often by commissions set up to be immune from crass public opinion—a model that elitists such as Sargent found attractive.

22 Photos of Biltmore under construction are in its museum, where I viewed them on January 29, 2018.

23 National Park Service, National Historic Landmarks Survey, "Biltmore Estate National Historic Landmark Nomination," 2003, 73. See also Laura Wood Roper, *FLO: A Biography of Frederick Law Olmsted* (Baltimore, MD: Johns Hopkins University Press, 1973), 416–19.

24 Pinchot diary October 14, 1891, box 10, GPP.

25 Pinchot to Pats of D'87, February 23, 1893.

26 Fernow to Pinchot, July 9, 1894, box 961, GPP.

27   Pinchot quoted in McGreary, *Forester-Politician*, 28.

28   Schenck claim quoted in James G. Lewis, "The Pinchot Family and the Battle to Establish American Forestry," *Pennsylvania History* 66, no. 2 (Spring 1999): 152.

29   Pinchot, *Conservation Diaries*, 48, 64.

30   Sargent quoted in Philip G. Terrie, *Forever Wild: A Cultural History of Wilderness in the Adirondacks* (Syracuse, NY: Syracuse University Press, 1994), 97.

31   Sargent quoted in Sutton, *Charles Sprague Sargent*, 103.

32   Karl Jacoby, *Crimes against Nature: Squatters, Poachers, Thieves, and the Hidden History of American Conservation* (Oakland, CA: University of California Press, 2014), 16–17. Louis S. Warren, *The Hunter's Game: Poachers and Conservationists in Twentieth-century America* (New Haven, CT: Yale University Press, 1999), 2–20.

33   Harold T. Pinkett, "Gifford Pinchot, Consulting Forester, 1893-1898," *New York History* 39, no. 1 (January 1958): 39–41.

34   Gifford Pinchot, "The Forest," *Garden and Forest* 8, no. 387 (July 1895): 298.

35   Robert Carrington Nesbit, *"He built Seattle": A Biography of Judge Thomas Burke* (Seattle, WA: University of Washington Press, 1961), 57, 413.

36   *Post-Intelligencer* quoted in Stephen Ponder, "Conservation, Economics and Newspapering: The Seattle Press and the Forest Reserves Controversy of 1897," *American Journalism* 3, no. 1 (January 1986): 54.

37   Stephen Ponder, "Gifford Pinchot: Press Agent for Forestry," *Journal of Forest History* 31, no. 1 (January 1987): 28. Pinchot, *Breaking*, 126.

38   Pinchot diary for September 5, 1897. It's transcribed in Pinchot, *Conservation Diaries*, 83, and typed in box 10, GPP—all but the "Not a clear day" note, which I read in a Grey Towers photocopy of the original handwritten diary.

39   "Rainier-Grand Hotel," Pacific Coast Architecture Database, http://pcad.lib.washington.edu/building/5542/, accessed January 13, 2018. "Victoria," *The Timberman* 15 (May 1914): 45.

40   Muir quoted in Wolfe, *Son of the Wilderness*, 274–75.

41   Pinchot diary for September 5, 1897.

42   Muir quoted in Wolfe, *Son of the Wilderness*, 275–76. Because these are a series of oral transfers of information—Muir to Colby, Colby to Wolfe—it's hard to know how or why they got embellished.

43   *Seattle Post-Intelligencer* (September 7, 1897), quoted in Char Miller, "What Happened in the Rainier Grand's Lobby? A Question of Sources," *The Journal*

of American History 86, no. 4 (March 2000): 1713. See also Miller, *Gifford Pinchot*, 119–25.

44 For the assertion that Muir felt betrayed by Pinchot, see, for example, "Chronology," in *John Muir: Nature Writings* (New York: Library of America, 1997), 847.

45 It's easy to find examples of Muir complaining about Pinchot, and thus to imply that Muir felt betrayed. For example, on October 16, 1897, after Charles Sargent forwarded Muir a letter in which Henry Abbot called Pinchot "a man of limited capacity" with a "lack of appreciation of proprieties usual among gentlemen," Muir told Sargent, "I think his estimate of Pinchot is just." And two weeks later, on October 28, Muir wrote Sargent that the appointment of "one feeble part of the Forestry Commission," Pinchot, to do forestry surveying work ("drygoods forestry") was "downright darkness and idiotic stupidity." But about that same appointment, Muir warmly congratulated Pinchot, saying, "You can do grand work for yourself and all of us." (Muir to Pinchot, July 8, 1897, box 964, GPP.) At best, Muir is consoling Sargent by mirroring Sargent's anger (rather than expressing his own anger). At worst, Muir is two-facedly telling his correspondents whatever they want to hear.

In a later example, on May 14, 1908, Muir wrote to R. U. Johnson that "Pinchot ou[gh]t to be ashamed of the false twaddle in the Collier's letter. He surrenders everything to politicians & rich schemers." And three weeks later, on June 2, 1908, Muir wrote to Johnson, "Pinchot is ambitious & never hesitates to sacrifice anything or anybody in his way." But both were in the context of consoling Johnson about an idea that Johnson believed Pinchot had stolen from him. Muir advised forgiveness; his next sentence in the June letter was, "Toss the miserable thing out of mind."

Finally, in November 1909, Muir wrote to Richard Ballinger, "Pinchot seems bent on stirring up barren strife to blot & becloud the good work he has hitherto done. Whom the gods wish to destroy they first make mad." Ten months later, on September 3, 1910, Muir wrote to Johnson, "I'm sorry to see poor Pinchot running amuck after doing so much good hopeful work—from sound conservation going pell mell to destruction on the wings of crazy inordinate ambition." But in these two examples Muir was bemoaning, in private, Pinchot's behavior in the so-called Pinchot-Ballinger Affair. Because that behavior got Pinchot fired from the Forest Service, it was much bemoaned in public by Pinchot's friends and enemies alike. (Except as noted, all letters quoted from JMP.)

Clearly, Muir believed, correctly, that Pinchot was ambitious. They disagreed on several important issues. They were rivals. But Muir never shied from an argument, and often overstated his case when writing. Now that Pinchot-phobes can no longer combine these and lesser examples with the alleged incident at the Rainier Grand Hotel, I am not persuaded that Muir found this rivalry emotionally upsetting, much less a "betrayal."

46 Muir to Johnson, March 27, 1898, JMP.

47 Of course, it's not easy to define "moderate." See William D. Rowley, *U.S. Forest Service Grazing and Rangelands: A History* (College Station, TX: Texas A&M Press, 1985), 33–37. See also Constance J. Burke, "Historic Fires In The Central Western Cascades, Oregon," https://andrewsforest.oregonstate.edu/sites/default/files/lter/pubs/pdf/pub567.pdf, accessed January 14, 2018, and Thomas G. Alexander, *The Rise of Multiple-use Management in the Intermountain West* (Washington, DC: USDA Forest Service, 1988), 17–20.

48 Muir to Johnson, March 27, 1898, JMP.

49 Reinhold Niebuhr, *Leaves from the Notebooks of a Tamed Cynic, 1929* (Meridian Books, 1957), xii–xiv.

5: The Tragedy of Gifford Pinchot

1 Pinchot, *Conservation Diaries*, 137.

2 This story is taken from McGeary, *Forester-Politician*, 66 (McCadden quote); Pinchot, *Conservation Diaries*, 137–38 (Pinchot quote); and Pinchot, *Breaking*, 317–18 (Bacon quote).

3 T. T. Munger quoted in Lawrence Rakestraw, "A History of Forest Conservation in the Pacific Northwest, 1891-1913," PhD diss., University of Washington, 1955, 37.

4 Johnson, *Yesterdays*, 307. Some skepticism may be warranted, because Johnson was using this quote as a way to blame Pinchot, and exonerate Roosevelt, for the Hetch Hetchy dam.

5 Roosevelt quoted in Miller, *Gifford Pinchot*, 35–37.

6 Pinchot, *Conservation Diaries*, 138.

7 Ponder, "Press Agent for Forestry," 26–27.

8 "This is my first attempt at administrative work," Pinchot wrote to Dietrich Brandis on June 1, 1898, as he decided on the Division of Forestry job (reel 4, series 10, GPP). His tone had a hint of insecurity, surprising and somehow reassuring given Pinchot's reputation for self-confidence.

9   Pinchot quoted in G. Michael McCarthy, *Hour of Trial: The Conservation Conflict in Colorado and the West, 1891-1907* (Norman, OK: University of Oklahoma Press, 1977), 226. See also https://www.loc.gov/resource/hhh .co0079.photos?st=gallery, http://www.historic-structures.com/co/denver /hotel_metropole1.php, accessed January 14, 2018.

10 The six states were Washington, Oregon, Idaho, Montana, Wyoming, and Colorado. This same bill renamed the reserves National Forests. Gerald W. Williams, *The USDA Forest Service: The First Century* (Washington, D.C.: USDA Forest Service, 2005), 25.

11 Convention speakers and newspapers quoted in McCarthy, *Hour of Trial*, 220–26.

12 Pinchot and newspapers quoted in McCarthy, *Hour of Trial*, 229–34.

13 "Flying Visit Is Made by Gifford Pinchot," *Great Falls Daily Tribune*, September 12, 1907, and various other 1907 western newspaper clippings, all in USFS series 6, box 36, ff 1, DPL.

14 Lewis, "The Pinchot Family," 151–52, 155, 157.

15 McGeary, *Forester Politician*, 161. In *Breaking* (451), Gifford recorded that the guest was General William Crozier. But McGeary cites Mary Pinchot's diaries.

16 John Vertrees (to a congressional committee) quoted in James Penick, Jr., *Progressive Politics and Conservation: The Pinchot-Ballinger Affair* (Chicago: University of Chicago Press, 1968), 155. Penick's great book is my major source for this section.

17 Pinchot, *Breaking*, 454.

18 Pinchot may have felt that he was defending himself. Robert Underwood Johnson's *Remembered Yesterdays*, published in 1923, was highly critical of Pinchot—largely because Johnson never forgave Pinchot for the 1908 Governors Conference on Conservation, an idea that Johnson believed Pinchot stole from him. And at least subconsciously, as Pinchot became dismayed at the increasingly extractive focus of foresters, he may have felt that forestry needed a personified moral hero to match the mythology of the "national park idea" (discussed in Chapter 6) and of his friend Muir.

19 Pinchot, *Breaking*, 322–23. Pinchot previously told the story in Gifford Pinchot, "How Conservation Began in the United States," *Agricultural History* 11, no. 4 (October 1, 1937): 255–65.

20 "Mr. Pinchot's 'Fight,'" *New York Times*, September 10, 1910. Gifford Pinchot, *The Fight for Conservation* (New York: Doubleday Page, 1910), 29, 110.

21 McGeary, *Forester Politician*, 56.

22 Ibid., 65–67.

23 Penick, *The Pinchot-Ballinger Affair*, 193.

24 Pinchot, *Conservation Diaries*, 200, 202.

25 "The land ethic simply enlarges the boundaries of the community to include soils, waters, plants, and animals, or collectively: the land," Aldo Leopold wrote in *A Sand County Almanac, and Sketches Here and There* (New York: Oxford University Press, 1949), 204. Leopold advocated a Pinchot-like multiple use with a re-ranking of uses to elevate preservation of habitat. Meanwhile, the Wilderness Society, founded in 1935, argued that some places should be preserved from any land-altering human activity—not only logging, mining, and damming, but also the roads and hotels that the Sierra Club had once proposed for Hetch Hetchy. Again, Pinchot's multiple-use framework was able to incorporate wilderness uses on Forest Service lands. As economist Terry Anderson noted (telephone conversation, March 30, 2017), Pinchot was interested in *how* to manage; Muir (and Leopold and wilderness advocates) in what to manage *for*.

26 Pinchot to Muir, August 20, 1899, JMP. Muir and Pinchot failed to arrange a government purchase of the Calaveras grove, but a new private owner kept its sequoia trees intact until 1931 when it became a California state park.

27 Thanks to Mather's work, the Park Service was founded in 1916. Mather served as its director until 1929. See generally Robert Shankland, *Steve Mather of the National Parks* (New York: Alfred A. Knopf, 1970).

Part II: The Birth of Public Lands
6: Bigger Stakes at Play

1 The phrase "national park idea" was rarely used before the 1916 founding of the National Park Service, which established a founding mythology around the alleged invention of that idea in Yellowstone in 1870. See John Clayton, *Wonderlandscape: Yellowstone National Park and the Evolution of an American Cultural Icon* (New York: Pegasus, 2017), 78–95. Thus this chapter charts the history of an idea that did not come to be known as an idea until long after it had succeeded.

2 U.S. Code, Title 16, Chapter 1, Section 48, June 30, 1864. See also Alfred Runte, *Yosemite, The Embattled Wilderness* (Lincoln, NE: University of Nebraska Press, 1993), 19–21.

3   Frederick Law Olmsted, "The Yosemite Valley and the Mariposa Big Tree Grove," https://www.nps.gov/parkhistory/online_books/anps/anps_1b.htm, accessed October 12, 2018.

4   Kathy S. Mason, *Natural Museums: U.S. National Parks, 1872–1916* (East Lansing, MI: Michigan State University Press, 2004), 7–11, 14. John C. Paige and Laura Soulliere Harrison, *Out Of The Vapors: A Social And Architectural History Of Bathhouse Row* (Washington, D.C.: National Park Service, 1988), 30–34.

5   A Constitutional debate has centered on whether the federal government has the right to supersede state laws on its lands, with courts generally saying that it does. But this is a question of whether the federal government is like any other landowner, a *proprietor* subject to state laws, or whether it has broader *sovereign* powers. Either way, the Constitution's "property clause" plainly declares that the government can own, retain, and manage land, even outside of the original thirteen states. Peter A. Appel, "The Power of Congress 'Without Limitation': The Property Clause and Federal Regulation of Private Property," https://digitalcommons.law.uga.edu/fac_artchop/785, accessed February 25, 2019; Elizabeth M. Osenbaugh and Nancy K. Stoner, "The County Supremacy Movement," *The Urban Lawyer* 28, no. 3 (1996): 497–516.

6   Rutkow, *American Canopy*, 33, 151.

7   Cole quoted in Aubrey L. Haines, *The Yellowstone Story: A History of Our First National Park*, Vol. 1 (Yellowstone National Park, WY: Yellowstone Library and Museum Association, 1977), 169–70. Cole understated the eventual size of Yellowstone, which is 63 by 54 miles, or (since it's no longer an exact rectangle) 3,471 square miles.

8   Trumbull and Dawes quoted in Haines, *The Yellowstone Story*, 170–71.

9   John Muir, "Yosemite Glaciers," *New York Tribune*, December 5, 1871. Note that I am making a conscious decision to quote from Muir's articles and letters, which portray his feelings and beliefs at the time, rather than memoirs, such as *My First Summer in the Sierra*, where the rhetoric is shaped by the political radicalization of his old age.

10   Muir (to Mrs. Ezra Carr, undated) quoted in Badè, *Life and Letters*, 271.

11   John Muir, "Modoc Memories," *San Francisco Bulletin*, December 28, 1874.

12   John Muir, "In the Yo-semite: Holidays Among the Rocks," *New York Tribune*, January 1, 1872. John Muir, "Yosemite in Spring," *New York Tribune*, May 7, 1872.

13 Muir to Louie, August 30, 1885, JMP.

14 In 1885, Yellowstone was the *only* national park. Technically, there was also Mackinac National Park in northern Michigan, which was run by an adjacent army fort. But it was rarely considered on the same level as Yellowstone, and indeed became a state park in 1895. Meanwhile, the Arkansas Hot Springs remained a *reserve*, not a national park, until 1921. (Mason, *Natural Museums*, 15, 29–42.)

15 For Muir's Yellowstone trip, I'm relying on Worster, *A Passion for Nature*, 298–300; Wolfe, *Son of the Wilderness*, 234; and Cohen, *Pathless Way*, 252; plus the letters, journals, and articles cited below.

16 Muir to Louie, August 12, 1885, JMP. The initial clause is too rarely included with this quotation; it shows that Muir is drawn to wilderness more than *Wisconsin*, not more than Louie or Martinez.

17 Muir to Louie, Aug 20, 1885, JMP.

18 Ibid. Worster, *A Passion for Nature*, 299, 333.

19 Haines, *The Yellowstone Story*, Vol. 1, 293–302. See also, generally, H. Duane Hampton, *How the U.S. Cavalry Saved Our National Parks* (Bloomington, IN: Indiana University Press, 1971).

20 John Muir journals, August 1885, JMP.

21 Muir to Louie, August 30, 1885, JMP.

22 John Muir, "The Yellowstone Park," *San Francisco Bulletin*, October 29, 1885. Probably by coincidence, Muir used the same angle that Charles Sargent had used two years previously in arguing for the preservation of what is now Glacier, where tributaries of the Missouri, Columbia, and Saskatchewan flow to the Atlantic, Pacific, and Hudson's Bay (Sutton, *Charles Sprague Sargent*, 96).

23 Muir, "The Yellowstone Park."

24 Ibid.

25 Muir to Louie, August 20, 1885, JMP.

26 Runte, *Yosemite*, 20. For the story of Sequoia National Park, I'm relying on Douglas H. Strong, "The History of Sequoia National Park, 1876-1926: Part I: The Movement to Establish a Park," *Southern California Quarterly* 48, no. 2 (June 1966): 137–67. See also Lary M. Dilsaver and William C. Tweed, *Challenge of the Big Trees: A Resource History of Sequoia and Kings Canyon National Parks* (Three Rivers, CA: Sequoia Natural History Association, 1990), chap. 4. General Grant National Park was subsumed into Kings

Canyon in 1940; the whole complex is now known as Sequoia/Kings Canyon National Park.

27 Schurz recommended reserving four sections. In surveying, a section is a square mile, or 640 acres. A township is thirty-six sections.

28 National Academy of Sciences, *A History of the First Half-century of the National Academy of Sciences, 1863-1913* (Baltimore, MD: The Lord Baltimore Press, 1913), 59–62.

29 Stiles (to R. U. Johnson, August 13, 1890, and in "National Parks," *Garden and Forest*, August 6, 1890), quoted in Hou, *The City Natural*, 175–76. Stiles was also likely referring to Arnold Hague's efforts to expand Yellowstone, discussed in Chapter 7. Muir basically agreed with Stiles about terminology: He preferred *reserve* to *park* (Cohen, *Pathless Way*, 296).

30 Craig H. Jones, *The Mountains That Remade America: How Sierra Nevada Geology Impacts Modern Life* (Oakland, CA: University of California Press, 2017), 160. While fighting the park designation, the Kaweah Colony collapsed under internal as well as external pressures.

31 John Muir, "A Rival of the Yosemite: The Cañon of the South Fork of King's River, California," *The Century Magazine* 43, no. 1 (November 1891): 77–97.

32 Ibid.

33 Muir to Johnson, July 14, 1891, JMP.

34 Jones, *Sierra Club*, 36–37, 57.

35 Muir to Johnson, July 2, 1891, JMP.

36 Robinson also derided Muir as a botanist with little "capacity as a 'Nature Lover.'" Norman L. Wilson and Lucinda M. Woodward, "C.D. Robinson and John Muir in the Kings River Canyon," in *John Muir in Historical Perspective*, edited by Sally M. Miller (New York: Peter Lang, 1999), 83–92. See also Adolph D. Sweet, "Meeting John Muir in King's Canyon," *Los Tulares*, Tulare County Historical Bulletin (September 1952).

37 Muir to Johnson, July 14, 1891.

38 Johnson (to Muir, May 1, 1891) quoted in Cohen, *Pathless Way*, 268. Robinson claimed to have given Johnson the idea of the Yosemite comparison; see Wilson and Woodward, "C.D. Robinson," 88.

39 Muir, "A Rival of the Yosemite." Muir to Johnson, August 15, 1891, JMP.

40 Muir, "A Rival of the Yosemite." Muir always spelled it King's River, but the Spaniard who camped on it on Epiphany, 1806, named it El Río de los Santos Reyes (the River of the Holy Kings).

7: Free Land for Many Uses

1 The anti-monopolist movement argued, persuasively, that by forming monopolies and syndicates, the robber barons gained undue market power, which they used to raise prices, lower wages, and alter government policies. For skepticism about Roosevelt's importance in carrying this argument, see, for example, Robert D. Atkinson and Michael Lind, "The Myth of the Roosevelt 'Trustbusters'," *The New Republic*, May 4, 2018.

2 Israel George Blake, "The Lives of William Steele Holman and His Father Jesse Lynch Holman," Ph.D. diss., Indiana University, 1940, 301, 309, 380, 387.

3 Cannon quoted in Blake, "William Steele Holman," 321.

4 Holman quoted in Blake, "William Steele Holman," 347, 385.

5 Charles Dana of the *New York Sun* quoted in Blake, "William Steele Holman," 302. Note that merely translating $100 million to $2.5 billion in 2017 dollars would understate Holman's effectiveness, because it would account only for inflation and not the growth of the federal budget—one-sixth of today's annual budget would be $630 billion.

6 W. S. Holman, "Economy and the Democracy," *North American Review* 154 (March 1892): 328, 331.

7 Thornton McEnery, "The World's 15 Biggest Landowners," *Business Insider*, March 18, 2011.

8 For American land policy and attitudes, see Benjamin Horace Hibbard, *A History of the Public Land Policies* (Madison, WI: University of Wisconsin Press, 1965) (reprint), 408–67.

9 Hibbard, *Public Land Policies*, 466.

10 From an ecological perspective, replacing a diverse native ecosystem, such as a tallgrass prairie, with an agricultural monoculture was a huge loss. But the science to articulate that perspective would not be understood until the twentieth century.

11 George Perkins Marsh, *Man and Nature* (New York: Charles Scribner, 1864), 36.

12 Mark Stoll, *Inherit the Holy Mountain: Religion and the Rise of American Environmentalism* (New York: Oxford University Press, 2017), 87–91. See also, generally, David Lowenthal, *George Perkins Marsh: Prophet of Conservation* (Seattle, WA: University of Washington Press, 2009).

13 Grinnell quoted, and others discussed, in Char Miller, "Deep Roots: The Late Nineteenth Century Origins of American Forestry," *Forest History Today*

(Spring/Fall 2005): 2. Olmsted discussed in Lowenthal, *George Perkins Marsh*, 541.

14 Arnold Hague, "The Early Tertiary Volcanoes of the Absaroka Range," *Science* 9, no. 221 (March 24, 1899): 426.

15 Arnold Hague, "The Yellowstone Park," in *American Big-game Hunting: The Book of the Boone and Crockett Club*, edited by Theodore Roosevelt and George Bird Grinnell (New York: Forest and Stream Publishing, 1893), 251–52, 255.

16 Hayden set Yellowstone's north boundary at the confluence of the Gardner and Yellowstone Rivers, and the west boundary ten miles west of "Madison" (apparently Shoshone) Lake. Mary S. Culpin, "Yellowstone and its Borders: a Significant Influence Toward the Creation of the First Forest Reserve," in *The Origins of the National Forests: A Centennial Symposium*, edited by Harold K. Steen (Durham, NC: Duke University Press, 1992), 276–83.

17 Arnold Hague, "The Yellowstone Park as a Forest Reservation," *The Nation* XLVI (January 5, 1888): 9–10.

18 Hague, "The Yellowstone Park" (in *American Big-game Hunting*), 254, 257. The actual headwaters of the Snake are within Yellowstone's boundaries, but as it quickly flows south, many of its early tributaries arise south of Yellowstone's southern boundary.

19 Not only was a forest's shade perceived as delaying snowmelt, but at the time some people even believed that forests could *cause* rain. If homesteaders would plant trees on the high plains of the Dakotas, for example, the forests would cause rain to increase and transform dry rangeland into profitable farmland. Forestry was an essential component of the then-faddish, now-discredited idea that "rain follows the plow." See, for example, Marc Reisner, *Cadillac Desert: The American West and Its Disappearing Water* (New York: Penguin, 1993) (reprint), 36.

20 Harold K. Steen, *The Beginning of the National Forest System* (Washington, DC: USDA Forest Service, 1991), 11. These categories differed slightly from those of the 1879 Public Land Commission; as Louise Peffer wrote, "nothing of any value came of the recommendations of the Public Land Commission, except numerous footnotes in later works." Prophecy fulfilled. See E. Louise Peffer, *The Closing of the Public Domain: Disposal and Reservation Policies, 1900-50* (Palo Alto, CA: Stanford University Press, 1951), 14.

21 51 Cong. Sess. II. Ch. 561 (1891), at https://www.loc.gov/law/help/statutes-at-large/51st-congress/session-2/c51s2ch561.pdf, accessed October 24, 2018.

22 Section 24 reads: "That the President of the United States may, from time to time, set apart and reserve, in any State or Territory having public land bearing forests, in any part of the public lands wholly or in part covered with timber or undergrowth, whether of commercial value or not, as public reservations, and the President shall, by public proclamation, declare the establishment of such reservations and the limits thereof." The president may set *what* apart? Note also that the president can only proclaim a reserve, not do anything with it. (Ron Arnold, "Congressman William Holman of Indiana: Unknown Founder of the National Forests" in *The Origins of the National Forests*, edited by Steen, 301.)

23 Arnold, "Congressman William Holman," 301–13. Steen, *The Beginning*, 11–23. John Ise, *The United States Forest Policy* (New Haven, CT: Yale University Press, 1920), 113–18. Blake, "William Steele Holman," 327–30, 336, 376. Richard F. Pettigrew, *Imperial Washington* (Chicago: C.H. Kerr, 1922), 13–16. John Noble to R. U. Johnson (May 14, 1908) quoted in Douglas H. Strong, "The Sierra Forest Reserve: The Movement to Preserve the San Joaquin Valley Watershed," *California Historical Society Quarterly* 46, no. 1 (March 1967): 8. Johnson, *Yesterdays*, 305.

24 Hague quoted in Steen, *The Beginning*, 16.

25 Arnold, "Congressman William Holman," 310–13.

26 Hague quoted in Steen, *The Beginning*, 24.

8: No Trespassing

1 A remarkably thorough account of Harrison's visit to Glenwood is in Angela K. Parkison, *Hope and Hot Water: Glenwood Springs from 1878 to 1891* (Glenwood Springs, CO: Glenwood Springs Legacy, 2000), 323–35.

2 "Laundry Trains to Glenwood," *Aspen Daily Times*, April 16, 1892. Cynthia Hines and the Frontier Historical Society, *Early Glenwood Springs* (Mount Pleasant, SC: Arcadia Publishing, 2015), 18, 76.

3 For Glenwood Springs history, see generally Hines, *Early Glenwood,* and Steven F. Mehls, *The Valley of Opportunity: A History of West-Central Colorado,* Colorado Cultural Resources Series Number Twelve (Denver, CO: Bureau of Land Management, 1982), chap. 8. For Devereux, see Len Shoemaker, "Roaring Fork Pioneers: Walter B. Devereux" in *Brand Book of the Denver Posse of the Westerners* (Denver: Denver Posse of the Westerners, 1962), and Jim Nelson, *Glenwood Springs: The History of a Rocky Mountain Resort* (Lake City, CO: Western Reflections, 1999).

4   Nelson (*Glenwood Springs*, 101) asserts that Harrison's personal observations led to the establishment of the nearby forest reserve, although given the distance of the reserved lands from Harrison's itinerary, I'm skeptical.

5   "It May Cause Trouble," [Leadville] *Herald Democrat*, October 6, 1891.

6   The Interior Department later acknowledged this concern by agreeing to honor claims within forest reserves of people who'd settled "in good faith" regardless of their paperwork. See James Muhn, "Early Administration of the Forest Reserve Act: Interior Department and General Land Office Policies, 1891-1897," in *The Origins of the National Forests*, edited by Steen, 259–75.

7   *Meeker Herald* (September 10, 1891) quoted in McCarthy, *Hour of Trial*, 31. "The Western Slope," *Aspen Evening Chronicle*, April 16, 1892. In claims that today seem both racist and farfetched, turn-of-the-century whites throughout the West complained that indigenous people regularly escaped their reservations to over-hunt wild game. See, for example, Esther B. Allan, "History of Teton National Forest" Bridger-Teton National Forest, https://www.fs.usda.gov/Internet/FSE_DOCUMENTS/fseprd534131 .pdf, accessed April 16, 2019, 1973, 131.

8   Devereux quoted in McCarthy, *Hour of Trial*, 32.

9   *Proceedings of the American Forestry Association*, Vol. 12 (1889), 5. George Bird Grinnell, *Trail and Camp-fire: The Book of the Boone and Crockett Club* (Washington, D.C.: Forest and Stream Publishing, 1897), 348–51.

10 Devereux quoted in McCarthy, *Hour of Trial*, 32. "Our National Parks," *Pueblo Daily Chieftain*, November 3, 1892. "The National Park," *Glenwood Avalanche-Echo*, October 16, 1891. "White River's Voice," *Aspen Evening Chronicle*, November 7, 1891.

11 John Muir, *Our National Parks* (Boston and New York: Houghton Mifflin, 1901), 39–40. Muir misstated the name of the Yellowstone Park Timber Land Reserve.

12 "Our National Park," *Aspen Weekly Chronicle*, March 25, 1889.

13 Edgar Ensign, "Forest Reserves and their Management," *Greeley Tribune*, July 7, 1892. Ensign was wrong about Colorado's future national parks: Mesa Verde was established in 1906, Rocky Mountain, 1915, Black Canyon of the Gunnison, 1999, and Great Sand Dunes, 2004.

14 Pinchot, *Breaking*, 85.

15 It's unclear how Fernow got the petition, although one conspiracy theory claimed that it was intentionally resurfaced by a timber company hoping to

corner the Sierra timber market. The following year the petition disappeared again, until historian Douglas Strong rediscovered it seventy years later. Strong, "The Sierra Forest Reserve," 8–9, 16.

16 Johnson quoted in Strong, "Sierra Forest Reserve," 11. Allen also excluded the Mount Whitney military reservation, discussed in Chapter 6; it would be folded into the Sierra Forest Reserve in 1905.

17 Strong, "Sierra Forest Reserve," 14. Muhn, "Early Administration."

18 Kiki Leigh Rydell and Mary Shivers Culpin, *Managing the "Matchless Wonders": A History of Administrative Development in Yellowstone National Park, 1872–1965* (Yellowstone National Park, WY: National Park Service, Yellowstone Center for Resources, 2006), 36–37. "Report of the Secretary of the Interior," *Congressional Serial Set* (Washington, D.C.: U.S. Government Printing Office, 1897), 796.

19 Some land functions were performed by non-GLO entities in the Interior Department, which has caused some scholars to refer to a vaguely defined super-set of the GLO called the Land Department. For simplicity's sake, I'll just refer to the GLO. See Muhn, "Early Administration," note 3.

20 In 1892, the GLO had ninety-five part-time special agents to investigate frauds, trespassing, timber theft, and other problems on 584 million acres of not-yet-homesteaded lands. Its budget allowed for only eighty-two special agents in 1893 and forty for the four years after that. Muhn, "Early Administration," note 39.

21 GLO documents quoted in Muhn, "Early Administration."

22 An Act to Set Apart a Certain Tract of Land Lying Near the Headwaters of the Yellowstone River as a Public Park, 16 U.S.C. § 21 (1872).

23 GLO memo quoted in Muhn, "Early Administration."

24 Harold K. Steen, *The U.S. Forest Service: A Centennial History* (Seattle, WA: University of Washington Press, 2013), 29–30. John Ise, *The United States Forest Policy* (New Haven, CT: Yale University Press, 1920), 119–28.

25 The cabin was near the present-day village of St. Mary. Gerald Allen Diettert, "Grinnell's Glacier," Graduate Dissertations, University of Montana, 1990, 84. Stephen Allan Germic, "Nature, Naturalism, American Exceptionalism: Nineteenth-century Designs To Obscure Class And Crisis," PhD diss, Wayne State University, 1997, 247.

26 Grinnell quoted in Diettert, "Grinnell's Glacier," 84. See also Sutton, *Charles Sprague Sargent*, 95.

27 Grinnell quoted in Deittert, "Grinnell's Glacier," 87. Andrew C. Harper, "The Crown and the Jewel: George Bird Grinnell, Louis Warren Hill,

and Glacier National Park," PhD diss., Northern Arizona University, 1999, 53.

28 Harper, "The Crown," 75. "Forest Reservations," *Garden and Forest* 4, no. 191 (October 21, 1891): 493.

29 For Norris, see Adolf Hungrywolf, *The Blackfoot Papers*, Vol. 4 (Skookumchuk, BC: Good Medicine Cultural Foundation, 2006), 1054; and http://abish.byui.edu/specialCollections/westernStates/westernStatesRecordDetail.cfm?recordID=407487, accessed April 6, 2018.

30 Harper, "The Crown," 83. The quote reveals a certain racial tension in the term *public lands*: Indian reservations were in fact public lands—but dedicated to a tribe's public rather than a white one.

31 Warren, *The Hunter's Game*, 135.

32 Christopher S. Ashby, "The Blackfeet Agreement of 1895 and Glacier National Park: A Case History," MS diss., University of Montana, 1985, 28–29.

33 John F. Rieger, "George Bird Grinnell and the Development of American Conservation, 1870-1901," PhD diss., Northwestern University, 1970, 156. George Bird Grinnell to Arnold Hague (December 14, 1896) quoted in Harper, "The Crown," 129. Mark David Spence, "Dispossessing the Wilderness: The Preservationist Ideal, Indian Removal, and National Parks," Ph.D. diss., University of Southern California, 1996, 197–200.

     Grinnell wrote to Pinchot, "I personally should like to have everybody kept off these reservations but I feel sure that [the Yellowstone reserve's No Trespassing] regulations . . . will make that reservation extremely unpopular with western men, and they will, of course, try to influence their representatives in Congress. I had a word with Hague about this, and he agrees with me." (George Bird Grinnell to Gifford Pinchot, December 31, 1897, box 964, GPP.)

34 Spence, "Dispossessing," 18.

35 Pinchot, *Breaking*, 87.

36 Phyllis Andersen, "'Master of a Felicitous English Style': William Augustus Stiles, Editor of Garden and Forest," https://www.loc.gov/preservation/about/prd/gardfor/essays/andersen.html, accessed April 4, 2018. See also Sutton, *Charles Sprague Sargent*, 77, 131.

37 Pinchot, *Breaking*, 88.

38 This and subsequent quotes from "A Plan to Save the Forests" and "Topics of the Time: The Need of a National Forest Commission," *The Century Magazine* 49 (February 1895): 626–35.

9: Lake McDonald's Delight

1 For the meeting: Pinchot, *Breaking*, 88, and Pinchot, *Conservation Diaries*, 71. For Holm Lea: Phyllis Andersen, "The Arnold Arboretum and the Early Years of Landscape Design Education in America," *Arnoldia* 62, no. 3 (2003): 2–9. Muir quoted in Badè, *Life and Letters*, chap. XVI.

2 B. June Hutchinson, "The Golden Age of Brookline Gardening," *Brookline Historical Society [Newsletter]*, Fall 1989, 3–4.

3 Pinchot, *Breaking*, 65. The fluid ambitions of the youthful Pinchot show a mix of egotism and selflessness—especially as filtered through the prejudices of the elderly Pinchot. See also Pinkett, "Gifford Pinchot, Consulting Forester," 42–44.

4 Howe, *Later Years of the Saturday Club, 1870-1920*, 45–48.

5 "The Coming Forestry Congress," *Garden and Forest* 6 (June 14, 1893): 251.

6 Pinchot to Dietrich Brandis, July 11, 1895, Letterbooks, box 411, Reel 3, GPP. Emphasis added.

7 Johnson (to Smith, November 11, 1895) quoted in *Pamphlets on Forestry*, Vol. 9, University of California, 1900, http://google.cat/books ?id=D8RDAAAAIAAJ, accessed November 20, 2018, 2. Smith's letter to Gibbs may have relied on a draft by Fernow rather than Pinchot; see Steen, *Centennial History*, 30-31.

8 William A. King, "The Private Forestry Movement in Massachusetts," in *Stepping Back to Look Forward: A History of the Massachusetts Forest*, edited by Charles H. W. Foster (Cambridge, MA: Harvard University Press, 1998), 105.

9 Gifford Pinchot, untitled lecture, November 30, 1895, Letterbooks, box 411, Reel 3, GPP.

10 Pinchot, untitled lecture, November 30, 1895. Today, science has demonstrated ecological benefits of old-growth forests, but at the time, Pinchot's position was science versus sentiment/beauty. For more on that distinction, see also Harold Pinkett, "Gifford Pinchot, Consulting Forester," 37–38, and Frederick Law Olmsted (to Pinchot, January 9, 1895), *The Papers of Frederick Law Olmsted: The Last Great Projects, 1890–1895* (Baltimore, MD: Johns Hopkins University Press, 2015), 889–91.

11 Nicholas C. Polos, "The Neo-Californians: John Muir, John Swett, and their Inner World," in *John Muir in Historical Perspective*, edited by Sally M. Miller, 68. Worster, *A Passion for Nature*, 282–87.

12 Wolcott Gibbs (to Smith, March 2, 1896) quoted in *Pamphlets on Forestry*, 6. In *Breaking*, 90, Pinchot wrote that he drafted a response for Gibbs, but "I do not recall" how much of it was used. He then quotes Gibbs's version at length. Given Pinchot's ego, if those were his words, he would have recalled.

13 Ahern quoted in Harper, *The Crown and the Jewel*, 94. On the nearby Sun River, Ahern said, "spring floods are earlier and disastrous," with midsummer flows inadequate, following massive timber cutting on public domain lands upstream. See also Sutton, *Charles Sprague Sargent*, 160.

14 Sargent to Pinchot, May 26, 1896, box 963, GPP. Johnson, *Yesterdays*, 298.

15 Pinchot, *Conservation Diaries*, 72. Sargent to Pinchot, May 26, 1896, box 963, GPP.

16 Months later, claiming that his surveys demonstrated the potential of the ceded strip as a forest reserve, Pinchot did try to submit his and Graves's expenses for reimbursement. Sargent, exasperated, rejected them. By then their feud was beyond salvage. (Sargent to Pinchot, June 21, 1897, Pinchot to Sargent, June 23, 1897, both in box 964, GPP.)

17 Sargent to Pinchot, n.d. [1896], box 963, GPP. See also Bernhard Fernow, "Recent Publications," *Garden and Forest* 9 (June 17, 1896): 249–50.

18 Constance Carpenter, *Forest Sustainability Assessment for the Northern United States*, (Newtown Square, PA: USDA Forest Service Northeastern Area State and Private Forestry, 2007), 21, 63.

19 Sutton, *Charles Sprague Sargent*, 113.

20 Muir to Pinchot, October 28, 1896, and December 17, 1896, box 963, GPP.

21. Pinchot, Hague, and Brewer were Yale graduates or faculty; Sargent, Agassiz, and Gibbs were current or retired Harvard faculty. Although Abbot graduated from West Point, his family had numerous Harvard connections.

22 Pinchot to Brandis, May 9, 1896, Letterbooks, box 411, reel 3, GPP.

23 Pinchot to Berthold Ribbentrop, May 20, 1896, Letterbooks, box 411, reel 3, GPP.

24 Johnson to Muir, January 9, 1896, JMP. Muir to Johnson, April 3, 1896, JMP. Again note Muir's interest in forest *management*, not wilderness.

25 Muir to Johnson, June 3, 1896, JMP.

26 Pinchot, *Conservation Diaries*, 72.

27 Pinchot, *Breaking*, 98–99.

28 "Jack Monroe's life bridges glamorous gap," *Sanders County* [Mont.] *Independent-Ledger*, August 19, 1942. Pinchot, *Conservation Diaries*, 72.

29 Muir to Louie, July 21, 1896, JMP.

30 Muir journal for July 16, 1896, JMP.

31 Pinchot, *Breaking*, 100.

32 Pinchot, draft manuscript, 99, box 973, GPP. Pinchot, *Breaking*, 100.

33 Muir journal for July 16, 1896, JMP. Muir to Louie, July 21, 1896, JMP.

34 Muir to Louie, July 15, 1896, JMP. Muir journal for July 16, 1896, JMP. The lake's majesty was little changed on my 2017 boat ride.

35 Albert Lewis Sperry, *Avalanche* (Boston: Christopher Publishing House, 1938), 38–46.

36 Muir journal for July 16, 1896, JMP. The sudden cool, birds, and alpenglow were not mentioned by Muir but instead come from my own 2017 and 2018 reenactments.

37 Muir journal for July 16, 1896, with original spelling.

38 Lyman Sperry, "Avalanche Basin, Montana Rockies," *Appalachia* 8, no. 1 (January 1896): 59, 65. C. W. Buchholtz, *Man in Glacier* (West Glacier, MT: Glacier Natural History Association, 1976), chap. 4.

39 Muir, "The Wild Parks and Forest Reservations of the West," 22.

40 Pinchot to parents, July 20, 1896, box 58, GPP.

41 Muir journal for July 17, 1896, JMP. Pinchot to parents, July 20, 1896.

42 Pinchot, *Breaking*, 100. Pinchot to parents, July 20, 1896.

10: The Public Good Forever

1 Pinchot handwritten diary for July 21, 1896, copy at Grey Towers.

2 Pinchot to parents, July 20, 1896, box 10, GPP. Muir diary July 20–21, 1896, JMP. Muir to Louie, July 21, 1896, JMP.

3 Pinchot, *Conservation Diaries*, 73. Muir to Pinchot, Jul 26, 1896, box 963, GPP.

4 Pinchot to Muir, July 23, 1896, JMP. Pinchot, *Breaking*, 101. The Washington and Olympic reserves are now the Mount Baker–Snoqualmie National Forest and Olympic National Park.

5 Pinchot, *Breaking*, 101. Pinchot to parents, July 20, 1896, box 10, GPP. Oddly, the commission did not recommend that Crater Lake become a national park, perhaps because its visit was clouded by rain.

6 Muir diaries, August-September 1896, 7, JMP.

7 Pinchot, *Breaking*, 103. John Muir, Linnie Marsh Wolfe, *John of the Mountains: The Unpublished Journals of John Muir* (Madison, WI: University of Wisconsin Press, 1979) (reprint), 357.

8   Pinchot, *Breaking*, 103.

9   Paul W. Gates, *History of Public Land Law Development* (Washington, DC: U.S. Government Printing Office, 1968), 568.

10   Hague to Pinchot, n.d., box 964, GPP. Pinchot did eventually implement military influences in the U.S. Forest Service.

11   To Pinchot, Muir said (December 17, 1896, box 963, GPP) that he had hoped Cleveland would make more forest reservations before leaving office. To Sargent, who disliked Cleveland, Muir said (February 24, 1897, quoted in Sutton, *Charles Sprague Sargent*, 164) that doing so would be Cleveland's last chance to redeem himself.

12   Sargent to Wolcott Gibbs, February 1, 1897, included as an attachment in Sargent to Muir, February 11, 1897, JMP.

13   Hague to Pinchot, February 6, 1897, box 564, GPP.

14   Sutton, *Charles Sprague Sargent*, 163.

15   Cleveland quoted in Pinchot, *Breaking*, 94. Some skepticism may be warranted: Although Pinchot claims to be quoting the commission report, Cleveland's words don't appear there. National Academy of Sciences, "Report of the Committee Appointed by the National Academy of Sciences Upon the Inauguration of a Forest Policy for the Forested Lands of the United States to the Secretary of the Interior," Government Printing Office, 1897.

16   Pinchot, *Conservation Diaries*, 76. Muir was not summoned because California was too far away, he didn't enjoy lobbying, and he wasn't an official commission member.

17   Muir to Johnson, March 6, 1897, JMP. Sargent to Muir, March 5, 1897, JMP. The impeachment allegation is in Bernhard Fernow, *A Brief History of Forestry in Europe, the United States and Other Countries* (Toronto: Toronto University Press, 1913), 485. Not only was there no time for impeachment proceedings, but it's the House, not the Senate, that initiates them.

18   Gates, *Public Land Law*, 569.

19   For extravagance and veto threats, see "Sundry Civil Bill Passed," *New York Journal*, March 1, 1897, 5.

20   "Congress and the Forest Reservations," *Garden and Forest*, March 17, 1897, 101–02.

21   Harper Barnes, *Standing on a Volcano: The Life and Times of David Rowland Francis* (St. Louis, MO: Missouri Historical Society Press, 2001), 100–101. In another version of the story, which strains credulity, Cleveland slammed the table for emphasis as he said, "Amend the Civil Sundry Bill, will they?

Well, if they do, I will veto the whole damned Civil Sundry Bill!" (Johnson, *Remembered Yesterdays*, 299–300.)

22 Johnson to Muir, March 8, 1897, JMP.

23 Pinchot, *Conservation Diaries*, 76. See also "Sunday Work in Senate," *New York Times*, March 1, 1897, 2, and "The Sundry Civil Bill," *New York Times*, March 2, 1897, 4.

24 This entire episode is detailed in Barnes, *Standing on a Volcano*, 101. Given the chaos, the events have received multiple interpretations. Sargent believed that the final draft of the Civil Sundry Bill didn't actually imperil the reservations ("Congress and the Forest Reservations," *Garden and Forest*, March 17, 1897, 102), and Johnson believed that Cleveland rejected it for other reasons (Johnson to Muir, March 8, 1897, JMP). But I find Barnes—relying on a 1919 letter from Francis to William Gorham Rice, who was then researching a never-published biography of Cleveland—more persuasive.

25 A skeptic would respond that Cleveland was just having a really bad day. After McKinley's inauguration, Cleveland left for three weeks of duck hunting in North Carolina, where companion Leonard Wood described him as "tired and worn" in Alyn Brodsky, *Grover Cleveland: A Study in Character* (New York: Macmillan, 2000), 407. Regardless of Cleveland's intentions, the ensuing national discussion proved valuable.

26 Johnson to Muir, March 8, 1897, JMP.

27 Page to Muir, March 5, 1897, JMP. Sargent to Muir, March 6, 1897, JMP.

28 Hague to Muir, March 9, 1897, JMP. Muir was not the only ally to whom the commission reached out. For example, Pinchot wrote to former president Benjamin Harrison, a family friend, hoping that Harrison could influence fellow Republican McKinley. (Pinchot to Harrison, March 10, 1897, reel 7, series 17, GPP.)

29 Johnson to Muir, March 8, 1897, JMP.

30 Sargent to Muir, March 6, 1897. Stiles and Sargent quoted in Sargent to Muir, March 10, 1897, JMP.

31 Muir to Walter Page, March 21, 1897, JMP. Although researchers have been able to identify only a couple of local articles, Muir likely played a role in others that didn't mention his name.

32 Sargent to Muir, April 6, 1897, JMP. Sargent to Muir, May 3, 1897, JMP.

33 Pinchot, *Breaking*, 108.

34 Ibid. Pinchot to Schlick, March 1, 1897, Reel 4, series 10, GPP.

35 Pinchot, undated draft of *Breaking*, 127, box 973, GPP.

36 John Muir, "The New Forest Reservations," *Mining and Scientific Press* 74 (April 3, 1897): 283 (cited by some sources as "Reservation" without the "s").

37 Muir to Pinchot, September 25, 1893.

38 "John Muir Is Here," *Portland Oregonian*, July 23, 1896, 4.

39 Muir, "The New Forest Reservations."

40 Muir to Theodore P. Lukens, March 15, 1897, JMP.

41 "Forestry Reserve Review: Commissioners Notified to Report to Secretary Bliss on Monday," *New York Times*, April 4, 1897, 17.

42 Sargent to Muir, April 6, 1897, JMP. See also: "Office Seekers in Force: Many Delegations See the President Concerning Appointments," *New York Times*, April 6, 1897, 2.

43 "Proceedings in Congress: The Senate Passes the Sundry Civil Bill," *New York Times*, May 7, 1897, 5. Ise, *Forest Policy*, 132–42. Technically, at this point Pettigrew was a Silver Republican, a short-lived Western faction.

44 National Academy of Sciences, "Report of the committee," 18, 21, 28. Sutton, *Charles Sprague Sargent*, 167. For the Forest Commission to take a position on the Grand Canyon was particularly ironic, given its relative lack of trees.

45 Gates, *Public Land Law*, 568. Rakestraw, "A History of Forest Conservation," 30.

46 Pettigrew, *Imperial Washington*, 16–17. Ise, *Forest Policy*, 122.

47 John Muir, "The National Parks and Forest Reservations," *Harper's Weekly* 41 (June 5, 1897): 563. Muir was fond of imaginary polling data; the "90 percent" here mirrors his later claim that 90 percent of San Franciscans would have opposed the Hetch Hetchy dam if they saw the valley (Worster, *Passion for Nature*, 424).

48 Muir, "The National Parks," 563–67. Muir, a great recycler, had used the right-and-wrong theme in an earlier speech to the Sierra Club (Muir, "The National Parks and Forest Reservations," November 23, 1895, discussed in Chapter 3) and repeated the metaphor of Eden as God's single-tree set-aside years later in the Hetch Hetchy argument (Muir to James R. Garfield, September 6, 1907, JMP).

49 Muir, "The National Parks," 566–67.

50 Nash, *Wilderness and the American Mind*, 138. Cohen (*Pathless Way*, 297–301) similarly argues that Muir quickly departed from Pinchotian forestry views, as does Miller in *Gifford Pinchot*, 138, Jones in *The Battle for Yosemite*, 18, and

William Cronon, as editor of *John Muir: Nature Writings*, Library of America, 1997, 863.

51 Muir, "The Wild Parks and Forest Reservations of the West." Portraying the loggers with sympathetic, sleepy-bear-cub imagery, Muir does call them "foes of trees," but primarily because there are so many of them, not because they are evil.

52 Muir, "The Wild Parks and Forest Reservations of the West." Emphasis added. Muir referred to the *Douglas spruce*, but *Douglas fir* is today more common. In effect, Muir's attitude toward public lands was like an evangelist toward a beautiful new church building: "This is great, but you still have to devote your life to God."

53 Muir to Johnson, June 18, 1897, JMP.

54 Harold K. Steen, "The Forest Service Organic Act," *Journal of Forestry* 103, no. 5 (July/August 2005): 235. The purposes are: to "preserve and protect the forest within the reservation . . . for the purpose of securing favorable conditions of water flows . . . [and] to furnish a continuous supply of timber for the use and necessities of the people of the United States." Given that the Organic Act prioritized managing water over managing trees, much less scenery, it should not be surprising that Pinchot favored a dam in Hetch Hetchy.

55 Samuel T. Dana and Sally K. Fairfax, *Forest and Range Policy* (New York: McGraw-Hill, 1980), 61.

56 Pinchot, *Conservation Diaries*, 78, 80.

Epilogue

1 The protection of antiquities was a new reason to set aside public land, and thus sparked a new public land format, the national monument.

2 Officially, BLM lands could have been homesteaded or otherwise "disposed" until the 1976 Federal Land Policy and Management Act, sometimes called the BLM Organic Act, which extended the concepts of permanent federal ownership and multiple use to what remained of the public domain. CRS, "Federal Land Ownership," 3–4.

3 Patricia Nelson Limerick, "The Forest Reserves and the Argument for a Closing Frontier," in *The Origins of the National Forests*, edited by Steen.

4 In 2018 and early 2019, the federal land transfer movement earned a lower public profile. Personally, I was pleased, although I couldn't dispute those who worried that it had merely gone underground.

5   For an introduction to USFS collaborative philosophies, see, for example, John Clayton, "Revisiting Muir and Pinchot," *Montana Quarterly* (fall 2017).

6   As timeless as it may feel today, even the Garden-of-Eden vision of unchanging wilderness is itself a change, a twentieth-century ideal that differed from the Sierra Club's 1907 vision for the Hetch Hetchy Valley.

BIBLIOGRAPHY

This is a bibliography of major sources. It excludes many valuable sources cited only once in the Notes. My most valuable sources were the John Muir Papers, online at https://scholarlycommons.pacific.edu/muir/; the Gifford Pinchot Papers, Library of Congress MSS36277; and the Sierra Club John Muir exhibit, http://vault.sierraclub.org/john_muir_exhibit/.

Arnold, Ron. "Congressman William Holman of Indiana: Unknown Founder of the National Forests." In Harold K. Steen, ed., *The Origins of the National Forests: A Centennial Symposium*, edited by Harold K. Steen. Durham, NC: Duke University Press, 1992.

Badè, William Frederic. *The Life and Letters of John Muir*. Boston and New York: Houghton Mifflin, 1924.

Barnes, Harper. *Standing on a Volcano: The Life and Times of David Rowland Francis*. Columbia, MO: Missouri Historical Society Press, 2001.

Blake, Israel George. "The Lives of William Steele Holman and His Father Jesse Lynch Holman." PhD diss., Indiana University, 1940.

Bradley, James G. "The Mystery of Gifford Pinchot and Laura Hough-teling," *Pennsylvania History: A Journal of Mid-Atlantic Studies* 66, no. 2 (Spring 1999): 199–214.

Cohen, Michael. *The Pathless Way: John Muir and American Wilderness.* Madison, WI: University of Wisconsin Press, 1984.

Congressional Research Service. "Federal Land Ownership: Overview and Data," CRS R42346, 2017.

Cronon, William, ed. *John Muir: Nature Writings.* Library of America, 1997.

Diettert, Gerald Allen. "Grinnell's Glacier." Graduate dissertations, University of Montana, 1990.

Felton, Lena. "Is America's 'Best Idea' at Stake?" *Atlantic Monthly,* November 27, 2017.

Fox, Stephen. *The American Conservation Movement: John Muir and His Legacy.* Madison, WI: University of Wisconsin Press, 1981.

Gates, Paul W. *History of Public Land Law Development.* Washington, D.C.: U.S. Government Printing Office, 1968.

Hague, Arnold. "The Yellowstone Park." In *American Big-game Hunting: The Book of the Boone and Crockett Club,* edited by Theodore Roosevelt and George Bird Grinnell. New York: Forest and Stream Publishing Company, 1893.

Haines, Aubrey L. *The Yellowstone Story: A History of Our First National Park,* Vol. 1. Yellowstone National Park, WY: Yellowstone Library and Museum Association, 1977.

Harper, Andrew C. "The Crown and the Jewel: George Bird Grinnell, Louis Warren Hill, and Glacier National Park." PhD diss., Northern Arizona University, 1999.

Hays, Samuel P. *Conservation and the Gospel of Efficiency.* Cambridge, MA: Harvard University Press, 1959.

Hibbard, Benjamin Horace. *A History of the Public Land Policies.* Madison, WI: University of Wisconsin Press, 1965 (reprint).

Hines, Cynthia, and the Frontier Historical Society. *Early Glenwood Springs.* Mount Pleasant, SC: Arcadia Publishing, 2015.

Hou, Shen. *The City Natural: Garden and Forest Magazine and the Rise of American Environmentalism.* Pittsburgh, PA: University of Pittsburgh Press, 2013.

Howe, Mark Antony De Wolfe. *Later Years of the Saturday Club, 1870-1920.* Freeport, NY: Books for Libraries Press, 1968 (reprint).

Ise, John. *The United States Forest Policy.* New Haven, CT: Yale University Press, 1920.

"John Muir Is Here," *Portland Oregonian,* July 23, 1896, 8.

Johnson, Robert Underwood. *Remembered Yesterdays.* Boston: Little, Brown, 1923.

Johnson, Robert Underwood, et al., "A Plan to Save the Forests" and "Topics of the Time: The Need of a National Forest Commission," *The Century Magazine* 49 (February 1895): 626–35.

Lewis, James G. "The Pinchot Family and the Battle to Establish American Forestry," *Pennsylvania History* 66, no. 2 (Spring 1999): 143–65.

Lowenthal, David. *George Perkins Marsh: Prophet of Conservation.* Seattle, WA: University of Washington Press, 2009.

Marsh, George Perkins. *Man and Nature.* New York: Charles Scribner, 1864.

McCarthy, G. Michael. *Hour of Trial: The Conservation Conflict in Colorado and the West, 1891-1907.* Norman, OK: University of Oklahoma Press, 1977.

McGeary, M. Nelson. *Gifford Pinchot: Forester, Politician.* Princeton, NJ: Princeton University Press, 1960.

Miller, Char. *Gifford Pinchot and the Making of Modern Environmentalism.* Washington, D.C.: Island Press, 2001.

———. "What Happened in the Rainier Grand's Lobby? A Question of Sources," *The Journal of American History* 86, no. 4 (March 2000): 1709–1714.

Miller, Sally M., ed. *John Muir in Historical Perspective.* New York: Peter Lang, 1999.

Muhn, James. "Early Administration of the Forest Reserve Act: Interior Department and General Land Office Policies, 1891-1897." In *The Origins of the National Forests: A Centennial Symposium,* edited by Harold K. Steen. Durham, NC: Duke University Press, 1992.

Muir, John. *A Thousand-Mile Walk to the Gulf.* Boston and New York: Houghton Mifflin, 1916.

————. *John of the Mountains: The Unpublished Journals of John Muir.* Madison, WI: University of Wisconsin Press, 1979 (reprint).

————. *Stickeen: The Story of a Dog.* Boston and New York: Houghton Mifflin, 1909.

————. *The Yosemite.* New York: The Century Company, 1912.

————. "Features of the Proposed Yosemite National Park," *The Century Magazine* 40, no. 5 (September 1890): 656–67.

————. "The National Parks and Forest Reservations," *Harper's Weekly* 41, no. 211 (June 5, 1897): 563–67.

————. "The National Parks and Forest Reservations," *Sierra Club Bulletin* 1, no. 7 (1896): 271–84 (reprint of a speech from November 23, 1895).

————. "The New Forest Reservation," *Mining and Scientific Press* 74 (April 3, 1897): 283.

————. "A Rival of the Yosemite: The Cañon of the South Fork of King's River, California," *The Century Magazine* 43, no. 1 (November 1891): 77–97.

————. "The Treasures of the Yosemite," *The Century Magazine* 40, no. 4 (August 1890): 483–500.

————. "The Wild Parks and Forest Reservations of the West," *Atlantic Monthly* 81 (January 1898): 15–28.

————. "The Yellowstone Park," *San Francisco Bulletin*, October 29, 1885, 37.

Nash, Roderick. *Wilderness and the American Mind.* New Haven, CT: Yale University Press, 2001 (reprint).

National Academy of Sciences, "Report of the Committee Appointed by the National Academy of Sciences Upon the Inauguration of a Forest Policy for the Forested Lands of the United States to the Secretary of the Interior," Government Printing Office, 1897.

Nelson, Jim. *Glenwood Springs: The History of a Rocky Mountain Resort.* Ouray, CO: Western Reflections, 1999.

Niebuhr, Reinhold. *Leaves from the Notebooks of a Tamed Cynic.* Meridian Books, 1957 (reprint).

Pamphlets on Forestry. University of California: 1900, http://google.cat /books?id=D8RDAAAAIAAJ.

Penick, James, Jr. *Progressive Politics and Conservation: The Pinchot-Ballinger Affair*. Chicago: University of Chicago Press, 1968.

Pinchot, Gifford. *Breaking New Ground*. Washington, D.C.: Island Press, 1988 (reprint).

———. *Fishing Talk*. Mechanicsburg, PA: Stackpole Books, 1993 (reprint).

———. *The Fight for Conservation*. New York: Doubleday Page, 1910.

Pinchot, Gifford, and Harold K. Steen. *The Conservation Diaries of Gifford Pinchot*. Durham, NC: Forest History Society, 2001.

Pinkett, Harold T. "Gifford Pinchot, Consulting Forester, 1893-1898," *New York History* 39, no. 1 (January 1958): 34–49.

Ponder, Stephen. "Conservation, Economics and Newspapering: The Seattle Press and the Forest Reserves Controversy of 1897," *American Journalism* 3, no. 1 (January 1986): 50–60.

———. "Gifford Pinchot: Press Agent for Forestry," *Journal of Forest History* 31, no. 1 (January 1987): 26–35.

Rakestraw, Lawrence. "A History of Forest Conservation in the Pacific Northwest, 1891–1913." PhD diss., University of Washington, 1955.

Righter, Robert W. *The Battle over Hetch Hetchy: America's Most Controversial Dam and the Birth of Modern Environmentalism*. New York: Oxford University Press, 2005.

Rothman, Hal. *Preserving Different Pasts: The American National Monuments*. Champaign, IL: University of Illinois Press, 1989.

Runte, Alfred. *Yosemite, The Embattled Wilderness*. Lincoln, NE: University of Nebraska Press, 1993.

Rutkow, Eric. *American Canopy: Trees, Forests, and the Making of a Nation*. New York: Scribner, 2012.

Smith, Michael L. *Pacific Visions: California Scientists and the Environment, 1850-1915*. New Haven, CT: Yale University Press, 1987.

Spence, Mark David. "Dispossessing the Wilderness: The Preservationist Ideal, Indian Removal, and National Parks." PhD diss., University of Southern California, 1996.

Steen, Harold K. *The Beginning of the National Forest System*. Washington, D.C.: USDA Forest Service, 1991.

———. *The U.S. Forest Service: A Centennial History.* Seattle, WA: University of Washington Press, 2013.

———, ed. *The Origins of the National Forests: A Centennial Symposium.* Durham, NC: Duke University Press, 1992.

Stoll, Mark. *Inherit the Holy Mountain: Religion and the Rise of American Environmentalism.* New York: Oxford University Press, 2017.

———. *Protestantism, Capitalism, and Nature in America.* Albuquerque, NM: University of New Mexico Press, 1997.

———. "'Sagacious' Bernard Palissy: Pinchot, Marsh, and the Connecticut Origins of American Conservation," *Environmental History* 16, no. 1 (January 2011): 4–37.

———. "Milton in Yosemite: *Paradise Lost* and the National Parks Idea," *Environmental History* 13, no. 2 (April 2008): 237–74.

Strong, Douglas H. "The History of Sequoia National Park, 1876-1926: Part I: The Movement to Establish a Park," *Southern California Quarterly* 48, no. 2 (June 1966): 137–67.

———. "The Sierra Forest Reserve: The Movement to Preserve the San Joaquin Valley Watershed," *California Historical Society Quarterly* 46, no. 1 (March 1967): 3–17.

Sutton, S.B. *Charles Sprague Sargent and the Arnold Arboretum.* Cambridge, MA: Harvard University Press, 1970.

Terrie, Philip G. *Forever Wild: A Cultural History of Wilderness in the Adirondacks.* Syracuse, NY: Syracuse University Press, 1994.

Thayer, James Bradley. *A Western Journey with Mr. Emerson.* Boston: Little, Brown, 1884.

Warren, Louis S. *The Hunter's Game: Poachers and Conservationists in Twentieth-century America.* New Haven, CT: Yale University Press, 1999.

Wiebe, Robert H. *The Search for Order, 1877-1920.* New York: Macmillan, 1967.

Williams, Dennis C. *God's Wilds: John Muir's Vision of Nature.* College Station, TX: Texas A&M Press, 2002.

Williams, Gerald W. *The USDA Forest Service: The First Century.* Washington, D.C.: USDA Forest Service, 2005.

Wilson, Norman L., and Lucinda M. Woodward. "C.D. Robinson and John Muir in the Kings River Canyon." In *John Muir in*

Historical Perspective, edited by Sally M. Miller. New York: Peter Lang, 1999.

Wolfe, Linnie Marsh. *Son of the Wilderness: The Life of John Muir.* New York: Alfred A. Knopf, 1947.

Worster, Donald. *A Passion for Nature*: *The Life of John Muir.* New York: Oxford University Press, 2008.

INDEX

A

Abbot, Henry, 166, 167, 170, 181, 183, 187, 190, 201, 237n45

Absaroka Mountains, 132

Adirondacks, 60–61, 73–76

African Americans, 128

Agassiz, Alexander, 166

Agassiz, Louis, 162, 166

The Age of Innocence (Wharton), 69

Agriculture Department. *See* Department of Agriculture

Ahern, George, 167

Alaska, 181, 182

Alaska National Wildlife Refuge, 100

Alhambra Valley, 26–29

Allen, B. F., 146

allotment policy, 153, 154

American Forestry Association, 12, 143, 145, 147, 149, 152, 161–162

animals, souls and emotions of, 11

anti-monopolism, 125–129

Antiquities Act, 52

Appalachian Mountain Club, 40

Arkansas Hot Springs, 105–106

Army Corps of Engineers, 157, 166

Army Forestry Corps, 157

army supervision, *see* military administration

Arnold, Ron, 138

Arnold Arboretum, 31, 159

Articles of Confederation, 127

Atlantic Monthly, 194–196, 202–204

Audubon Society, 150

Avalanche Lake, xxii, 177–178

B

Bacon, Robert, 84

Ballinger, Richard, 54, 58, 92–95

Bidwell, John and Annie, 25–26

Biltmore estate, 12, 43, 68–73, 91

Bitterroot Forest Reserve, 182

Blackfeet Indian Reservation, xiv, 152–155, 172

Bliss, Cornelius, 199

Bloomberg, Michael, xvi

Boone and Crockett Club, 41–42, 43, 68, 135, 143, 150

Brandis, Dietrich, 63–64, 68, 162, 170, 175, 181

Brewer, William, 166, 167, 170, 181, 183, 187, 190, 200

Brower, David, 49

Bull Moose party, 94

bully pulpit, 87

Bureau of Forestry, 43, *see also* U.S. Forest Service

Bureau of Land Management, xiii, xiv, 209
Burke, Thomas, 77–78
Burns, Ken, xviii
Burns, Robert, 8, 21
Burroughs, John, 9, 43, 56

C
Calaveras Grove, 116–117
California, 19, 189, 195
California Sierra, 21, 29, 34, 116–120, *see also* Sierra Nevada, High Sierra
Campbell, Alexander, 20
Cannon, Joe, 126
capitalism, 90, 110, 125–126, 202, 213
Carnegie, Andrew, 56
Carr, Ezra, 66
Carr, Jeanne, 23, 26, 27, 108
Carter, Thomas, 88
Catlin, George, 74
Central Park, 43, 70, 103
The Century, 35, 37, 38, 121, 122, 155, 156, 162, 195
Christianity, 11, 21, 63
cities, 14, 22
civilization, 28, 29
Civil Sundry Appropriations Bill, 188–191, 194, 200–202
Civil War, 18
class system, 6, 75, 89, 143
Clay, Henry, 59
Cleveland, Grover, 141, 147–148, 185–192, 194, 201
climate change, xxi, 213–214
Cody, William F. "Buffalo Bill," 8
Colby, William, 45, 46, 54, 79
Cole, Cornelius, 106, 121
Colorado, 87–91, 140–145, 189
Colvin, Verplanck, 74
community, xxi, 4, 85, 131
Congress
    forest policy and, 66, 137–138, 185–198

Hetch Hetchy dam and, 54, 58
homesteading and, 129–130
national parks and, 38–39, 42, 103–105, 107, 123–124, 144
conservation, xvii–xviii, 52, 67–68, 80
    definition of, xvii, 193
    federal policy on, 96
    forests and, 130–132
    ideals of, 97–98
    Native Americans and, 152–155
    Pinchot and, 95–96, 193
    politics of, 88
    preservation-versus-conservation divide, xix–xx, 52, 56, 75, 79–82, 99–100, 148, 203, 212
    supporters of, 118–119
cowboy mythology, 110
Crater Lake, 182–183
Crown of the Continent, 151, 155, 168
Cumberland Plateau, 20

D
Darwin, Charles, 56
Dawes, Henry, 106
Dawes Act, 153
deforestation, 66, 130
Delta, 118
Denver Public Lands Convention, 87–90
Department of Agriculture, 52, 85, 92, 117
Desert Land Act, 129–130
Devereux, Walter, 141, 143
Dinosaur National Park, 49
dog story, 7–11

E
Emerald Necklace, 23, 31, 70
Emerson, Ralph Waldo, 6, 7, 21–25, 162
Emory River, 19–21
Ensign, Edgar, 144–145, 149
environmental movement
    in 1800s, 131–132
    grassroots, 54
    split in, 79–82

Europe, 128
executive power, 92, 138, 164–165, 192

F
federal land policy, 78, 88–89, 141,
    165–166, 183
    See also forest policy
federal land transfer, xiv–xv, 209–210
Fernow, Bernhard, 65, 70, 91, 132
    on army management, 157
    forestry policy and, 137, 138, 146, 152
    Marsh and, 131, 132
    National Forest Commission and, 161,
        182
    Pinchot and, 60, 68, 73, 170
The Fight for Conservation (Pinchot), 96
Fisher, Walter, 54, 58
Forest and Stream, 118, 134, 151
Forest Management Act, 205
forest policy, 77–78, 137–138, 146,
    183–203
Forest Reserve Act, 76, 137–139, 141,
    145, 148, 205
forest reserves, 137–139, 182
    critics of, 78
    debates over, 142–145
    establishment of, 31–32, 76, 147
    management of, 83, 206
    National Forest Commission and,
        184–198
    policies on, 146–158
    Roosevelt and, 43, 88, 92
forestry, 59–65, 68
    education, 73, 85, 157
    Pinchot and, 91, 98–100, 156–158,
        163–165
    practical, 14, 91
    profession, 61–62, 85, 164
    profitable, 91
    scientific, 14, 91, 163–164
forestry schools, 73, 85
forests
    See also forest reserves

conservation of, 130–132
management of, 157–158, 163–165
old growth, 164
preservation of, 31–32
protection of, 66–68, 136–138,
    146–147
uses of, 149, 184–185
Forest Service. *See* U.S. Forest Service
Fox, Stephen, 19
France, 62–63
Francis, David, 184, 186, 188–191
Free Timber Act, 130
French National Forestry School, 63–64

G
Garden and Forest, 31, 118, 152, 156, 160
Garfield, James, 47, 49, 52, 54
Garfield Grove, 119
Garr, Henry H., 177
Garrison, William Lloyd, 82
General Grant National Park, 119–120,
    145–146
General Land Office (GLO), 39, 110–
    111, 118, 141–142, 145–150, 200, 206,
    209
Geology of the Yellowstone National Park
    (USGS), 133
Giant Forest, 118, 119
Gibbs, O. Wolcott, 160–161, 165–166
Gifford, Sanford, 7
Gilded Age, 59, 69, 75, 125
Glacier National Park, xiii, xvi–xvii, 8,
    155, 176, *see also* Lake McDonald,
    Crown of the Continent
glaciers, 9, 13, 29, 31, 79, 107, 114, 176, 178
Glavis, William, 93, 94
Glen Canyon, 49
Glenwood Springs, Colorado, 140–145
God, 11, 18, 21, 78, 108, 115–116
gold, 141
gold rush, 79
Gramercy Park, 6
Grand Canyon, 70, 183–184, 201, 204

Grand Sentinel, 120
Grange, 165
Grant Grove, 117, 118
grassroots environmentalism, 54
Graves, Henry, 169, 171, 172, 182, 183
grazing, 79–81, 110, 146–147, 193
Great Northern railroad, 77, 173, 178
Grey Towers, 12, 32–33, 69
Grinnell, George Bird, 41, 67, 68, 118, 131, 134, 150–155, 168

H

Hague, Arnold, 132–136, 139, 145, 154, 166, 167, 181, 186, 195, 196, 200, 206, 212
Half Dome, 23
Harper's Weekly, 202–203
Harriman, Edward, 56
Harrison, Benjamin, 39, 119, 138, 140–141, 144, 147
Hayden, Ferdinand, 107
Hayden Valley, 113
Hetch Hetchy Valley, 36–37, 94
  debate over damming of, xvii–xviii, xix, 46–50, 53–58
  Muir and, 33, 53–58, 204
High Sierra, 146, *see also* California Sierra, Sierra Nevada
Hill, James J., 77
Holman, William S., 126–129, 136–139, 145, 149, 193
Holm Lea, 159–160
Homestead Act, 39, 128
homesteading, 36, 39, 64, 109–111, 127–130, 136–138, 141–142, 148, 153
Hot Springs National Park, 105–106
Hough, Franklin, 66
Houghteling, Laura, 13, 76, 78
Hudson River School, 7
Humboldt, Alexander von, 56
Hunt, Richard Morris, 69
hunters, 67–68, 150–151
Hutchings, James, 144

I

income inequality, 125, 127, 128–129
Indian reservations, 152–155
indigenous populations, 128, 152–153
individualism, xxi, 4, 61, 81, 165
industrialization, 75
Industrial Revolution, 125, 129
interest groups, xiv
Interior Department, 47, 52, 54, 76–78, 92
Irrigation Congress, 90

J

Jackson, Billy, 168, 171–172
Jardin des Plantes, 62–63
Jeffersonian society, 128
Johnson, Robert Underwood, 46, 81, 118–119, 151, 161–162
  forest policy and, 156–158, 189–190
  Hetch Hetchy and, 54
  Muir and, 7, 34–42
  National Academy of Sciences and, 171
  national parks and, 121–124
John the Baptist, 41
Jordan, David Starr, 56

K

Kaweah Colony, 118, 119, 144
Keith, William, 30, 50, 53, 121
Kent, William, 50–53, 56, 58, 212
King, Clarence, 107
Kings Canyon National Park, 120–123, 144
Klondike Gold Rush, 79

L

Lacey, John, 190
Lacey Amendment, 190, 191
Lake Eleanor, 48–49, 55
Lake McDonald, xvi, xviii, xxii, 175–179, 181, 207–208, 212–214
land
  See also public lands

Native American, 152–155
  ownership of, 127–129
land ethic, 99, 209
landscape architecture, 70
land transfer, xiv–xv, 209–210
Lane, Franklin K., 58, 94
LeConte Memorial Lodge, 46
Lembert, John Baptiste, 39, 42
Leopold, Aldo, 209
Limerick, Patricia Nelson, 209
Lincoln, Abraham, 82
locusts, 37
logging, 66, 67, 74–76, 130, 136–137
Louisiana Purchase, 128
lumber camps, 13–14

M
Malheur National Wildlife Refuge, xv
Mammoth Hot Springs, 114
Man and Nature (Marsh), 131–132
Manson, Marsden, 47, 48, 58
Mariposa Grove, 103, 116
market failures, 193
Marsh, George Perkins, 66, 131–132,
  156, 163, 197
Martinez, California, 26–27, 35, 53, 108,
  122
Massachusetts, xiv, xix, 159–160, 162–
  165, 171
Mather, Stephen, 100
McCadden, Mary, 85
McCarthy, Michael, 88
McClintock, Walter, 172
McKinley, William, 184, 191, 194
McRae, Thomas, 149
Meister, Ulrich, 64, 65, 72, 91, 175
middle class, 129
midnight reserves, 88, 92
military administration, of forest reserves,
  133, 156, 157, 161, 185, 201
Miller, Char, 80
Milton, John, 21, 22–23
mining, 141, 155, 200

Mining and Scientific Press, 198, 199
Mirror Lake, 23
monopolies, 48, 55, 67, 77, 89, 92, 99,
  125–126, 129–130, 137
Monroe, Jack, 168, 172–173, 174
Montana, xiv, 105, 110, 134
Mountain Shoshone tribe, 104
The Mountains of California (Muir), 33
Mount Rainier, 30–32, 201, 204
Mount Shasta, 111–112
Mount Tamalpais, 50
Mount Whitney Military Reservation,
  117
Muir, Daniel (father), 4, 8, 12, 15–20,
  56–57, 111–112
Muir, Helen (daughter), 40, 53, 57, 111
Muir, John, xvii
  achievements of, 33
  biographical background on, 15–19
  blindness of, 18–19
  career of, 4
  death of, 57–58
  dog story of, 7–11
  Emerson and, 21–25
  faith of, 17–18
  family background of, 3–4
  final years of, 53–58, 95
  on forest management, 158
  friendship between Pinchot and, 50,
    170, 174–179, 181–184
  at Gramercy Park dinner, 3–14
  Hetch Hetchy and, xvii–xviii, 33,
    49–50, 53–58
  on Holm Lea, 159
  on human society, 28–29
  as introvert, 5
  inventions by, 16, 18
  Kings Canyon National Park and,
    120–123
  letters between Pinchot and, xix,
    13–14, 32–33, 181, 185, 198, 237n45
  Marsh and, 132
  Mount Rainier climb by, 30–32

National Forest Commission and, 171, 173–184

patronage network of, 6–7, 27–29, 53, 56

personality of, 19, 26

physical appearance of, 3, 27, 36

Pinchot and, 50, 170, 174–184

power and, 5

religion and, 20, 21

rivalry between Pinchot and, xviii–xxii, 79–82, 99–100, 165, 207–210, 212–215

Sargent and, 32, 108, 158, 167, 171, 178, 181, 194

sequoia groves and, 116–120

Sierra Club and, 40–42, 53

solo journeys by, 25–27

storytelling ability of, 7–8, 18, 36

support for forest reserves and, 195–199, 202–206

tragedy of, 34–58, 98

views of nature of, 5, 14, 18, 28–29, 55–56, 113–116, 165, 193

writings of, 55–57, 107–109, 121–123, 198–199, 202–205

Yellowstone and, 111–116, 144

Yosemite and, 34–40, 42–46, 107–111

Muir, Louie (wife), 27–28, 35, 53, 111

Muir, Wanda (daughter), 40

Muir-Johnson Yosemite bill, 119

Muir Woods, 50–53, 56, 92, 212

multiple-use agencies, xiv

My First Summer in the Sierra (Muir), 57

mysticism, 61

N

Nash, Roderick, 203

National Academy of Sciences, 161–162, 165–167, 192

National Forest Commission, 165–187, 192–203

national monuments, xv, 52, 88, 209

national parks, 88

See also specific parks

birth of, 103–124

proponents of, 151

public perceptions of, 123–124

purpose of, 104

The National Parks: America's Best Idea, xviii

National Park Service, 209

Native Americans, 128, 143, 152–155, see also Blackfeet Indian Reservation

natural resources, 65–68, 99–100, 149

natural science, 107

nature

God and, 108, 115–116

individuals and, 165

Muir's views on, 5, 14, 18, 28–29, 55–56, 113–116, 165, 193

public lands and, 193–194

public perceptions of, 123–124

science and, 27

society's relationship with, xv, xvi, 211–212

spiritual insights provided by, 10, 18, 29, 43

Transcendentalist's view of, 22

Nature Conservancy, xv–xvi

New Testament, 21

Niagara Falls, 106

Niebuhr, Reinhold, 82

Noble, John, 138, 139

North Coast Water Company, 51, 52

No Trespassing policy, 148–150, 154, 156, 187

O

oil, 66–67

O'Laughlin, John Callan, 92

Old Faithful, 111, 114

old growth forests, 164

Olmsted, Frederick Law, 23, 51–52, 59

Biltmore estate and, 69–73

legacy of, 70

Marsh and, 131, 132

Muir Woods and, 51–52

public parks and, 31, 43, 103–104
Yosemite and, 38, 39–40
Olney, Warren, 48, 56, 58
Olympic Forest Reserves, 182
Organic Act, 205
overgrazing, 67, 110, 146, 193
Overhanging Rock, 44

P
Page, Walter, 194–195, 196
Paradise Lost (Milton), 21–23, 55
Parsons, Edward, 53
Pelton, Emily, 16, 17
Pettigrew, Richard, 138, 200–202
Pettigrew Amendment, 200–202,
205–206
Phelan, James, 42, 47, 58
Phelps Dodge company, 70
Phillips, William Hallett, 135, 139
Phillips Exeter academy, 4
Pinchot, Gifford, xvii
Adirondacks and, 73–76
biographical background on, 59–65
career of, 4, 13–14
conservation and, 131, 193
criticism of, 80–81, 90–91, 95, 99
at Denver Public Lands Convention,
87–90
egoism of, 95–96, 170
as extrovert, 5
family background of, 4, 12–13
fiancée of, 13, 76, 78, 95
forest policy and, 187–198
forestry and, 59–65, 98–100, 145,
156–158, 163–165
in France, 62–63
at Gramercy Park dinner, 12–14
as head of Forest Service, 87–93,
98
Hetch Hetchy and, xvii–xviii, 47–50,
54–55, 58
at Interior Department, 76–78, 206
leadership of, 85

letters between Muir and, xix, 13–14,
32–33, 181, 185, 198, 237n45
media skills of, 90
mentors of, 72–73, 97, 160, 175
Muir and, 50, 170, 174–184
Muir Woods and, 51–53
National Forest Commission and,
166–167, 171–179, 180, 182–184
personal life of, 95
physical appearance of, 3
politics and, 86–87
power and, 5
rivalry between Muir and, xviii–xxii,
79–82, 99–100, 165, 207–210,
212–215
Roosevelt and, 83–87, 93, 96–98
Sargent and, 160–162, 166–170, 196–
197, 212
at Saturday Club, 163–165
Sierra Club and, 46
statesmanship and, 59–60, 82, 91, 129
tragedy of, 98–99
views of nature of, 5
Pinchot, James (father), 7–8, 11–12,
60–61, 65, 131, 180
Pinchot, Mary (mother), 4, 7, 13, 60,
91–96, 131, 160, 180
Pinchot-Ballinger affair, 92–96
pocket veto, 191, 194
political corruption, 39, 74–75, 93–94,
113, 153
politics, 86–88, 205
See also Congress, individual politicians
Post-Intelligencer, 78, 79
Powell, John Wesley, 107
practical forestry, 14, 91, 207
Prairie du Chien, Wisconsin, 16–17
preservation, xvii–xviii, 56, 67–68, 74–75,
158
definition of, xvii
and parks, 119, 139, 155
and Pinchot, 164, 199
in Yosemite, 104

preservation-versus-conservation divide,
  xix–xx, 52, 56, 75, 79–82, 99–100,
  148, 199, 203, 212
professions, 61–62, 85, 164
Progressivism, 35, 36, 40, 47, 51–52, 56,
  77, 98, 164
property rights, 110–111, 142, 149, 192,
  201
prophet-versus-statesman, 82
Prospect Park, 70
Protestantism, 20
public domain, 36, 110, 127, 136, 155,
  165, 176, 188, 191, 193, 201, 203,
  222n1
public lands, xiii–xiv, 36
  Antiquities Act and, 52
  boundaries of, 77
  debates over, xvii–xviii
  deforestation of, 130
  expansion of, 209, 211
  forest reserves and, 88–89, 204–205
  homesteading and, 127–129
  management of, xiv–xvi, 100, 135, 193,
    212
  midnight reserves of, 88, 92
  nature and, 193–194
  need for, 211–212
  ownership of, 105–106
  redefining, 192–194
  shortage of, 129–130
  trespassing on, 148–150
  uses of, xv–xvi, 149–150, 210
  views on, 208
public parks
  idea of, 103–104
  purpose of, 104
public schools, 165
Puritanism, 22, 131

R
railroads, 41–42, 44, 77, 119–120, 135–
  136, 173
Rainier Grand Hotel, 79–80, 203

ranchers, 146–147
rational forest policy, 160, 165–166
recession, 43–44, 45–46
Redwood Creek valley, 50–52
religion, 4, 11, 19, 20, 21, 61
Republican Party, xiv–xv, 98
reservoirs, need for, 50–51
Revolutionary War, 105, 127
robber barons, 125, 131
Robinson, Charles D., 120–122, 231n22
Rockefeller, John D., 67
Roosevelt, Theodore, xvii, xxi, 41, 208, 212
  Boone and Crockett Club and, 41–42,
    43, 68
  Bull Moose party and, 94
  environmentalism of, 43, 98
  Hetch Hetchy and, 54, 58
  midnight reserves and, 88, 92
  Pinchot and, 83–87, 93, 96–98
  as trust-buster, 125–126
  Yosemite camping trip of, 42–46
Root, Elihu, 86

S
San Francisco, water needs of, 46–48
Sargent, Charles, 7, 31–32, 65, 67, 68, 71,
  151, 156
  Adirondacks and, 74–75
  Holm Lea of, 159–160
  Marsh and, 131, 132
  National Forest Commission and,
    166–167, 173–174, 184–186, 194–196,
    200, 201, 205
  Pinchot and, 81, 160–162, 166–170,
    196–197, 212
Saturday Club, 162–165
Schenck, Carl, 73, 91
Schlick, William, 197
Schurz, Carl, 68, 117
scientific forestry, 14, 91, 163–164
Scotland, 3, 7, 20
Seattle, 77, 78, 79
Section 24, 137–139, 145, 147–150, 205

Sellers, Alfred and Fay, 113, 115
sequoias, 116–120, 123
Sequoia National Park, 38, 119–120, 145–147
sheep grazing, 37, 67, 79, 80, 81, 146–147
Sheridan, Phillip, 134
Sherman, William T., 63, 68
Sierra Club, xvii, 15, 40–42, 44–50, 53, 55, 58, 195
Sierra Forest Reserve, 146
Sierra Nevada, 6, 108, *see also* California Sierra, High Sierra
silver, 141
Skull and Bones, 4, 51
Smith, Hoke, 147–148, 162, 168, 171, 184, 192
Snagjumper, 26
Snagjumper II, 26
society, Muir's view of, 28–29
Society for the Preservation of National Parks, 54
Society of American Foresters, 85
Soda Springs, 34, 36, 39–42
South America, 20
Southern Pacific Railroad, 44, 120
Sperry, Lyman, 177–178
Spring Valley Water Company, 47, 53, 58
state government, 43–44
statesmanship, 59–60, 82, 91, 129
Stewart, George, 118, 145–146
Stickeen (dog), 8–11
Stiles, William, 118–119, 156, 160, 196
Stimson, Henry, 77
The Story of My Boyhood and Youth (Muir), 57
Strentzel, John and Louisiana, 27–29
Strentzel, Louisa. *See* Muir, Louie
Sutton, S. B., 169
Swannanoa Bridge, 68, 69
Swan Valley, 172, 174
Swett, John, 53, 165

T
Taft, William, 54, 58, 86, 92–94, 126
Tammany Hall, 74
Teller, Henry, 88
Thoreau, Henry David, 21, 22
Timber and Stone Act, 138
Timber Culture Act, 129–130
timber industry, 67, 73, 75, 77, 118, 130, 136–137
tragedy of the commons, 110–111
Transcendetalists, 21–22
Travels in Alaska (Muir), 57
Trumbull, Lyman, 106
Trump administration, xiv–xv
Tulare County, 117
Tuolumne Meadows, 34
Tuolumne River, 36–37, 48–49
Turner, Ted, xv
Twain, Mark, 125

U
U.S. Capitol, 70, 210–211
U.S. Forest Service, xiv, xvii, 85, 86, 88, 92, 93, 98, 164–165, 205, 209
U.S. Geological Survey (USGS), 133, 135, 200, 206, 208

V
valuation surveys, 168–169
Vanderbilt, George, 12, 68–71
Vandever, William, 118, 119
Vest, George, 134
Visalia, California, 26, 117–120, 145–146

W
Walcott, Charles, 200, 206
War Department, 158, 190
Washington's Birthday Reserves, 182, 186–191, 195, 197, 201, 205
water companies, 51, 52, 53, 58
water supplies, 46–48, 50–51, 67
Wharton, Edith, 69
Wheeler, Benjamin Ide, 56

The White Pine (Pinchot), 169–170
White River Plateau Timber Land
    Reserve, 142–145
Whitman, Walt, 33
Whitney, Josiah, 107, 122
wilderness, xix, 14, 19, 28–29, 43, 65, 99,
    104, 112, 115, 119, 155, 198, 203–204,
    211, 224–225n17
wildlife habitat, 134–135, 150–151, 154
wildlife refuges, xiii, xv, 88, 100, 209
Wilson, Woodrow, 55, 58, 94
Wolfe, Linnie Marsh, 79–80
women, 128
wood, 66
Wyoming, 105, 111, 134

Y
Yale School of Forestry, 73, 85
Yale University, 3, 4, 12, 50–51, 61–62,
    73, 77, 85, 87, 133, 150, 156, 166, 170
Yellowstone National Park, 37–38, 42, 74
    boundaries of, 134–136
    creation of, 104–107, 211
    enforcement at, 147

as first national park, 103
    Hague and, 132–136
    management of, 113
    Muir and, 111–116
    purpose of, 148
Yellowstone Park Timber Land Reserve,
    139, 144
The Yosemite (Muir), 57
Yosemite National Park
    boundaries of, 42, 45
    creation of, 34–40, 119
    as first national park, 103
    management of, 104
    Muir and, 107–111
    Pinchot and, 70
    purpose of, 104
Yosemite Valley, 22–23, 24, 28, 29,
    34–40, 43
Young, S. Hall, 8–9
Young Men's Christian Association
    (YMCA), 61

Z
Zinke, Ryan, xv